Dark Sides of Business and Higher Education Management

Dark Sides of Business and Higher Education Management

Volume I

Edited by

Agata Stachowicz-Stanusch and Gianluigi Mangia

BEP BUSINESS EXPERT PRESS

Dark Sides of Business and Higher Education Management, Volume I

First published in 2016 by
Business Expert Press, LLC
222 East 46th Street, New York, NY 10017
www.businessexpertpress.com

ISBN-13: 978-1-63157-355-2 (paperback)
ISBN-13: 978-1-63157-356-9 (e-book)

Business Expert Press Principles for Responsible Management Education Collection

Collection ISSN: 2331-0014 (print)
Collection ISSN: 2331-0022 (electronic)

Cover and interior design by Exeter Premedia Services Private Ltd., Chennai, India

First edition: 2016

10 9 8 7 6 5 4 3 2 1

Printed in the United States of America.

Abstract

Contemporary management studies usually concern positive and desirable solutions that increase the organizational effectiveness and performance. That is why graduates of higher business schools, equipped with idealistic views on business environment, need to face the dark side of business practice without the appropriate preparation. Their unawareness of the risk associated with management misconduct results in corrupt scandals, erosion of public trust to their organizations, or even the collapse of profitable corporations. Underestimation of unethical behaviors may lead to severe consequences.

The last decade, in fact, has been abundant in numerous examples of corruption scandals in modern organizations and instances of management misconduct that have eroded public faith (such as Enron, WorldCom, Tyco, Adelphia, Arthur Andersen, and Parmalat). These repeated misconducts have led scholars to pay more attention to the so-called "dark side" of organizations.

In the current book and journal publications, the "dark side" is pursuit as abnormal, dysfunctional, or pathological aspects of business and education. Indeed, we should say that the "dark side" is not exceptional: it is a part of the normal community of everyday organizational activities.

There are three main reasons for this book. First, since there is a highly active dark side to the organizations, which is quite unknown in management studies, this book attempts to shed the light on the practical challenges for business practice and for higher education management that come from misconduct occurring in various aspects of business and educational environment.

Second, research on the "dark side" is a new, emerging source of research in the area of business and higher education management.

Finally, it is virtually impossible to carry all the works and research on the development of positive, bright sides of business and higher education without a thorough knowledge and understanding of the destructive, dark sides of organizations that have led and still lead to the collapse of many organizations and a decline in public confidence in the corporations and their leaders.

Keywords

business ethics and integrity, business misconducts, dark side, higher education

Contents

Acknowledgments

We thank all chapter authors who met deadlines, engaged ideas, responded to feedback, and wrote magnificent chapters that make this book amazing. We are proud to have had the opportunity to work with all of them. We are indebted to our reviewers for their valuable and thoughtful suggestions that have enriched this book. We are greatly indebted to Anna Sworowska and Andrea Tomo—our research associates and colleagues—whose editorial acumen is reflected on every page of this volume.

Especially, we would like to thank Oliver Laasch, Editor of the United Nations Principles for Responsible Management Education Collection (PRME) and Rob Zwettler, Executive Acquisitions Editor, Business Expert Press, for their continuous support.

PART I
Introduction

CHAPTER 1

Dark Sides of Business and Higher Education Management

Agata Stachowicz-Stanusch and Gianluigi Mangia

There are several reasons for this book. The very first reason has been provided by the knowhow (practice) in management, since the last decade has been abundant in numerous examples of corruption scandals in modern organizations and instances of management misconduct that have eroded public faith (such as Enron, WorldCom, Tyco, Adelphia, Arthur Andersen, and Parmalat). It made us realize that there is a highly active dark side to the organizations, which is quite unknown in management studies. However, majority of the research and scientific publications on business and education management have been focusing on the positive, even romantic aspects of the organizations, leaders' behavior, the analysis of the positive influence of these behaviors on the members of a given organization, and organizations as a whole.

In the current book and journal publications, the "dark side" is recognized as abnormal, dysfunctional, or pathological aspects of business and education, while the "dark side" is not exceptional; it is a part of the normal community of everyday organizational activities. Secondly, research on the "dark side" is a new, emerging source of research in the area of business and higher education management.

Thirdly, one can observe a significant gap in the market for scientific publications, both non-serial publications and periodicals on the aforementioned topics. Based on our personal experience, it could be the first book (and for sure it is one of the few books) on this subject, in the world.

Fourth, it is virtually impossible to carry all the works and research on the development of positive, bright sides of business and higher education without a thorough knowledge and understanding of the destructive, dark sides of organizations that have led and still lead to the collapse of many organizations and a decline in public confidence in the corporations and their leaders.

The book is divided into two separate volumes, each of which consists of three parts.

The first volume starts with this introduction: "Dark Sides of Business and Higher Education Management" by the editors.

In the second part "Theorizing in the Shadow (of Higher Education Management)," Rosalie Holian's chapter "The Emperor's New Clothes: Learning How to Deal with the Undiscussable" explores theory and practice in ethical decision-making behavior and links to management education, including change and development, individual reflection, and learning. This is made through the use of a story about an Emperor who was tricked into parading naked in public after his, and his advisors' better judgment was compromised by vanity and delusion. There are parallels between this tale and the ways in which leaders may not only lack insight about how their behavior appears to others, but also prevent others from providing important feedback. The chapter describes examples of what can go on in the dark side of the organizations, some reasons these situations occur, and suggests some possible solutions.

In the third chapter, "Whistle-Blowing and Education Management," Raimondo Ingrassia analyzes the personal, organizational, juridical, social, cultural, and political factors influencing the decision-making process of denunciation of wrongdoings. Then, the issues related to the implementation of a whistle-blowing training program are addressed. The features related to the various phases of the program, such as needs analysis, objectives and contents, teaching methods, and evaluation of results, are discussed. The author concludes that the aim of a whistle-blowing training program should be to create potential and build up awareness regarding the subject, rather than to convert into action what might be an absolutely extraordinary and undesirable episode in the life of an organization.

Tomo et al. in the chapter "Integrity and Ethics in Higher Education: The Role Played by Teachers and Theories in Forming New Managers," aim to understand the role of professors in forming future managers. This is done by analyzing the perspective of business students on the relevance of ethical issues in their present work and in their future as managers and to have a better understanding of how students assess ethics in comparison with others manager traits. In this way, the authors aim to underline that management education should respond to the need of training the managers able to recognize that their authority also requires an understanding and acquisition of responsibility. This means that management education should move beyond a technical view of management, and should increasingly show concern for its ethical dimension and its impact on the society and natural environment.

The third part "Light and Darkness in Higher Education Management" opens with the contribution by Fabiola Gerpott and Sven C. Voelpel "The Dark Side of the Transformational Leadership Paradigm: Why Leadership Education Curricula Need to Be Reconsidered." In this chapter, the authors systematically reviewed the last three years (2012–2014) of literature on new teaching methods published in the journal *Academy of Management Learning and Education*. Their work concludes that although some promising avenues have been explored, there is a need of highly innovative concepts that not merely regard leadership as an "add-on" topic to general management education but that integrates human resource management into other disciplines.

In the chapter "Bullying and Single Cases of Harassment in Higher Education Organizations: Managerial Solutions to Eliminate the Problem," Jolita Vveinhardt analyzes the destructive relationships between the employees of higher education institutions as organizational problems that prevent the staff of the organizations from revealing themselves and from realization of their potential. The aim is to analyze the prevalence of bullying in relationships between the employees of higher education institutions, distinguishing the most frequent methods of terrorization of co-workers in higher education organizations, and form managerial solutions to eliminate the problem. Unethical, destructive actions used in relationships between the employees of higher education institutions are identified; possible individual and organizational causes and consequences are discussed. The mechanism of making managerial decisions in dealing with the problems of destructive relationships between the employees of higher education institutions is presented; recommendations on improvement of the system based on the qualitative research are provided.

In McInerney and Mader's chapter "The Dark Side of Higher Education Administration: The Untold Story of Women in Leadership." the authors attempt to shed light on the hidden dark side of higher education administration and its impact on women in leadership roles. Through the personal stories of women who ventured out of their faculty roles and entered academic administration, issues of communication and power as well as undertones of trust and mistrust, manipulation, leadership, and gender stereotyping emerge. The personal and anecdotal descriptions of the experiences show remarkable consistency in their pattern, as the women move from excitement and enthusiasm to frustration and understanding. While new female administrators grow professionally, they also become more cynical as they transition from the brightness and newness of their positions to the shadows of the darkness. Although the learning curve was steep and painful among those women sampled, most chose to stay in administration and are quite effective in their role.

Kamal Tandon and Soma Kamal Tandon in their chapter "Conspiratory Maneuverings: Tackling Them in Educational Institutions" discuss the "evil somebody" and attempt to understand the concept of conspiracy at work. The authors try to identify the reasons for conspiracy, the types of conspiracy, and the impact thereof. Conspiracy at work is an unethical strategy adopted for personal and professional gain. The impact of conspiracy is manifold: it has a negative as well as positive impact; it has an impact on productivity, discipline, employee retention and recruitment cost, brand image, and the psychological mindset of the employees. The chapter, then, culminates with ways to tackle these conspiracies with instances of conspiracy in educational institutions.

The second volume of this book concerns specific problems of business and higher education management and focuses on individual behaviors and perceptions developing our knowledge of the dark sides of the discussed issues in different organizational contexts.

This book is authored by a range of authors from all over the world. They provide us with examples of some irregularity in the business and in the education management context. Some theoretical and practical contributions into the topic of organizational social irresponsibility, corruption, and unethical behavior were included. We hope it will be a worthy inspiration for struggling with the dark sides of business and higher education management.

PART II

Theorizing in the Shadow (of Higher Education Management)

CHAPTER 2

The Emperor's New Clothes: Learning How to Deal with the Undiscussable

Rosalie Holian

College of Business, School of Management, RMIT University

Introduction

In order to understand the ethical issues, dilemmas, and outcomes, it is important to consider the context in which the norms and values exist, the past history and current setting, place where, and time when actions are played out. It is also necessary to pay attention to the perceptions of and the impacts on the people directly and indirectly involved, which may include organizational members and other stakeholders. In a global world of work and in local workplaces with members from diverse backgrounds, traditions, and cultures, there can be more than just one right way to do things. While holding true to one's values can still be seen as having personal integrity, in some situations, this can be perceived as rigidity and imposing the values of a dominant group on others who may not agree that this is the best available option. There may be alternative options that are equally good, equally bad, or have mixed implications. So, how should we choose? In many cases, the answer may be "that depends" on the context and people involved; there is often no simple solution, short-cut, or checklist to make a good decision.

While aspects of business ethics can be "taught" from a general theoretical or philosophical perspective, and this can assist with the generation of options and judgment of competing factors, ethical management decisions also often need to be based on the first principles, taking into consideration the specific context, history, and stakeholders involved. This requires attention to be placed on emotions and processes as well as the cognitive content of thinking with reflection, evaluation, critique, and understanding not only what we think is "right," but also how it is that we know this.

Paying attention to the ethical issues can raise awareness of dilemmas, emergent problems that cannot easily be described, and concerns about these may cause some feelings of stress until these are addressed or resolved. However, being aware of the nature of the ethical issues can also help reduce anxiety and uncertainty by providing individuals with some clarity about what is right and wrong, particularly when they are asked to cross a line, when they are not comfortable to do so. Facing ethical dilemmas can provoke feelings of worry related to the need to take actions that involve some risk or uncertainty. While having laws, rules, and guidelines may generally help reduce uncertainty about what is acceptable as "right," at times, acting within the law can still be regarded as unethical, and in order to be ethical can sometimes involve bending, if not breaking rules.

The Emperor's New Clothes

In the children's nursery story usually entitled "The Emperor's New Clothes," based on the translations of the original tale penned by Hans Christian Andersen, not only the Emperor, but also the trusted advisors and members of the court are hoodwinked by confidence tricksters who claim to weave a beautiful cloth that is visible only to those who are wise and well-informed. These confidence tricksters pretend to be master weavers as well as tailors, require expensive resources, fine silks, and gold thread, and go to elaborate lengths over a period of time to create the illusion that they are creating a spectacular set of garments, which does not exist in reality. Not only are they able to maintain this illusion, they are also bestowed awards and titles, acknowledging the excellence of their invisible work output. They appeal to vanity and use flattery to deceive the leader, senior advisors, and members of the community that they are seeing something that does not actually exist. While some observers may have doubts because they cannot see what others describe, none have the courage to say they cannot see it.

This pattern of human behavior is similar to what was much later described as symptoms of processes involved in "Group Think" (Janis 1972; Sims 1992b; Sims and Sauser 2013). The members of the group assume or imagine that others understand and agree with what is being done, and although they see things differently, they do not feel free to admit that they don't understand or don't agree. When advisors have doubts, but do not express these, this can allow the leader to make serious or embarrassing mistakes, the advisors can neglect their duty if they do not offer fearless, full, and frank feedback. In the children's story, there is widespread collusion to pretend the imaginary cloth is real, until a child, as the *voice of innocence*, speaks this out loud and the message is heard. Only then do people in the crowd and the members of the court allow themselves to accept the truth, although even then they continue to maintain the pretense in order to finish the parade. The children's story usually ends at this point, leaving it to the imagination as to what happens to the confidence tricksters when the Emperor and advisors return to the palace, and how the Emperor deals with the loss of face and reputation from having paraded naked in front of the populace.

This children's story also illustrates how the confidence tricksters can be charming and manipulative; they are aware of the weaknesses of others and use them to appeal to their vanity, using flattery, and lead their marks to believe that they are being offered a unique new opportunity, when in reality, they are being lied to and cheated. The confidence tricksters want what is best for themselves and know how to manipulate others' thoughts and feelings to get them to agree to do things that will benefit them. They can read other people and get them to like and trust them. The tricksters know that they are using others to get what they want, but can justify this by saying that the others have agreed, it was legal, even if the way they got them to agree was unethical. The mark and their advisors have the opportunity to say no; however, they get caught up in the promise of something too good to be true, and set aside their intelligence to go along with it. Those being deceived, and their key advisors, choose to "turn a blind eye," so that they do not have to see, admit, and challenge what is going on. This creates shared collusion between those who want to be aligned with those in power. To question those in power is to risk becoming the object of their anger, to be marginalized and expelled from the inner chamber. When the illusion is shattered and deception revealed, they may not admit that they were tricked, that they trusted those they should have avoided; it may be easier to call it a "mistake" or a new idea that didn't work out. There are similarities between the confidence tricksters in the story of the Emperor's New Clothes and how pathological narcissists behave in organizations. What they ask to be done is to their advantage, often at a cost to others. They can be charming and manipulative, using flattery and peer pressure to mold others to support what they want. In order to reduce the impact of falling prey to the confidence tricksters, leaders need to have a "bull dust" detector turned on full power, and encourage key advisors to have the courage to openly question assumptions, raise concerns, and address areas of doubt. If leaders are approachable, they may be able to be told anything reasonable when this is well-intended and in their best interests, including that they seem to be acting in an unreasonable way.

Narcissistic Managers and Leaders

For the purposes of this chapter, pathological narcissistic behavior is defined as actions that are remorseless, without conscience or concern for others, lacking empathy and human values, self-absorbed with an inflated self-image, cold and exploitative, and with a strong need to be in control and not criticized (Holian 2006). Pathological narcissism is not found only in those in leadership roles in organizations; if it is role modeled by those in the senior executive positions, it can spread across all levels and into all work teams. The ways people work in such dark places sit in stark contrast to those striving to embrace "Authentic Leadership" (Avolio 2011), where inspirational motivation, intellectual stimulation, individualized consideration, and idealized influence are grounded with transparency, self-awareness, balanced processing, and moral/ethical behavior. If the senior leaders display ethical leadership, this contributes to the development of an ethical culture (Schaubroeck et al. 2012), which in turn promotes shared expectations about and norms that support ethical cognitions and behaviors in subordinates.

Despite the long history of promoting "good" leadership practices in management education programs, both those conducted by skilled consultants to industry and those offered as part of postgraduate academic qualifications, leaders are still selected and rewarded for "Anti-Leader" behaviors, which can be manipulative and perverse. Not only individuals but also organizations can be seen as having a narcissistic culture or identity. Duchon and Drake define "extreme narcissistic organizations" as those with:

> Self-obsessed identities such that collective self-aggrandizement, a profound sense of entitlement, and denial become normal. Such an identity makes cynicism, exploitation, and a lack of empathy acceptable. Such an identity is morally flawed: It does not contain a predisposition to act virtuously. (Duchon and Drake 2009, 305)

The "Bathsheba Syndrome" described by Ludwig and Longenecker (1993, 265–69) is related to the story of King David in which a "good, bright, successful, popular, and visionary king, David, was nearly destroyed because he could not control his desire to have something that he knew it was wrong for him to have—Bathsheba." As part of the "cover up" following this impropriety, Bathsheba's husband, an officer away in battle, is first recalled by the King and then sent to the battlefront to die. Ludwig and Longenecker suggest that success can be an antecedent to ethical failure because it carries with it not only the benefits, such as privileged access and control of resources, but also a "dark side" with negative by-products, which can lead to poor decisions, including a loss of strategic focus due to complacency and neglect and an inflated belief in one's own personal ability to manipulate outcomes. They identify similar patterns of behavior in modern media stories about "good, respected, successful leaders, men and women of intelligence, talent, and vision, who suddenly self-destruct as they reach the apex of their careers." While they do not suggest that success will necessarily lead to such negative behaviors, there could be powerful temptations, and therefore, the potential for this to occur.

Can sociopathic members of organizations be identified and stopped before it is too late? asked Pech and Slade (2007, 264), and their answer was "probably not," as the applicants for management roles may be able to display behaviors that appear to be "oozing with wit, charm, audacity, and enthusiasm" and may even stand out in interviews as appearing to have "attractive personal qualities." They suggest that the best ways to address this may not be increased attempts to avoid wrong selection decisions, which can be difficult to do given the clever manipulative skills of such individuals, but rather to develop organizational cultures that promote and practice values and expectations that do not foster or tolerate sociopathic management behavior, do not reward such behaviors, and where the organizational members will not stand by silently as they manipulate others for their own purposes. As Clements and Washbush (1999, 170) have asked, "if there is a dark side to leadership, isn't it also likely that there is a dark side to followership, as well?" They go on to argue that followers have a responsibility to recognize, understand, and deal appropriately with the darker sides of behavior, both their own and also that of others, including managers and leaders. If sufficient numbers of organizational members are involved, then organizational resistance to unethical behavior can be effective. Godkin and Allcorn (2011, 568) outline how awareness of destructive narcissistic leadership behavior can foster resistance, so that instead of standing up against wrongdoing becoming a "career-ending decision" for an individual, they are protected by their colleagues in a similar way to how a "herd of buffalo comes to the defense of a calf set upon by lions." In the children's story of the Emperor's new clothes, the "whistleblower" was heard, and through the act of speaking out, enabled others to acknowledge what was wrong.

Emotional Intelligence and Ethical Behavior

Emotional Intelligence or EI can be defined (Caruso and Salovey 2004) as having sets of skills, which go beyond being able to be rational, logical, calm, and straightforward (which alone may be ineffective), and these include:

> Identifying how all of the key participants feel, themselves included; using these feelings to guide the thinking and reasoning of the people involved; understanding how feelings might change

and develop as events unfold; and managing to stay open to the data of feelings and integrating them into decisions and actions. (Caruso and Salovey 2004, xiv–xv)

EI can be seen as a form of maturity or wisdom. It does not simply mean (Goleman 1998, 6–7) "being nice," particularly if being nice would involve avoiding tough, but necessary feedback or conversations, or allowing "free rein" to openly express feelings. EI is associated with being able to understand and appropriately manage both one's own and others' emotions. The published literature on EI to date only briefly mentions the aspects of ethics, such as moral character, integrity, honesty, justice, and spirituality. Caruso and Salovey (2004, 171–72) discuss how an emotionally intelligent manager may not necessarily be a good manager, as this expertise can be used to manipulate others; however, true EI includes empathy for others, which they hope means a well-developed moral perspective. Mesmer-Magnus et al. (2008, 234) provide empirical support for a positive relationship between EI and both individual ethicality and individual perceptions about the ethics of others. Their findings suggest that the development programs that result in enhanced EI may also increase integrity and ethical behavior and reduce wrongdoing.

Many approaches to learning how to enhance the ethical interpersonal behavior have focused on the use of cognitive skills or "ethical maturity" (Wickham and O'Donohue 2012), drawing on what can be observed rather than underlying attitudes and feelings. Gaudine and Thorne (2001, 176) outline how "the cognitive-developmental perspective on ethical decision making has been grounded in a tradition, which focuses on cognitive processes" with a lack of attention to the influence, impact, and importance of emotions. They argue that positive and negative emotions, level of emotional arousal, and mood or feeling state have an impact on the processes of ethical sensitivity, prescriptive reasoning, ethical motivation, and ethical character, which in turn impact the outcomes: identification of an ethical dilemma, prescriptive judgment, ethical intention, and ethical behavior. Emotions can have an impact on decision making, whether this is recognized and wanted or not, and to deny, ignore, or discard these influences as irrational factors can result in poor outcomes. The ethical components of business, education, training, and development programs need to consider the impact of the issues associated with emotions, individual values and beliefs, personality variables, interpersonal relationships, organizational culture, and group dynamics.

Despite the calls for EI, and ethical intelligence (Wickham and O'Donohue 2012), to be considered as important as cognitive intelligence, there seems to be a continuation in industry and educational institutions to value those who have narcissistic tendencies over those with more well-rounded authentic leadership skills. Where organizations and communities privilege logic and rationality, and ignore the positive contribution of intuition and values, there is a loss of access to understanding the impact of fear and hope, perceptions and dreams, on individual and group behavior. This can create a hostile environment in which pathological narcissism is accepted by members and leaders, with detrimental impacts on the internal and external working relationships and productivity.

Research on the potential relationship between high or low scores on measures of EI and behaviors related to workplace-based ethical issues and values has only recently started to emerge (such as Angelidis and Ibrahim 2011; Athota and O Connor 2014; Deshpande and Joseph 2009; Perryer and Scott-Ladd 2014). A limitation of many investigations of ethical behavior in organizations has been a tendency for university-based researchers to draw on students as participants. It can be argued that part-time postgraduate business students, typically those undertaking an MBA, who work full-time in middle-level roles in organizations may be able to be considered as similar to typical managers. Although the popular image of a manager may indeed be similar to the student profile of many MBA classes, in terms of both gender and age, this may be more a stereotype than an accurate representation of the population of all those in the management roles. If one is prepared to accept the argument that business students are a reasonable source of research participants, there still remains doubt as to whether how they respond to surveys and questionnaires administered in class, as part of their course of study is similar to how they would respond in their work setting. The postgraduate students in a university setting may not be as willing and able to be honest and open about issues as participants in the in-organization management development programs engaged in learning with work peers. Which responses may be more accurate and closer to the actual attitudes and behavior in organizations remains to be seen.

Nevertheless, the outcomes of research involving students, such as Angelidis and Ibrahim (2011), which was part of a larger cross-national study of business ethics is of potential interest and value to the management educators and also organizations and managers seeking to enhance skills in ethical decision making. They gathered information from managers enrolled in MBA programs across five universities in the United States using an instrument to measure EI as well as the ethics position questionnaire based on the work of Forsyth (1980), which has four categories related to the high or low scores on the two dimensions of idealism and relativism: absolutists, situationists, subjectivists, and exceptionists. They found that those with high idealism (absolutists and situationists) had similar EI scores (greater than 4.0 on a 5-point scale), while those with low idealism (subjectivists and exceptionists) had lower EI scores (below the neutral point of 3.0), which they interpreted as suggesting "strong evidence that the level of EI is strongly correlated with ethical behavior."

If aspects of EI can be learned, and training and development can enhance some of these skills, can this contribute to better ethical behavior in the workplace? This is also still in need of further investigation, as while having a high score on EI may correlate positively with the scores on questions related to ethical behavior; this may simply indicate well-developed social awareness, understanding of culture and norms, and the ability to identify the emotions of others as well as one's own. While this provides a basis for knowing what "should" be done, it does not necessarily follow that the highest values of most good-for-all will necessarily be followed. In the previous research (Holian 2002, 2006), the participants reported that their values and behavior may vary depending on the context, and there could be a difference in how they thought and behaved at work, and how they operated in their family, social setting, and community. Just because they may be aware that there was a "higher" way to behave, did not mean that they would choose that option; this depended on their evaluation of "what is in it for me," the potential risks and rewards, and who else may benefit or be harmed.

Understanding the feelings and motivations of others can be used to engage, manipulate, and convince them to alter their preferred behavior for self-serving and unethical reasons. Like the confidence tricksters in the children's story, narcissists can be charming and persuasive when they see this as a way to get what they want, and may be able to fool others for quite some time as they are prepared to postpone immediate gratification for longer term, greater, personal gains.

Ethical Issues and Management

Managers need to make decisions under conditions of uncertainty, and deal with the outcomes of these actions. The ideal amount and type of information available before a decision needs to be made may not always be available, and so, there can be some risk involved. Ethical dilemmas can arise in gray areas where there are no clear guidelines, where the existing rules offer conflicting points of view, where the ways things have been done may no longer seem to apply due to the changes in the internal or external environment, and when there are diverse approaches that are valid alternative ways of operating.

Ethical issues can become a problem for managers, work groups, and organizations when the decision makers involved do not have sufficient skills to deal with the ethical dilemmas they face. This includes those who are indecisive and can't make a decision, as well as those who can't see the ethical dimensions of situations, who do the wrong thing themselves, allow wrongdoing to occur, and indeed, may order others to act illegally and unethically. Practicing managers deal with ethical issues on several fronts, including human resource management, provision of information to senior management, doing what is necessary to meet the organizational targets and goals, dealing with external stakeholders, clients, and customers, and maintaining their own personal values. Ethical issues they may need to deal with in the organizations can include bullying and harassment, nepotism and unfair favoritism in work assignments, job promotions, and workplace rewards. In order to get things done on time, they may cut corners on materials or Occupational Health and Safety standards, offer bribes and incentives, breach confidentiality, and deliberately mislead others, perhaps by omitting to provide key information or by lying and cheating. Taking these actions may be a calculated risk, which if discovered, can be dealt with by an apology and seemingly made right, or may be able to be covered up with no requirement to revisit and change what was done.

The development and maintenance of good working relationships characterized by trust can be regarded (McAllister 1995, 30) as having both cognitive and affective foundations, and "some level of cognition-based trust may be necessary for affect-based trust to develop." Trusting in an authority figure, such as a manager, can help to reduce employees' concerns about dealing with uncertainty and complexity; however, as Colquitt et al. (2012, 5) point out, "choosing to do so also opens the door to potential exploitation." The findings reported by Colquitt and Rodell (2011, 1202) suggest that while perceptions about integrity based on the past experience can influence expectations, in order to be seen as fair, it is also important that managers continue to behave honestly, use sound values and principles to guide actions, "stick to their word" and demonstrate that they care. Where trust has been established, and a level of vulnerability allowed to develop, there can also be a potential for the betrayal of that trust. Elangovan and Shapiro (1998, 563–64) identified and defined three types of betrayal: accidental, premeditated, and opportunistic, and propose that "what leads employees to betray others in organizations" is related to the organizational, interpersonal, and intrapersonal characteristics.

Unethical managers may be able to "act as if" they have integrity and concern for others, when this is not genuine, and by doing so, may be able to establish working relationships (at least temporarily) where others come to accept them to be trustworthy. When this deceit and manipulation is revealed through later betrayal, the effects on those who allowed themselves to become vulnerable may be devastating. It would be useful to be able to examine if there are differences in the processes used in the development and betrayal of trust between the employees and managers who display extremes of negative or pathological, behavioral characteristics and managers whose range of good and poor behaviors fall more within a mid or "normal" range. Discovering this may depend on continuing research that uses what Goldman (2006, 409) described as the "golden bridge under construction linking leadership, management, and psychology under the shared umbrella of toxic individuals and systems."

Why Do Leaders Behave Badly?

Narcissistic leaders can have attractive qualities and interpersonal skills that make them appear to be worthy of emulating, and perhaps, this is one of their most dangerous characteristics. Not all leaders who are self-confident and optimistic are both emotionally intelligent and ethical. While it is possible to devise laws and codes that cover the key areas of prohibited behavior, point to cases of publically known "ethical failures," and share inspirational "heroic" ethical behavior stories about the choices between good and evil, between these extremes there is a continuum with many shades of gray. While making a profit may be good, making more profit at the expense of honesty or by exploiting the vulnerable is not a greater good. Where do you draw the line? How do you learn how to draw your own lines, and how to communicate and collaborate to agree on what is reasonable to expect of each other in this particular setting? What worked in the past may not be what is needed now, but it is also possible that what we have been doing is better than what we are being asked to change to do instead.

The dark side of organizations and leadership can be the other side of the same coin, the side that is hidden from view, or the side we are not currently paying attention to. While we may like to shine a light on what we prefer to be on view, we know there are other things going on in the shadows. If we do not recognize this, then we may not be prepared to deal with the necessary problems. If the issue is too large and too public, the key decision makers and organization may be humiliated and scapegoated in the public media. We could all become part of the next case study to be used in business management ethics classes as an example of what not to do, and may agree with others that the problems and outcomes are now clear in hindsight.

If we stop and reflect on what seems to have gone wrong in the case studies we use, can we really know for sure that those managers were all that different from others making similar decisions elsewhere? If so, will punishing them help prevent others from making the same type of choices, or does this make them more careful and better at covering things up? Will teams exclude members who may have different values, which could challenge assumptions about what it is OK to do? Will the "voice of innocence" be intimidated into silence, ignored, or heard? Some executive teams may choose to have a role for a devil's or angel's advocate to help avoid "group think;" however, this can also be used to bullet proof rationalizations and justifications, and plan how to create distance and deniability, rather than to reconsider options based on wider considerations, possible and probable consequences.

Business and management ethics education may overly rely on the "horror" stories of what went wrong in publically named and shamed companies, with players being singled out for personal investigation and punishment. Is this much different from the stocks in the market square, heads on poles, stripping of goods, and banishment of an entire family line, which may have taken place in medieval or ancient times? Did this work then, and will it work now? Unfortunately, the problem is that these stories can be gripping; how the mighty and powerful have fallen or been toppled. They can get the attention of those we think may need to learn a lesson from others' mistakes, to avoid repeating these. Organizations fear that the same could happen; they may set up training and development and clarify internal written codes and procedures. The purpose of these changes may not only be to try to prevent wrongdoing, but also to have a firm basis on which they can shift blame to individuals who are found guilty, having documented that the organization has stated that these actions are not allowed.

However, in some cases, this may be well-known to be merely the official "espoused theory," rather than what the organizations know and allow to happen in practice as "theory in use" (Argyris 1991). These mixed and conflicting messages can make it even more difficult for the managers and organizational members to work out what to do, and can simply lead to double dealing and hidden cover ups. As Argyris (1991) argues, "smart" people can have difficulty learning if they are either not aware or do not accept feedback that their current behavior is suboptimal because of errors associated with the "single loop" thinking, defensive routines, and other "undiscussables" (Argyris 1986, 1990). Many groups and organizations have undiscussables; these may be small (we don't comment on that person's hair) or they may be large (behavior that is unethical and illegal), but we don't talk about it. We also don't talk about how we don't talk about it, so, if you are new or not in the know, we don't tell you that we don't talk about it, and when you try to talk about it, we ignore, deny, or cover it up. In other words, the undiscussability of the undiscussable is not discussable, perhaps because we think that if we don't admit there is a problem, then we won't have to do anything to try to change it, even if we wanted to.

What Can Go Wrong: Examples from the "Dark Side" of the Organization

The undiscussables present in work groups, management teams, and boards are part of the fabric of business as usual in organizations, whether public or private, including higher educational institutions. As aforementioned, the "theory espoused" by an organization about internal decision making, including human resource management practices, can be very different from the "theory in use" (Argyris 1991). The behavior of members of an executive group can reflect values associated with a shared understanding to not "rock the boat," get away with what you can, and let others get away with not being called to account either. There may be an assumption that rewards and recognition will be related to who you know rather than how well you perform, the antithesis to "putting people first" and practicing what we preach.

These differences between what the senior management says they want others to do and what they do themselves may be openly acknowledged and discussed behind closed doors. The aspects of organizational strategies, policies, codes, and procedures may be regarded as part of a façade or "window dressing," largely irrelevant to the day-to-day practice. Other ethical issues may be seen as the personal "hobby horse" of one senior leader, which one has to pay at least some lip service to, particularly if records are kept, and it could be reported to the head office.

Power, Influence, and Decision Making

There can be an undercurrent of desire for power and what seems to be an open invitation by those who hold power extended to others to seek to influence their decisions. This can apply to interactions and decisions made within the organization as well as work with external agencies or individuals. A long-term detailed account may be kept of favors "banked" as well as slights that are owed revenge. Personal and professional secrets can be held as a type of ransom that is used to force actions and decisions that may not otherwise have been taken. Relationships and liaisons with other staff, personal likes and dislikes, hopes and fears, and past successes and mistakes can all be considered as legitimate inputs into decision making.

It can be difficult to make decisions at an executive level when there are many hidden as well as some not-so-hidden agendas, competing interests, and potential repercussions on the balancing of accounts as to whether favors are owed or would be owed, and this can lead to considerable delays in decision making, for many months or indefinite periods. These delays can take so long that an opportunity passes by or other factors arise to change the situation, so that negotiations and discussions need to be revisited, resulting in further delay. For example, while a human resource management decision, such as a key promotion, could be made on the basis of knowledge, skills, and merit, and following appropriate rules and regulations, there may be other factors that are also considered. When giving a reason for a decision is considered necessary, which may not be always, the official reasons given may often not be the true story or whole picture, but rather justifications chosen from a range of ideas about how it could "best" be presented to those outside the decision-making group.

Secrecy and Solidarity

There can be strong norms of "cabinet solidarity" within a board of directors or senior executive team regarding the details of deliberations. However, individual members of these groups may still pass on some information about the "real" reasons for decisions, in strict confidence, to their "inner circle" of managers who report directly to them. This can socialize those managers to comply with the senior executive's wishes by teaching them how the power grid works, who is "in," and who is "on the way out," how to "get ahead," what might alarm or annoy the members of the board or executive, and the punishments or rewards passed out to people who have either displeased or pleased them.

Senior executives may hold meetings with their own management team in private, where arguments about judgment and integrity based on law, rules, or fairness are counteracted with other information about the effects on those who were owed or would be owed favors as a result. Having information about the real reasons for decisions can have an effect of reducing the opposition of those charged with implementing decisions and ensuring compliance by others. Knowing these real reasons and having discussed alternative options that were rejected, although unable to disclose these outside the management team, can involve collusion and bind the members firmly to protect and support the decisions by the board or top executives.

Improper Decisions

"Improper" decisions can range from those contrary to law to those in breach of local guidelines. At times, such decisions can be made despite individual members having expressed full knowledge of the nature, content, and intent or spirit of relevant legislation, rules, codes, or policies. However, the predominant reason for having paid close attention to these may have been in order to find "loop-holes," which permit the chosen action to be taken. This rather "legalistic" approach to problem solving can be based on the assumption that written proscriptions are "objective facts," which need to be addressed, while perceptions and opinions about what was appropriate in a given case are more "subjective" and can be ignored.

The focus on identifying "loop-holes" that could justify decisions, while often clever and useful from the "intended decision makers" perspective, does not always promote an ethical approach to problem solving. A board or top executive team may seek "expert" interpretations and additional information from the external or internal specialists or professionals in regard to the application of laws or rules to a particular case and the range of the possible outcomes of alternative decisions. This advice can be used to smooth the path for the intended decision by identifying pockets of resistance, which can then be lobbied or neutralized, and to identify the expected "price" of a complaint, if one were to be made and found proven. Where there is full knowledge of what "ought" to be done, the decision makers may deliberately choose to make contrary decisions, ranging from the illegal to those "merely" contrary to espoused organizational policy and values. These decision-making processes may be less than optimal, from not only an ethical perspective, if members of a board or top executive team address problems or issues by first asking "what do we want to do?" rather than properly investigating the context, considering the possible causes of the apparent problem, and the full range of alternative options available.

Some decision makers may have extensive personal networks, and as a result of this, be able to obtain advance knowledge about emergent issues, which allow them to come prepared with what may seem to be "objective facts" to significantly influence decisions in a particular direction. It is also possible to imply or embellish information about situations and use this to lobby relevant parties to achieve desired outcomes. Lobbying may be very selective and not involve seeking input from all those effected by a decision, but rather a selected few informants or confidents trusted to keep the issues secret.

Discussing the Undiscussable?

The message about making even a mild internal complaint, as distinct from whistleblowing to an external regulator or the media, about what appears to be a deliberate and unambiguous breach of law, policy, or rules may be quite clear: "don't bother." The organizational members may understand fully well the reasons why they should "put up with the heat or get out of the kitchen," no one likes a trouble maker, team players don't talk out of school, and in the end, "nothing will happen, except to you." Pointing out the "undiscussables" may not only be not appreciated, but actively discouraged, and those who try to be too open and too honest can be punished (Sims 1992a). In the children's story, the Emperor's advisors may have been afraid to tell him that he had been tricked into wearing no clothes.

Those who complain about improper practices may no longer be trusted with information about what is really going on in the organization. They can be "frozen out" of informal networks that not only make it easier to get work done, but also alert people to dangers and opportunities, and offer social support to soften the effects of the day-to-day hassles. While friendly colleagues may still provide some assistance off the record, this may not extend to backing them up in writing or putting their own career on the line. One effect of labeling the internal whistleblowers as "troublemakers" is that, it allows those who participated or turned a blind eye to avoid feelings of guilt about doing so, by justifying it as "loyalty" to superiors and the organization. The effect on those who complain or are left in difficult situations can be increasing hopelessness or cynicism, either continuing to protest although no one seems to listen, or accepting the situation and refraining from complaining again, and not supporting protests by others in the future.

Intimidation and Cover-up

When a senior executive observes what they believe to be illegal, unethical, or inequitable decisions and behavior, and wants to examine ways to reduce or eliminate these, they may arrange a private meeting with the Chair of the board or CEO. Prior to such a meeting, they may collect evidence and prepare a report that they pass on in advance of their face-to-face discussion, where they may provide additional detail. However, when such a meeting finally does take place, it may become clear that the purpose is not to address the reported problems, but rather to determine how these could be "covered-up." They may be asked to suggest answers as to how what was done, or not done, can be justified if it becomes publically known. There may be little concern about an ongoing pattern of the reported past offences and lack of ethical outcomes, or that improper actions will continue to occur, as there may be no intention to investigate complaints. The purpose for bringing potentially embarrassing ethical issues to the attention of the Chair or CEO may only be to mitigate the dangers of exposure.

When the improper behavior involves senior executives, they may be made aware that a complaint has been made, and in some instances, this may involve "counseling" them that certain actions are not appropriate. However, it could also be a way of warning them to be more careful about what they say and do in the presence of the person who raised these (albeit legitimate) concerns. For example, a CEO may arrange for the issue to either be listed as a topic on a formal meeting agenda, or if it is sensitive, call an informal meeting of the members of the board or executive. While this may be a way to confront those involved and "resolve" the issues, it could also be seen as an attempt to intimidate the person who made the report. There may be no warning that the issue is going to be raised and it may come as an ambush, at least to the person who thought they had raised the problem in confidence. They may be asked to withdraw their report and complaint, and even to apologize to those seen as engaging in wrongdoing, or sign a "statement of support" for those who were responsible for the offence(s). The problem may then be considered as having been "resolved," with the issue(s) raised having been squashed, and a clear message given to all those involved that this is how complaints about ethical issues are likely to be dealt with in this organization in the future.

Can People Learn How to Make More Ethical Decisions?

In a study that involved both college freshmen and seniors, Allen et al. (2005) discovered that those earlier in their college career regarded "heart" values as more important than those who had experienced more years of tertiary education. Allen et al. (2005) ask if this may be related to how business and ethics were taught and if it:

> May be a function of our desire as business instructors to teach students to be critical thinkers. We stress the importance of using logic and reason, not emotion, in making decisions. Ultimately reinforcing the importance of using their heads and not their hearts. (Allen et al. 2005, 178)

Some years ago, I was a senior executive in a national organization, and was responsible for leading an in-house management development program working with intact work groups for a total of over 200 managers, where we explored theory, practice, and group dynamics of decision making. I also undertook a study that included gathering information from managers in a range of other organizations, exploring questions, including: what is the nature of organizational decision making involving ethical issues? What are the differences between decision makers in the ways in which they define, recognize, and address perceived ethical issues? Who are the role models for practicing managers and what do they do? and How can managers enhance their ethical decision making behaviors?

As an outcome of this work, five modes of management approaches to ethical decision making were identified: navigation, legalistic, entrepreneurial, worried, and narcissistic (Holian 2002, 2006). These modes were alternative strategies used rather than a classification of individuals into a particular category, although some showed a preference for often using a particular mode. The sets of skills underlying the different modes were comprised of combinations of high to low levels of *judgment, integrity, courage,* and *humanity.* The most commonly used mode overall was legalistic, which involved *judgment, integrity,* and *courage,* and this could well be quite a sufficient basis for decision making for the straightforward day-to-day operations. However, some, often at the most senior levels, also operated as navigators; these were able to incorporate *humanity,* a capacity for great understanding that included having a sense of humor, appreciating how it can be impossible to control the wider environment, and predict the behavior of others, allowing people "the benefit of the doubt," and a willingness to forgive and forget, rather than dwell on the past mistakes. Developing *humanity* could enhance decision making by bringing this from a rather legalistic approach to one that was closer to navigation, and this can be one aim of management development. Having developed and being able to choose combinations of the skills associated with *judgment, integrity, courage,* and *humanity* can increase the repertoire of choices and options available to decision makers, and therefore hopefully enhance decision making.

Problems dealing with ethical issues arose most often for those who were missing sufficient levels of *integrity*, leading to the use of narcissistic or entrepreneurial modes of behavior, and those lacking *courage*, who became trapped in a worried mode, knowing what should be done, but unable to take action to do it. Increased knowledge of laws, rules, and codes could raise levels of compliance, even if attitudes may not have changed, which while not yet the same as acting with *integrity* could help improve behavior in the desired direction. With practice and social reinforcement, this could produce better behavior in the workplace. However, helping people to develop *courage* when they are not ready to do what they know they should do can be more difficult. *Judgment, integrity, courage,* and *humanity* require both heart and head values to operate well. To navigate through the ethical dilemmas, we need to have a range of rational and emotional skills, judgment, and integrity, with courage and humanity (including a sense of humor).

Role Models and Leadership

When we consider who we see as "good" leaders, those we see as role models for ourselves and others, what is it about them and their behavior that makes us see them this way? If I want to be more like them and to help others to be more like them, then I need to work out what they do that attracts and inspires me. I can observe the messages they communicate both verbally and nonverbally, the content of what they say, and whether they act consistently in line with their espoused values.

Authenticity, in the sense of being centered and acting from your values, rather than an image of how you would like to be or how you think you should act–acting "as if" this were truly the case already when you are not there yet, is part of this; however, this alone is not enough. Authenticity needs to be more than that; Avolio's (2011) extended "full range leadership" model suggests that an authentic foundation includes moral/ethical behavior, balanced processing, self-awareness, and transparency. Leaders do not always act authentically; they can lie to others as well as to themselves, cheat and then cover up the cheating or pretend it isn't cheating, that it is strategy or how business is done. They may split off their authentic self, and personal values, which they may still try to operate from outside work. They can act "as if" what they do is OK, right, and even proper, as if they are the leader they think others want to see. The problem with acting is that it is not authentic or sustainable. When a mask such as this cracks what is revealed can be surprising; if you cannot hold on to your role, a dark shadow side can begin to leak out, becoming visible to both yourself as well as to others.

When I reflect on my own behavior and how I view Avolio's (2011) inspirational motivation, intellectual stimulation, individualized consideration, and idealized influence grounded with transparency, self-awareness, balanced processing, and moral/ethical behavior, I realize that this may differ from how others see things. Perhaps, this would not matter so much if workplaces had regular open dialog about our views and perceptions. Sometimes we choose to assume that what we believe we have observed with our senses is the "truth" and factual; however, others who observe the same behavior may come to a different conclusion because our observations are not value-free, they are influenced by our experiences and assumptions. Much as we may like to measure accurately and reliably and know for sure that what we know is correct, human behavior and the thinking that goes before, during, and after human action cannot be accurately measured by another person, even if it is audio- and video-recorded, even if we "scientifically" record their heart rate, respiration, and galvanic skin response.

If we have developed a good sense of self-awareness, then knowing why we think we behave in a particular way under certain circumstances can help us form hypotheses about others actions; however, their reasons may differ from ours. We may not always act in a consistent manner ourselves, so how do others interpret this? If I receive feedback that my behavior is a problem for others and accept that this is valid and want to learn how to react and behave differently, how do I do this? What needs to change? Will additional information alter my cognition, and rational thinking change my beliefs about what I notice or see, or do I also need to learn how to better regulate my emotions?

In the cognitive behavior theory, this dilemma can be approached by considering what was the activating event, our beliefs about this, what we think and feel, and how we behave based on those thoughts and feelings. Emotions and cognitions happen at the same time; sometimes, one leads to the other; however, there is no agreement as to whether there is a primacy of emotions over reason or cognitions before feelings. To look at one to the exclusion of the other is artificial and limited; however, when trying to untangle what seems to be going on, it is useful to try to slow down the process between what is observed to happen and the response, to try to work out if the response was warranted and if it helped us to achieve the best outcome.

Human behavior is influenced by emotions; humans who do not experience "normal" emotions, including empathy, can have difficulties getting along with others. The literature on social intelligence and EI and competence (Caruso and Salovey 2004; Goleman 1998) suggests that individuals can be "alexithymic," lacking understanding of and how to communicate about feelings, which makes it difficult for them to learn how to change their behavior or to attend to emotions that may be experienced by others. Feelings are natural and need to be understood in order to be dealt with, rather than denied or covered-up. Cognitive therapy (Beck 1976; Beck and Dozois 2011; Leahy 2003) pays attention to the interaction between thoughts and feelings. The "emotional schema model" developed by Leahy, Tirch, and Napolitano (2011) includes both normalized as well as negative interpretations as an outcome of paying attention to emotions that are present. When emotions can be accurately identified, and regarded as normal, people are able to accept and express these, and this can lead to experiences of validation and learning.

Leading Management Education—Values for Improvement?

What can we do in business and management education, particularly in higher educational institutions, about learning how to balance thoughts and feelings that impact the ethical behavior? As educators, how well can we promote ethical behavior in others if we are not aware of our own shortcomings? Are we afraid to speak out about what is wrong in our own industry or organization? Are we able to speak up and point out when the "Emperor" has no clothes? In an academic setting, we can be tempted to fly to theory and literature, scholarly books, and journal articles that have a limited grounding in practice. Rather than try to look at the integrated role of a manager holistically, this is broken up into small pieces that can be examined in isolation. We design a questionnaire and send it to hundreds of people in order to have empirical data, then we have counts of something(s) to analyze statistically. This is fine when measuring facts, if we asked the height and weight and age and gender of those perceived to be "good" managers (and such factors may be more correlated than we like to think). When we don't have facts, yet act as if we do, are we wearing invisible clothing?

We ask about the perceptions and subjective views about the behavior of others; however, we need to go beyond the observable facts. In the traditional academic settings, we may appear to privilege ideas over action and abstract critique from an "ivory tower" perspective over understanding and enhancing practice. This may come from considering there to be a dichotomy between what is "empirical" or "rational" versus values, meaning and emotions. Emotions may be downplayed as not as relevant because they are unpredictable and variable, and yet feelings and emotions influence what we are interested in, how we perceive it, what we acknowledge as relevant information, and what we choose to ignore or discard, as too difficult, too hard, too messy. The observable, measurable information is only a part of the whole picture, and alone, it lacks substance and coherence. Academics may admit that an overly rational approach to business strategy can be too narrow in practice, so perhaps we could acknowledge that the cognitive abilities are not all there is to being a good ethical leader.

Does this also play out in the divide of teaching versus research? While there are academic staff members (maybe more likely to be teaching faculty), who argue that one should not have to choose between being a teacher or a researcher, that you can be both and good at both, this does not seem to be the majority or dominant view in institutions of higher education. To be seen as a good researcher, there is still a strong leaning toward positivism and the concept of an objective researcher who can observe facts and arrive at "truth," which can be verified by others (valid and reliable) and replicated elsewhere. While this may be true in the areas of pure science and mathematics, when people become the objects of investigation, not only as individuals, but also how they act in large and small groups, things get more complicated.

Humans have a will, or free will, perhaps influenced by experience, peers, family, organizational culture, preferences, and attitudes which impact their behavior. Where these have been learned, they may be changed with further learning. Behavior may be able to be changed in some circumstances to fit with and meet the local requirements (and this can be a good thing); however, the underlying values and bias may not change to meet these, and this can result in cognitive dissonance. One force associated with unethical behavior in higher education institutions has been the increasing level of emphasis placed on the academic research publications and attracting external income at the expense of time and effort spent on designing and delivering teaching and learning experiences for students. While students continue to compete for entrance into limited university places, where they pay high fees for what they expect to be a professional standard of education, income available to provide these services may be diverted to fund projects that have little to do with students or teaching programs. Are higher education students no longer getting enough of what they have paid for? Is this due to poor consumer awareness, or are they being short-changed and defrauded by "confidence tricksters" promises in misleading promotional materials? As a result, are there staff and students in higher education institutions who are "wearing no clothes?" Business educators, who become aware of such issues, may face ethical dilemmas in their organization; will we able to be authentic leaders and practice what we preach about ethical behavior when this occurs?

Summary and Conclusion

To demonstrate ethical decision making, it requires both well-developed cognitive and emotional skills; these operate in conjunction and simultaneously impact each other, to seek to focus on either at the expense of the other would be short-sighted.

While there is not a universal way to address any ethical dilemma, a general approach that is useful in business settings has been described by Coghlan (2010, 2012, 2013), put simply, this process requires four components or steps: be attentive, be intelligent, be reasonable, and be responsible. It involves attending to the relevant information, including thoughts and feelings, considering the information gathered intelligently, taking into account the available knowledge and theory, weighing up what is reasonable given the particular context and circumstances, and finally choosing to act and taking responsible action. The process requires informed choice, and is not only, theoretical but also practical, as it seeks to help individuals and groups of decision makers to address the question "what should I do?"

References

Allen, W., P. Bacdayan, K. Kowalski, and M. Roy. 2005. "Examining the Impact of Ethics Training on Business Student Values." *Education + Training* 47, no. 3, pp. 170–82.

Angelidis, J., and N. Ibrahim. 2011. "The Impact of Emotional Intelligence on the Ethical Judgment of Managers." *Journal of Business Ethics* 99, no. 1, pp. 111–19.

Argyris, C. September/October 1986. "Skilled Incompetence." *Harvard Business Review*, no. 5, pp. 74–79.

Argyris, C. 1990. *Overcoming Organizational Defenses*. Boston: Allyn and Bacon.

Argyris, C. May/June 1991. "Teaching Smart People How to Learn." *Harvard Business Review*, pp. 99–109.

Athota, V., and P. O'Connor. 2014. "How Approach Avoidance Constructs of Personality and Trait Emotional Intelligence Predict Core Human Values." *Learning and Individual Differences* 31, pp. 51–58.

Avolio, B. 2011. *Full Range Leadership Development*. 2nd ed. Thousand Oaks: Sage.

Beck, A. 1976. *Cognitive Therapy and the Emotional Disorders*. New York: International Universities Press.

Beck, A., and D. Dozois. 2011. "Cognitive Therapy: Current Status and Future Directions." *Annual Review of Medicine* 62, pp. 397–409.

Caruso, D., and P. Salovey. 2004. *The Emotionally Intelligent Manager*. San Francisco, CA: Jossey-Bass.

Clements, C., and J. Washbush. 1999. "The Two Faces of Leadership: Considering the Dark Side of Leader-Follower Dynamics." *Journal of Workplace Learning* 11, no. 5, pp. 170–75.

Colquitt, J., and J. Rodell. 2011. "Justice, Trust, and Trustworthiness: A Longitudinal Analysis Integrating Three Theoretical Perspectives." *Academy of Management Journal* 54, no. 6, pp. 1183–206.

Colquitt, J., J. LePine, R. Piccolo, C. Zapata, and B. Rich. 2012. "Explaining the Justice-Performance Relationship: Trust as Exchange Deepener or Trust as Uncertainty Reducer?" *Journal of Applied Psychology* 97, no. 1, pp. 1–15.

Coghlan, D. 2010. "Interiority as a Cutting Edge Between Theory and Practice: A First Person Perspective." *International Journal of Action Research* 6, nos. 2–3, pp. 288–307.

Coghlan, D. 2012. "Understanding Insight in the Context of Q." *Action Learning: Research and Practice* 9, no. 3, pp. 247–58.

Coghlan, D. 2013. "What Will I Do? Toward an Existential Ethics for First Person Action Research Practice." *International Journal of Action Research* 9, no. 3, pp. 333–52.

Deshpande, S., and J. Joseph. 2009. "Impact of Emotional Intelligence, Ethical Climate, and Behavior of Peers on Ethical Behavior of Nurses." *Journal of Business Ethics* 85, no. 3, pp. 403–10.

Duchon, D., and B. Drake. 2009. "Organizational Narcissism and Virtuous Behavior." *Journal of Business Ethics* 85, no. 3, pp. 301–8.

Elangovan, A., and D. Shapiro. 1998. "Betrayal of Trust in Organizations." *The Academy of Management Review* 23, no. 3, pp. 547–66.

Forsyth, D. 1980. "A Taxonomy of Ethical Ideologies." *Journal of Personality and Social Psychology* 39, no. 1, pp. 175–84.

Gaudine, A., and L. Thorne. 2001. "Emotion and Ethical Decision-Making in Organizations." *Journal of Business Ethics*, 31, no. 2, pp. 175–87.

Godkin, L., and S. Allcorn. 2011. "Organizational Resistance to Destructive Narcissistic Behavior." *Journal of Business Ethics* 104, no. 4, pp. 559–70.

Goldman, A. 2006. "Personality Disorders in Leaders: Implications of the DSM IV-TR in Assessing Dysfunctional Organizations." *Journal of Managerial Psychology* 21, no. 5, pp. 392–414.

Goleman, D. 1998. *Working with Emotional Intelligence.* London: Bloomsbury.

Holian, R. 2002. "Management Decision Making and Ethics: Practices, Skills and Preferences." *Management Decision* 40, no. 9, pp. 862–970.

Holian, R. 2006. "Management Decision Making, Ethical Issues and 'Emotional' Intelligence." *Management Decision* 44, no. 8, pp. 1122–38.

Janis, I. 1972. *Victims of Groupthink.* Boston: Houghton Mifflin.

Leahy, R. 2003. *Cognitive Therapy Techniques a Practitioners Guide.* New York: The Guilford Press.

Leahy, R., D. Tirch, and L. Napolitano. 2011. *Emotion Regulation in Psychotherapy.* New York: The Guilford Press.

Ludwig, D., and C. Longenecker. 1993. "The Bathsheba Syndrome: The Ethical Failure of Successful Leaders." *Journal of Business Ethics* 12, no. 4, pp. 265–73.

McAllister, D. 1995. "Affect-and Cognition-Based Trust as Foundations for Interpersonal Cooperation in Organizations." *Academy of Management Journal* 38, no. 1, pp. 24–59.

Mesmer-Magnus, J., C. Viswesvaran, J. Joseph, and S. Deshpande. 2008. "The Role of Emotional Intelligence in Integrity and Ethics Perceptions." In *Research on Emotions in Organizations: Emotions, Ethics, and Decision-Making*, eds. W. Zerbe, N. Ashkansky, and C. Hartel, 225–40. Vol. 4. Bingley, UK: Emerald Group Publications.

Pech, R., and B. Slade. 2007. "Organizational Sociopaths: Rarely Challenged, Often Promoted, Why?" *Society and Business Review* 2, no. 3, pp. 254–69.

Perryer, C., and B. Scott-Ladd. 2014. "Deceit, Misuse and Favours: Understanding and Measuring Attitudes to Ethics." *Journal of Business Ethics* 121, no. 1, pp. 123–34.

Schaubroeck, J., S. Hannah, B. Avolio, S. Kozlowski, R. Lord, L. Trevino, N. Dimotakis, and A. Peng. 2012. "Embedding Ethical Leadership Within and Across Organizational Levels." *Academy of Management Journal* 55, no. 5, pp. 1053–78.

Sims, R. 1992a. "The Challenge of Ethical Behavior in Organizations." *Journal of Business Ethics* 11, pp. 505–13.

Sims, R. 1992b. "Linking Groupthink to Unethical Behavior in Organizations." *Journal of Business Ethics* 11, pp. 651–62.

Sims, R., and W. Sauser. 2013. "Toward a Better Understanding of the Relationship Among Received Wisdom, Groupthink, and Organizational Ethical Culture." *Journal of Management Policy and Practice* 14, no. 4, pp. 75–90.

Wickham, M., and W. O'Donohue. 2012. "Developing an Ethical Organization: Exploring the Role of Ethical Intelligence." *Organization Development Journal* 2, no. 2, pp. 9–29.

CHAPTER 3

Whistle-Blowing and Education Management

Raimondo Ingrassia

University of Palermo

Introduction

The term *abuse of office* is used in this article in the sense of wrongful behavior by a member of an organization. The term also tends to include juridically relevant semantic cases, for example, crimes, offences, misdemeanors, illegalities, and suchlike. Abuse of office constitutes, first of all, anti-moral behavior with subsequent juridical repercussions. The distinction between abuse of office and crime is, in fact, quite flimsy and ambiguous; only in the wake of culturally based, ethical, and political opinions is it becoming possible to outline its boundaries more clearly. In certain circumstances of time and place, it is very likely that behavior that is questionable on the ethical plane also ends up by being considered a crime by the general public.

In public and private organizations, acts of abuse of office of every kind, and on every level, are perpetrated. Conduct of this type cannot always be construed as an offence in the juridical sense, but should actually be interpreted as a criminal offence; it, therefore, needs to be severely censured since it extensively harms not only the society, but also the organizations themselves. The defining characteristic of this kind of wrongdoing is that it is not committed by deviant organizations or individuals (organized or everyday crime), but rather under the protective shield of legal activity carried out by organized labor.

The organizational matrix of these wrongdoings has come under the spotlight in a wide range and variety of literature. Sociological studies have tackled the issue under the term *white-collar crimes* (i.e., crimes committed by respectable people as a result of the power with which they have been entrusted, in positions that they hold at the heart of an organization) (Sutherland 1949; Wickman and Dailey 1982). Philosophy of law has talked of *cheating* (i.e., offences against moral and material norms), conceived in order to regulate social cooperation based on fraud or deception (Green 2006). Many types of misconduct enter into this category, such as corruption, embezzlement, coercion, exploitation, perjury, and *regulatory offences*.[1] Various studies of management have examined corporate crimes and occupational crimes (Clinard and Quinney 1973; Clinard and Yeager 1980; Kramer 1982; Windolf 2004). The former refer to abuse of office carried out in the interests of the organization, whereas the latter refer to the wrongdoing committed in the personal interests of whoever has a job. From this point of view, one might consider as wrongdoings those acts committed by the employer to the detriment of the employee (and vice versa) and those committed by an organization and damaging its stakeholders.

Therefore, an organization may represent not only a driving force for the benefit of society, but also a source of danger and damage. The question is, therefore, asked as how the society might defend itself from such threats. There are many ways in which the society is able to defend itself from detrimental abuse of office carried out by an organization. Because of the quality of information that it can provide and its capacity to restrict internal misconduct, one of these is protection for *personal denunciation of abuse of office*, a special form of control in the hands of extraordinary forces for combating corruption in the organization (Peters 1995, It. trans. 417; Transparency International 2013).[2]

---

[1] Regulatory offenses are those committed in breach of regulatory norms for social or economic phenomena, such as financial markets, transport, trade, health, environment, safety of products and the workplace, competition, discrimination in the workplace, and so on.

[2] Peters has long been dealing with instruments controlling administrative responsibility of public organizations. With opportune adaptations, his analysis is also valid for the profit and nonprofit organizations. For a deeper examination of the subject, q.v. his 1995 study (It. trans. 1999, 408–50).

Section I

The Whistle-Blowing Phenomenon

Definition and Measures

Personal denunciation of abuse of office has only become an object of interest and study relatively recently (the first studies were carried out about 30 years ago).[3] Known in the Anglo-Saxon world as *whistle-blowing* (WB), this term can be defined as denunciation by persons working in organizations and being in possession of facts or circumstances connected with it (Miceli, Near, and Dworkin 2008).[4] On the basis of studies and the existing legislation, whoever denounces (i.e., the *whistle-blower*— WBr) is a person who: (a) has a collaborative relationship with an organization as, for example, an administrator, consultant, manager, employee, blue-collar worker, and so on; (b) has not participated in any way in the wrongdoing and discovers it accidentally or in the wake of well-founded suspicions and personal investigation; (c) is not intended to be responsible for control, inspection, verification, denunciation duties, and so on; (d) is driven by ethical or also utilitarian motives. In other words, the WBr is a person who is familiar with the wrongdoing, is in good faith, is not institutionally responsible for bringing a denunciation, and is in possession of adequate motivation for doing so (Devine and Maassarani 2011; Fraschini, Parisi, and Rinoldi 2011; Miceli, Near, and Dworkin 2008; Rothschild and Miethe 1994).

---

[3] Although there are those who espouse the possibility of denouncing abuse of office collectively (Rothschild and Miete 1994), in reality, WB remains an individual act (Mansbach 2009).

[4] From the linguistic point of view, the term WB had its origins in other contexts. The picturesque image of the old-time London bobby has been evoked, blowing his whistle to signal everyday crimes and misdemeanors committed in the local city streets. Others suggest the football referee blowing his whistle to signal a foul committed by the players and still others, forestry units signaling forest fires. However, the difference between these figures and the WBr is substantial, because whereas the former are denouncing in accordance with strict professional and institutional duties, the WBr is acting for other (moral or utilitarian) reasons, not being personally in charge of controlling or combatting abuse of office.

It is not easy to assess the extent of WB because of the covert, secre-
tive dimension of the phenomenon, which hampers the collection and
processing of reliable judiciary statistics.[5] However, for a few years now,
there have existed public and private organisms carrying out surveys and
monitoring the WB phenomenon throughout the world (and confirming
its constant growth).

The *Securities and Exchange Commission* (SEC) in the U.S. states that
it received 3,238 tips and complaints from WBrs in the year 2013, with
an 8 percent increase over the year 2012 and +90 percent when compared
with August 2011, the time in which the WB program was launched.
The Commission paid out $14 million to WBrs as "recognition of their
contributions to the success of enforcement actions pursuant to which
ongoing frauds were stopped in their tracks" (SEC 2013, 1). Tip-offs
arrived from every state in the Union, but with greater frequency from
California, Texas, Florida, New York, New Jersey, and Washington. From
the rest of the world, tip-offs to the SEC arrived from 68 countries, above
all from the United Kingdom, China, Canada, Russia, India, and Ireland
(SEC 2013).

The *Defense Department* (2013) in the United States also announced
that tip-offs to the department from WBrs also rose by 125 percent
between 2009 and 2013. The Government Accountability Project (GAP),
a nonprofit organization, with the task of promoting and sustaining WB
in the world, communicated that it had assisted more than 6,000 WBrs
since its foundation in 1977 (www.whistleblower.org).

The international consultancy firm *PricewaterhouseCoopers* (PwC),
which has, for several years, been involved in research into financial
criminality, found that, out of a sample of 5,128 organizations operating in 95 countries worldwide, 5 percent of the methods of detection

---

[5] Anonymous denunciation to judicial authorities cannot be considered a WB
action because of the impossibility of identifying the authors. Internal personal
denunciation, on the other hand, when this does not give rise to external verification procedures, remains within the workplace in which it has been reported, as
we shall see later in this article. All this makes it difficult to implement a system
of systematic statistical monitoring.

of wrongdoing could be linked to WB systems, and the 62 percent of these organizations had adopted compliance programs in this regard.[6] An interesting fact emerging from the PwC research is that 56 percent of the economic frauds are perpetrated internally in the organizations by middle management, who have been in service for three to five years, male, aged between 31 and 40 years, and with educational qualifications ranging from secondary school leaving certificate to university degree, as if to say that the threat of economic crime emerges to a considerable extent from internal risk factors and from a potentially broad base of employees (PwC 2014a, 23–24, 2014/b, 2–3).

A *YouGov* survey, carried out for *Public Concern at Work* in the UK in August 2013, on a representative UK population sample of 2,017, over 18 years old, revealed that: (a) 42 percent of those interviewed stated that today their employers operated a company policy on WB (while in 2007, the figure was only 29 percent); (b) 10 percent of those interviewed had witnessed, in the previous two years, cases of corruption, danger, or serious negligence in the workplace, and (c) 66 percent of the latter mentioned that they had reported their personal preoccupations to their employers (www.pcaw.org.uk).

As we said before, WB has been the subject of in-depth studies over the last few years. The results of studies regarding certain critical aspects of the phenomenon are presented in the first section, that is, the decision to denounce, the identity profile of the WBr, the organizational context that influenced the denunciation, reprisal, effectiveness of the denunciation, the juridical discipline, and the sociocultural and political dimension of the phenomenon.

Deciding Whether to Denounce

The decisional process urging a person to report a wrongdoing in the workplace has been reconstructed in three phases (Gundlach, Douglas,

---

[6] The sample has the following characteristics: 50 percent of those responding are senior executives, 35 percent quoted companies, and 54 percent organizations with over 1,000 employees.

and Martinko 2003; Miceli, Near, and Dworkin 2008). *Phase 1*. In order for the wrongdoing to be perceived as such, it needs to be concerned with facts and circumstances with which the bystander interacts directly and with which he is familiar, it being a part of his work. Furthermore, the person will evaluate whether other persons in the organization have the responsibility of acting to halt the abuse of office; only then might he decide to intervene. *Phase 2*. Anyone witnessing wrongdoing assesses whether the organization is well-disposed toward tolerating such conduct, and whether the declared policy is not merely formal adherence with no real desire to suppress. Another important component in this second phase is the psychological impact of the wrongdoing; the measure in which this might lead to demotivation at work, or a fall in personal commitment increases the probability of denunciation by the bystander. *Phase 3*. Anyone witnessing wrongdoing assesses whether he/she has a formal responsibility to act and whether there is a likelihood of success in putting a stop to this abuse of office. The observer knows that the organization is the source of material resources and existential gratification, which risk being reduced or nullified by actions that find no general consensus or are manifestly opposed in the working environment. Therefore, whoever observes wrongdoing must carefully weigh up the costs and benefits of the denunciation, such as, for example, the risks of social exclusion in the workplace, a reduction in the probability of promotion and career, the possibility of dismissal, the absence of financial reward, the real probability of halting the wrongdoing, and so on.

Identity Profile of the Whistle-Blower

Certain personal characteristics affect the previously mentioned decision-making process. There are, above all, four that empirical research has examined in depth: (1) personality factors, (2) demographic variables, (3) perception of one's work, and (4) ethics and personal values.

With regard to *personality, negative affectivity* factors, such as inclination to suspect, hypercritical nature, anger, fear, aggression, or guilt would seem to favor the perception of wrongdoings in the first phase,[7] whereas factors of *positive affectivity* or *proactive* personality, such as self-esteem, an elevated internal *locus of control,* conscientiousness, or extroversion would seem to influence the evaluation of the perceived pros and cons (phase 3) (George 1992; Miceli, Near, and Dworkin 2008, 33–66). Those who believe in their own personal worth (self-esteem), who think that events depend on their own actions (internal locus of control), who are serious and competent in their work (conscientiousness), open, communicative, and persuasive in their social relations, feel they can carry out a significant role in the process of denouncing, and have greater probability of success in bringing it to a conclusion. The results of empirical research, however, have not yet been confirmed with regard to the WBr personality. Furthermore, there are other bases for ambiguity. For example, a proactive personality may express sentiments and behavior that are opposed to denunciation. This person might show no interest in the organization's wrongdoings so as not to prejudice his success and career ambitions in the work environment (Crant 2000).

With regard to *demographic variables*, extensive research has demonstrated significant correlation between denunciation decisions and elevated positions in the hierarchical scale. With regard to gender, men tend to denounce more than women. The key to interpreting this item should be sought in the dominance of gender. Men, still today, have a higher socio-organizational and professional status than women. This leads to their having a greater likelihood of influencing the organizational decisions regarding the cessation of wrongdoings, and consequently, in denouncing them (Miceli, Near, and Dworkin 2008, 59–62).

With regard to *perception of work*, it has been noted that if one carries out one's work in a satisfying and involving manner and if the wrongdoing is in conflict with the interests of the organization, then there is a higher likelihood that the person might tend to denounce; this is because

---

[7] American psychologist Clark maintains that an employee with a history of aggressive behavior sees this exacerbated in environments where wrongdoing has taken place (Jones and Pettigrew 2005), tending to undertake unauthorized personal initiatives (Frese and Fay 2001).

the employee relishes his/her relationship with the organization in harmonious, gratifying, and involving fashion. He/she perceives the misdemeanor as a dissonant element and tends to try to eliminate the causes (Festinger 1957).

Ethics and *personal values* seem to be predictive values for WB, although research in this field has not been very thorough. In general, we know that personal convictions regarding models of behavior, and aims deemed to be fair, condition one's evaluation and behavior, and are firmly resistant to change (Rokeach 1973). Given the types of abuse of office, their seriousness, their impact on the organization, and the persons affected by the wrongdoing, ethical evaluations seem to have a significant role in the decision whether to denounce or not (Miceli, Near, and Dworkin 2008, 58–59), to the extent that the decision to denounce will be deemed as behavior geared toward the interest and well-being of the organization *prosocial organizational behavior* (POB) (Brief and Motowidlo 1986).

The Organizational Context Influencing the Decision to Denounce

Several variables in the organizational context, which influence the decision whether to denounce or not, and above all, the *characteristics of abuse of office*, were the object of empirical investigation. Research has highlighted the fact that poor management in a business or sexual harassment in the workplace are felt more deeply than wrongdoings, such as theft, wastage, security problems, and issues of sexual discrimination (Near et al. 2004). Other research has found the seriousness of the wrongdoing is positively correlated with the decision to denounce, and the "normalized" wrongdoings (i.e., those of the system) are positively correlated with the utilization of external channels for denunciation (Miethe 1999). In general, it is maintained that the type of wrongdoing interacts with two other features: the seriousness and the evidence (e.g., the extent of the damage and the presence of incontrovertible proof). In its turn, the proof is correlated with the decision as to whether or not to utilize the external channels of denunciation.

Secondly, the *type of organization*. Public bureaucracy, through its very nature, ought to be more inclined to discourage WB practices, being linked to a more deep-rooted convention of acceptance of power (a marked hierarchical bureaucratic configuration) and of a cultural or environmental order, such as a certain tendency toward self-referencing. However, public organizations can also be more inclined than private ones to respect the WB practices when tutelage norms are imposed on them, with accompanying protection from denunciation (laws, regulations, procedures, formal bodies, and codes of ethics). This is a response not only to precise duties of administrative transparency and procedural justice, but also to sophisticated strategies of institutional formalism introduced with the objective of achieving social legitimacy and approval (Meyer and Rowan 1977). Research in the United States examined the current affairs journalism about WB in the 30 most-important national daily newspapers over a period of seven years, revealing that 70 percent of WB episodes took place in the public sector, whereas a mere 20 percent of the American workforce was occupied in that sector in the same period. The data were interpreted as meaning that the presence of norms advocating civil liberties provides protection from acts of reprisal, and in general, works in favor of the WB activity (Brewer 1996).

Thirdly, another factor that might influence decisions to denounce is the management's capacity to undertake *captious strategies of action and communication* in response to the denouncer's behavior. The likelihood of success in ending abuse of office may well be impaired by: covering up wrongdoings and reprisal, segregation, and delegitimization of the WBr, attempts to find a scapegoat, ability to transform a legitimate tip-off into a complex legal issue (Martin and Rifkin 2004), persuasive and reassuring organizational communication regarding the cessation of wrongdoing or attempts to downsize the perceived gravity, and public relations geared toward creating support networks, alliances, and political and emotional involvement in favor of the organization (Bies 2013).

Lastly, a final factor that may influence denunciation is the *normalization of abuse* of office within the system (Aguilera and Vadera 2008; Ashforth and Anand 2003). Wrongdoings can be rationalized, that is to say, justified, by the wrongdoer who might well claim that he/she had no choice, that he/she did not damage anyone and that he/she redressed an unfair situation, and so on. Wrongdoings may also be socialized by becoming part of a wider process of corruption geared toward embroiling others in gross misconduct via forms of co-opting, involvement, compromise, and coercion. Research into the socialization of wrongdoings has documented a greater incidence of the phenomenon in organizations with a high turnover, weak cultures, and mediocre social norms for dealing with wrongdoings (Robinson and Kraatz 1998). Wrongdoings may also be institutionalized. Abuse of office can be said to be institutionalized when a process of collective corruption is verified to be running rife in the formal structures, administrative procedure, and the history of the organization, which affects the ethics of the system profoundly. The procedures of filing away superficial documents, verification and checks that hardly scratch the surface, disjointed role models, and ineffective preventive norms might also be indicators of institutionalized abuse of office. In all three cases of normalization, the results show a scanty perception of wrongdoing, leniency of judgment, collective self-censuring, and self-sufficient corruptive phenomenon (Malem Seña, 2002 It. trans. 57) with a consequent reduction in the likelihood of voice *of* and *in* the system (Hirschman 1970).

Reprisals

One of the most important issues to be faced by the person denouncing a wrongdoing in the workplace is the reprisal, (i.e., the action carried out against the WBr as a direct response to his WB) (Miceli, Near, and Dworkin 2008, 119). The settling of scores may be linked to the working relationship, including immediate or postponed dismissal, undesired transfer, downsizing of duties, assignment of deskilled duties, removal of financial incentives (no bonuses or opportunities to do overtime), manifestly unfair promotion of colleagues, or forms of social relations, such as harassment, verbal abuse, ostracizing, scolding, threats, or silent treatment. Research has reported high levels of reprisal, especially informal (up to 87 percent of the total) (Rehg et al. 2008). The effects on the life of the denouncer can be alarming. Abundant research shows the difficulties encountered by WBrs in finding new jobs, loss of primary assets, such as housing, serious marital problems, and symptoms of psychological breakdown in the form of stress, depression, anxiety, and attempted suicide (Cortina and Magley 2003; Rehg et al. 2008).

The reprisal phenomenon can be synthesized in the following way. If the *person being subjected to reprisals* (i.e., the WBr) has prestige and organizational powers (French and Raven 1959), he also has a greater probability of avoiding reprisals, in accordance with the Moscovici and Nemeth (1974) "theory of influence of minority." The Pfeffer and Salancik (1978) "theory of dependence of resources" provides quite an interesting explanatory key to interpretation of the reprisal phenomenon. In an organization, the person controlling "critical" resources for the survival or prosperity of the system (strategic skills, social relations, or privileged clients, and so on) runs less risk of being the target of reprisals. Theories of power are also true for *whoever is committing abuse of office*. In an organization, if the wrongdoer has the key to resources or privileged power, then he/she also enjoys the possibility of going unpunished when carrying out reprisals. The utilitarian theory of dependence of resources consents an explanation as to why organizations persist in abuse of office. If the total expected benefits are superior to the "costs of discovery" of the wrongdoing (legal costs, delegitimization, and loss of reputation or market value), the organization will continue to persist in its misconduct, regardless of the gravity of the actual wrongdoing. Certain wrongdoings (e.g., embezzlement or sexual harassment) are considered less important under this aspect than others, such as financial offences, or, more generally, all those wrongdoings geared toward augmenting a company's resources. Therefore, anyone denouncing wrongdoings, including serious but vital cases for the survival of the organization, will have a greater likelihood of being the object of reprisal.

Effectiveness of Denunciation

The real aim of WB is to put an end to the wrongdoing in the working environment over a limited period of time, and not to provoke alarmism, sensationalism, external scandal, nor to perpetrate persecutory behavior toward other individuals or one's employer (Miceli, Near, and Dworkin 2008, 16). The requisite conditions for denunciation to be effective have not been the object of as much in-depth empirical research as those regarding reprisals. It seems that the effectiveness of denunciation once again depends on the "position of power" of whoever is denouncing. Research has concentrated mainly on the theory of dependence of resources (already discussed with regard to reprisals). According to Pfeffer and Salancik (1978), the human resources on which organizations might depend are: (a) hierarchy, (b) degree of specialization of work, and (c) market price of one's skills. A high hierarchical position, highly technical duties, and much sought-after professional skills endow an individual with power, increasing the probability of putting an end to the denounced wrongdoing.

Juridical Disciplining of WB

There are two types of legislation with regard to WB: (a) laws that safeguard denunciation and (b) laws that provide incentives for denunciation. Laws of the first type regulate the object of the signaling, the levels of protection, and the privacy provided to the WBr, protection from reprisal, potential specific sectorial aspects, the spread to connected organizations, the organisms and procedures for communication and reception of signaling, a right to compensation for damages, and much else. Laws of the second type, apart from being laws of tutelage, have an additional specific discipline of incentives. In the United States, where incentive laws are more advanced, the law stipulates that both the denouncer and the institutional figure handling the investigation (such as state attorney or state department) may draw benefit from incentives. The sources of financing for these financial benefits may come from either the organizations or the persons responsible for the wrongdoing, from obligatory contributions or public financing, and may be adapted to match the entity of the damages ascertained or avoided.

The most highly developed system with regard to WB is at present deemed to be the American one (Miceli, Near, and Dworkin 2008, 154). The WB issue worldwide oscillates between two types of laws, with a clear majority of legislation for tutelage over incentive laws. The most advanced legislation is to be found in countries boasting democracy and developed economies, or emerging countries, such as Canada, Japan, Israel, Australia, New Zealand, United Kingdom, South Africa, Romania, and South Korea, even though there is no shortage of activity in the developed countries without systematic and comprehensive legislation regarding

WB, for example, Austria, Belgium, Italy, France, Holland, Germany, Portugal, and Poland in Europe and India, Singapore, and Malaysia in Asia (Siddiquee 2010). The larger international organizations, such as UNO, EU, Council of Europe, and Organisation for Economic Co-operation and Development, (OCED) have specific norms with regard to WB. In general, countries with less democratic political systems do not have norms regarding WB (e.g., China, Russia, or Nigeria). Italy still does not have a systematic law for WB, and still, today, has a normative framework that continues to privilege professional secrecy and loyalty to one's employer. In 2012, a specific norm regarding WB was issued, denominated "Tutelage of the civil servant who signals misconduct" (Law no. 190/2012, clause 51). The norm stipulates that a civil servant finding out about illicit conduct should report it to the judicial authorities, to the Court of Auditors, or to one's hierarchical superior. To this end, there is provision for tutelage of anonymity and from direct or indirect discriminatory acts resulting from the denunciation.

The Sociocultural and Political Dimension of WB

WB has a strong roots in the culture and politics of a society. Wherever the culture acknowledges (Goffman 1963) public denunciation as deplorable and the person doing the denouncing as a treacherous figure betraying relations of loyalty and the logic of belonging (i.e., the spy) or as a feather-headed and dangerous scaremonger (i.e., the bell-ringer) or perhaps a pathetic social outsider (i.e., the lighthouse-keeper), there is an increase in the paroxysmal assessment of risks and a propensity toward inaction on the part of whoever witnesses wrongdoing (Johnson 2002).

Particularly interesting was an attempt to correlate WB with national cultures in accordance with Hofstede's (1980) widely known analytical dimensions. In a completely generalized fashion, it was claimed that *collectivist cultures* ought to be frowning upon WB activity since it is experienced in actual terms of betrayal of logic of belonging and loyalty. However, it was also noted that cultures of this type might well-encourage WB when the interests of national economy, for example, are brought into the question, or the individual company or specific groups within it, following the rational logic of pro-sociality (Brief and Motowidlo 1986) and organized citizenship (Organ 1990). Cultures that are *hostile to risk and uncertainty* and the ones that are more acquiescent toward the hierarchy (e.g., India and China) should be more conformist, and thus frown upon deviant behavior such as WB.

As far as reprisals are concerned, the considerable *distance from positions of power* should increase the likelihood that this may be tolerated by the system, and paradoxically, accepted by those subjected to it, whereas collectivist cultures, in contrast to individualistic ones, might legitimize reprisals for the simple reason that the "tip-off" was taken as betrayal of the group or the organizational community. On the other hand, denunciation is evaluated positively when it defends national interests or those of a single enterprise. Research carried out on the organizational methods highlights the fact that organizations geared toward results and in particular, profit, tend to favor denunciation (and a reduction of reprisals), if the actual denunciation is functional to economic improvement; on the other hand, organizations geared toward norms and legality only tend to act when there are existing formal regulations that combat reprisals; in the absence of these reprisals, there is a tendency for conformism and blind obedience to prevail, thus encouraging retaliatory actions (Kerr and Slocum 2005). These empirical observations cannot help but confirm the assumptions laid out in the theory of dependence on resources.

The *political dimension* of WB is also of considerable importance. In the contemporary world, corporations are having an ever-growing influence on public life and government policy. The society needs to find a way of regulating and defending itself against this enormous power of influence via instruments that demand social responsibility, ethics, legality, and honest professional managerial behavior. This assumption of responsibility is particularly strongly felt in democratic societies whose very existence is founded on the ideals of freedom of opinion and expression,[8] respect for the law, political pluralism, the participation of civil society,

---

[8] Freedom of speech was already a deep-rooted value in ancient Greece, where what is known as *parrhesia* was practiced, a sort of verbal activity through which a citizen expressed publicly his/her particular perception of the truth in order to encourage (through personal and public exposure) public information and truth (Foucault 2001).

and administrative transparency. In the light of these considerations, WB should be seen and promoted as an act of democratic and responsible collaboration for all organizations and society. With regard to organizations, it would safeguard its direct stakeholders, who are the principal source of support; with regard to the society, it would represent an act of social citizenship aimed at protecting the society from potentially deviant actions on the part of organized interests (Alford 2008; Mansbach 2009; Vandekerckhove 2006).

Section II

Education Toward Whistle-Blowing

Training Program for Whistle-Blowing

In this second section, we shall be dealing with pursuable policies for educating the members of an organization toward this important practice of organizational control.[9] Traditionally, the training process is divided into four phases: needs analysis, objectives and contents, teaching methods, and evaluation of results (Noe et al. 2010, It. trans. 2012, 182 and following). Subsequently, we shall be examining in detail the characteristics that these four phases assume when implementing a training program for WB.

Needs Analysis

On the basis of neo-institutional theories, training needs may emerge from the impetus of three forces: the emulation of best practices from other organizations, with the aim of establishing a reputation, in the eyes of the outside world, as an outstanding organization (mimetic force); on the basis of norms and public directives (coercive force); and being induced by ethical rules emanating from specific bodies or professional communities (normative force) (DiMaggio and Powell 1983; Engwall

---

[9] In this article, we use the terms *education* and *training* as near-synonyms, since both indicate (albeit in different ways) a course of teaching and learning geared toward a person's acquisition of cognitive, cultural, aesthetic, and moral elements (www.treccani.it).

2007). Empirical evidence seems to bear witness to the propulsive role of the coercive forces in determining awareness of the educational needs and initiatives with regard to WB. The federal Medicaid program in the USA, in perfect accord with the country's tradition of compliance programs, demands that suppliers who receive $5 million in annual payments should create focused training programs for their employees, suppliers, and agents, geared toward the denunciation of wrongdoings, wastage and fraud, as well as including a specific chapter on WB in the employee handbook (Miceli, Near, and Dworkin 2008, 166–67).

Objectives and Contents

The defining of objectives and contents of a training program becomes gradually more complex when the program provides for certain aspects, such as attitude, ways of resolving problems, relations with others, activation of emotional components, capacity to tackle new situations, and unforeseeable cultural changes (Associazione Italiana Formatori [AIF] 1988, 158–59). A WB educational program certainly presents characteristics of this type; the aims and the contents of such a program should, therefore, provide for aspects linked to technical knowledge of wrongdoings (Morrison and Milliken 2003) as well as aspects linked to the psychological, behavioral, and value-based reaction of the person studying the abuse of office.

From the perspective of technical knowledge about wrongdoing, certain issues appear to be indispensable for sound WB training, cleverly summed up in "one cannot be a supporter of something that one does not understand" (Gauthier 2006). The following are the suggestions regarding the contents that should be included in a WB training program: (a) Knowledge under the technical, penal, and deontological profiles of wrongdoings relative to a company's core business; for example, financial wrongdoings in the case of banks; environmental wrongdoings in the case of businesses operating in the energy and environment sectors; misconduct regarding the quality of product in industrial and commercial businesses; administrative wrongdoings in the public sector, and so on; (b) Knowledge under the technical, penal, and deontological profiles of wrongdoings relative to the auxiliary organizational functions and staff duties; for example, wrongdoings related to the regulations for working relations, accountancy, purchase of goods and services, tutelage of company assets, institutional communication and so on;[10] (c) Knowledge of the normative framework and procedures regulating WB; and (d) Knowledge of principles and techniques of *risk management* with particular reference to corruption (quantitative and qualitative analyses of risk, statistical processing, methods of risk management, and so on).

From the perspective of psychological, behavioral, and value-based reactions to wrongdoing, the following disciplines seem particularly important: elements of social psychology, organizational behavior, cultural anthropology, sociology of deviance, public ethics, and political science. All are chosen and developed with specific reference to the issues of personality, social responsibility of organizations, and personal responsibility of individuals, civil protest, anticorruption policies, loyalty to the group, and legality.

Teaching Methods

Teaching methods need to be suited to the type of training program and learning approach being applied (Noe et al. 2010, It. trans. 2012, 213). Attitudes and knowledge are the priority areas of learning in a WB educational program. To this end, teaching instruments based on the actual learning of concepts seem to be more suitable than instruments based on doing, for example, on-the-job training and action learning, or on relationships, such as the T-Group or the Community of Practices. In fact, instruments based on the learning of concepts enable one to act not only on knowledge of the phenomenon, but also on convictions and attitudes with regard to it. Subsequently, we shall be illustrating the characteristics of a collection of teaching instruments that are more likely to

---

[10] Green (2006, It. trans. p. 43) maintains that criminal norms carry out an educational function, supporting and promoting certain styles of life. The decision to criminalize certain behavior reflects the dominant moral rules in a given moment in society; it follows that the general perception of wrongdoing is conditioned by the choices, made by society, as to whether to criminalize behavior and the extent to which these choices are known by those members of society.

be utilized by trainers and accepted by trainees and clients in a WB education program. It should be noted that, the order in which these are presented is based on an increasing degree of interactivity guaranteed by the instrument.

Texts

The textbook has always been the teaching instrument *par excellence* since it fosters the systematic acquisition of knowledge, critical reflection regarding its contents, introspection, and individual learning. With regard to WB, there is, nowadays in the market, a wide range of reading material (scientific, vocational, journalistic, and instructional texts) that provides information from various points of view and with a level of in-depth examination that will satisfy the interests of the most varied readers. As well as the numerous scientific texts and articles, several of which are listed in the bibliography at the end of this chapter, we might mention: *The Corporate Whistleblower's Survival Guide: A Handbook for Committing the Truth* by Devine and Maassarani (2011) and a few journalistic works such as *The Informant (a True Story)* by Eichenwald (2001), *The Smartest Guys in the Room: the Amazing Rise and Scandalous Fall of Enron* by Bethany McLean and Elkind (2004), and *All the President's Men* by Bernstein and Woodward (1974). In the category of texts, one might include journalistic articles, legal texts, and jurisprudential interpretations, widely published in international juridical fields and the media.

Thematic Portals

Thematic portals are an important instrument for studying and learning about the principal issues inherent to WB, while, at the same time, constituting an important gateway for access to, and communication with, independent bodies in this delicate field. The thematic portals are websites. Here, we might mention the most significant: www.whistle-blower.org of the GAP and www.pogo.org of the *Project on Government Oversight* (POGO) (the latter is devoted in particular to federal administration), both operating in the United States; www.pcaw.org.uk of *Public Concern at Work* in the UK; www.canadians4accountability.org of *Canadian for Accountability* in Canada; www.internationalwhistleblowers.com of the homonymous New Zealand organism; www.whistle-blowing.it, the Italian site of *Giorgio Fraschini*; www.transparency.org, site of the homonymous international organization, which, in its databank, reports 276 results of WB.

These sites are promoted by nonprofit organizations or ordinary persons, and have the goal of providing information, consultancy, support, and legal and training services to those (persons and organizations) who are tackling issues linked to WB. The most frequently recurring contents in this site are: (a) information regarding the identity of administrators and collaborators, (b) mission and goals as pursued by the organization, (c) suggestions as to how to propose personal and institutional affiliation, offer professional or financial collaboration via donations and gifts, (d) documentation services (norms, procedures, texts, studies, useful advice, recommendations, press releases, newsletters, online book shops), (e) presentation of video clips of WBrs, administrators, witnesses, and consultants who have had experience of WB, (f) training and consultancy services on the payment and legal assistance, (g) political support and lobbying activity, (h) celebratory events and public encounters, (i) reserved channels of communication (contacts and hotlines), (j) models of compliance programs, and (k) FAQs, blogs, and many other items of multimedia support (Wankel 2009).

Filmography

In-service company training is nowadays characterized ever more frequently by the adoption of artistic and multimedia forms that are supplementary to the traditional techniques of classroom management. The audiovisual tools constitute a great resource for training since they offer the possibility of benefitting from communicative devices that are quite different from the traditional forms of teaching based around the written word in textbooks or the teacher's spoken word (films, shorts, documentaries, videos on the web, and so on) (Awasthi and Staehelin 1995; Bogliari 2007; Rivoltella 2001). In the last few years, probably due to the growing sensitivity toward the issues of the social responsibility of organizations, WB has aroused interest in the film industry, as demonstrated by important films that have come out regarding this topic, including: *The Whistleblower* (2010), *The Informant* (2009), *Enron: The Smartest Guys in the Room* (2005), *The Insider* (1999), *Erin Brockovich* (2000), without forgetting the *ante-litteram All the President's Men* (1976).

The evocative and communicative force of the film, its capacity to offer realistic images of human behavior, the emotional impact that it can spark off, its ability to stimulate the spectator's critical interpretation and opinion, the power of its images, the possibility of being confronted by events and problems that are not easily encountered elsewhere, and the practical advantage of being able to interrupt scenes in accordance with class requirements (thus consenting repeated and retrospective viewing of the narration) represent highly significant features of audiovisual devices; the overall aim being to sensitize consciences with regard to such out-of-the-ordinary material.

Lessons in the Classroom

The classroom lesson is one of the most important and common teaching approaches in the field of education, and at the same time, one of the most (unfairly) criticized. In reality, the effectiveness of the lesson depends not so much on the nature of the instrument itself as on certain subjective characteristics of the person conducting the lesson, for example, credibility of the source; communicative and organizational capacity of instructor in terms of timing, clarity of explanation, and aims of contents; quality of rapport established with the class; ability to stimulate interaction between the members of the learning group; and capacity to involve. Apart from being a valid instrument for transfer of information, capable of augmenting knowledge of a specific phenomenon, the lesson is also a potential instrument of persuasive communication, which is traditionally considered to be particularly effective in changing attitudes (Hovland, Janis, and Kelly 1953).

The person giving a classroom lesson in a WB education program might be a teacher, a professional, or an institutional figure, with sufficient experience with regard to study, research, teaching, and professional work in the field. A specific role might also be taken on by internal, organizational figures, whose task would be to prepare training and development programs for the personnel, based on the issues of *bad behavior* in working organizations, as supervisors of organizing units, specific authorities, workgroup coaches, company counselors, project managers, and so on (Porath and Pearson 2010; PNA 2013). An Italian anticorruption law (no. 190/2012) has instituted the figure of Person responsible for prevention of corruption (clause 7) with one of the tasks being to select personnel for specific sectors at risk of corruption and to sensitize and train civil servants with regard to anticorruption.

WB Stories

From the theoretical perspective, WB stories represent an autonomous way of learning, in that they enable one to obtain knowledge of events, acts, and people, that have really existed. Obviously, every story does not have an aseptically objective content, but is still the result of the storyteller's perception and interpretation, the means utilized to tell it, the rigor with which the information to reconstruct it is acquired, and the social context in which it has matured and taken place. Any historical reconstruction is, therefore, the fruit of the subjectivity of the doer and teller (Egan 1985). On the practical level, learning through stories is usually entrusted to other, previously encountered, communicative instruments such as written texts, the teacher, filmography, or direct testimony. In this sense, WB stories can be conveyed effectively through written scripts or video-recorded interviews, case studies written by journalists or academics, or rigorous analysis carried out exploiting judicial deeds and sentences.

Testimony

Testimony is a familiar teaching instrument widely used in training programs. Generally speaking, a testimony has a great informative value if it is chosen prudently within the framework of the training program in question (Lackey 2008). More than any other instrument, a testimony from a person who has undergone experiences in this field (mismanagement, denunciation of wrongdoings, reprisals, trials, mobbing, and so on) constitutes an instrument capable of touching a person's conscience, and enhances a training program dealing with WB. The protagonists in the first person (i.e., the WBrs), lawyers who have defended legal cases on the subject, magistrates, company representatives, public authorities, or also the simple presentation of personal cases on the part of the learners, can contribute in decisive fashion to learning and the success of the course.

Self-Directed Learning

By self-directed learning, we mean a series of activities connected to the educational process and carried out autonomously by that person (Knowles 1975). With self-directed learning, the learner grows accustomed to seeking out for himself the various requirements, materials, information, and training opportunities handy for a greater understanding of the phenomenon in question (Mezirow 1991). According to Hoban et al. (2005), the people most inclined toward self-directed learning are those who see education as an opportunity for personal growth, who are curious about new experiences, and have an adequate sense of their self-efficacy regarding their learning ability. Considering the considerable implications that WB entails for an individual's life, the utilization of an educational mode that encourages introspection, personal research, discretion, autonomous processing of knowledge, and judgment may well-constitute a better way of tackling the existential questions of such complexity.

Evaluation of Results

As we saw in the first section of this chapter, the aim of WB is to put a stop to abuse of office within an organization, and not that of retaliation and personal interests, social scaremongering, and media scandals. In this regard, a training program should not envisage a practical transfer to the field of what has been learned, as might fairly be expected at the end of a normal training course; this is because the denunciation of the wrongdoing (and the wrongdoing itself) needs to be considered as extraordinary and undesirable events in the life of an organization, and also because the transfer itself requires a favorable response from the social and organizational context that the denunciation is threatening and destabilizing (bosses, colleagues, support networks, opportunities for practice, and handling of feedback) (Aguilera and Vadera 2008; Broad and Newstrom

1992; Kirwan and Birchall 2006; Van den Bossche Segers and Jansen 2010).

According to Kirkpatrick's scale (1996), the process of evaluating the training course should, therefore, end with a survey of opinions regarding the program or a verification of an altered emotional and cultural assessment of the phenomenon from the perspective, not so much of expectations of concrete behavior in the workplace, as of the capacity to influence the trainees' fundamental attitudes (Noe et al. 2010, It. trans. 2012, 214). The aims and results of a WB education program should, therefore, be formulated and evaluated with regard to the capacity to inform about the features of the phenomenon, to reduce prejudices toward it (Aronson, Wilson, and Akert 2005, 316), to propose to the trainees a line in public ethics in fresh terms with regard to the objectives of building up a person's potential, rather than his operative capacity. From this type of perspective, an isolated act of denunciation over a long time span or no act would not be assessed negatively in educational terms.

Summary

In the first section of this chapter, we saw how denunciation of wrongdoings depended on personal, organizational, juridical, social, cultural, and political factors that interact with the phases of the decision-making process being denounced. As for personal factors, research has found a certain regularity, but also many uncertainties. There are several definite correlations between the demographic variables, perception of one's own work, personal values, and the decision to denounce, whereas the correlations between the personality factors and decisions to denounce appear to be more ambiguous and contradictory. The organizational factors have an even greater influence than the personal factors in deciding whether to denounce. The seriousness of the wrongdoing, its relationship with the interests of the organization, the public or private nature of the organization, its managerial strategies in response to initiatives of WBrs, the degree of normalization of the wrongdoing within the organizational system, the potential impact of reprisals on the WBr's psychological condition and professional life, and the position of power of the denouncer in an effective WB course, profoundly affect the decision-making process, influencing the general perception of the abuse of office, its psychological impact on the observer, and evaluation of the costs/benefits ratio of the act. Over the last few years, the juridical factors have had a growing influence on the spread of the phenomenon. The existence of norms regarding WB is the first element for evaluating a country's politics. A second element is the quality of the laws passed. Alongside the presence of evermore focused and accomplished protective laws, a legislation for incentives is being developed, aiming to offer material (and moral) rewards to whoever might decide to denounce.

Although, in the organizational behavior theory, the ethics and personal values are considered as exclusive to the person, they are greatly influenced by a country's (or an organization's) social, political, and cultural factors. In those countries (and organizations) where the values of collectivism are more widespread and the pressure to conform is greater, WB seems to denote negative connotations. The actual distance from the positions of power seems to be a factor in favor of leniency toward reprisal, whereas the alignment between the organizational interests, abuse of office, and the decision whether to denounce is a decisive factor in tolerating the wrongdoing, or on the contrary, in the consensus regarding the denunciation. Lastly, the political factors appear to be particularly influential with regard to the existence of the phenomenon. Many of the countries that have a civic tradition or normative systems geared toward safeguarding denunciation of wrongdoings are also the most democratic countries, where debate between institutions, politics, and the citizen tends to encourage the principles of responsibility, active participation, personal integrity, and administrative transparency. The political factor, therefore, represents something particularly influential in the debate about public acknowledgement of the phenomenon.

In the second section of the chapter, we dealt with how to pass on knowledge about the WB phenomenon from the perspective of implementing a training program. In this way, a needs analysis, as well as considering the requirements dictated by specific norms imposed by the public anticorruption policy, should also seriously take into account the requirements resulting from the organization's needs to gain credence in the eyes of its own stakeholders. The aims of the training program should be limited to an understanding of the WB phenomenon in all its manifestations and an altered basic approach toward it, rather than imagining the undesirable practical applications of what has been learned. The contents of the program present several original aspects, but also a high level of complexity due to the marked interdisciplinary nature of the proposed training modules. The contents refer to both elements of technical, juridical, and deontological knowledge of the wrongdoings, with the aim of creating in the subject a capacity for critical judgment and also elements for eliminating the psychological, political, ethical, and cultural stigma attached to public denunciation of wrongdoings. The choice of teaching method is dictated by the instruments selected in function of the educational objectives being pursued. In this sense, teaching aids, such as textbooks, thematic portals, filmography, classroom lessons, stories, testimony, and self-directed learning, take on a particular importance. Finally, the evaluation of results of the program should be carried out on the basis of parameters of participant satisfaction and a modified awareness of the issues in question, rather than from the perspective of material transfer of contents.

Conclusions: Knowing When to Throw Light on an Organization's Dark Side

One cannot be the advocate of something that one does not understand. The meaning and aim of this work of ours might be expressed in these few words: knowing and judging before acting, knowing how to assess people, behavior, the facts and the circumstances, before blowing the whistle. This is probably the real function of education with regard to such a thorny issue as denunciation of wrongdoings in the workplace. In order to consent the acquisition of information and to express value judgments, it is, however, necessary to understand the phenomena that one is intending to suppress. As we have seen in the course of this study, WB is a growing phenomenon, at least in its modern guise, because of a change in sensitivity toward an organization's social responsibility and legislation that is ever-more attentive toward the phenomenon. Knowing is not acting. Education management geared toward public denunciation of wrongdoings should set itself the goal of creating potential and building up awareness in such a way that a person feels it to be a duty, whenever the need to protest presents itself, and to shout it out loud, so that others, worried about the values that are being sacrificed, might come to his/her aid and help throw light on the organization's deeper and darker side.

References

Aguilera, R.V., and A.K. Vadera. 2008. "The Dark Side of Authority: Antecedents, Mechanisms, and Outcomes of Organizational Corruption." *Journal of Business Ethics* 77, no. 4, pp. 431–49. doi:10.1007/s10551-007-9358-8

Alford, C.F. 2008. "Whistleblowing as Responsible Followership." In *The Art of Followership: How Great Follower Create Great Leaders and Organizations,* eds. R.E. Riggio, I. Chaleff, and B.J. Lipman. San Francisco: Jossey-Bass.

Aronson, E., T.D. Wilson, and R.M. Akert. 2005. *Social Psychology.* Reading, MA: Longman (It. trans. *Psicologia sociale.* Bologna: il Mulino, 2006).

Ashforth, B.E., and V. Anand. 2003. "The Normalization of Corruption in Organizations." In *Research in Organizational Behavior,* eds. R.M Kramer, and B.M. Staw, 1–52. Amsterdam: Elsevier.

AIF (Associazione Italiana Formatori). 1988. *Professione Formazione (Training Profession).* Milano: Franco Angeli (ristampa 2002, 13ª ed.).

Awasthi, V.N., and E. Staehelin. 1995. "Ethics and Management Accounting: Teaching Note for a Video Case. The order: A Progressive disclosure Vignette." *Journal of Accounting Education* 13, no. 1, pp. 87–98. doi:10.1016/0748-5751(94)00023-9

Bernstein, C., and B. Woodward. 1974. *All the President's Men.* New York: Simon & Schuster Paperbacks.

Bies, R.J. January 2013. "The Delivery of Bad News in Organizations: A Framework for Analysis." *Journal of Management* 39, no. 1, pp. 136–62. doi:10.1177/0149206312461053

Bogliari, F. (a cura di) 2007. *Il grande libro del cinema per manager [The Big Book of Cinema to Manager].* Milano: Etas.

Brewer, G.A. 1996. *Incidence of Whistle-Blowing in the Public and Private Sectors.* Athens, GA: Department of Political Science, The University of Georgia.

Brief, A.P., and S. Motowidlo. 1986. "Prosocial Organizational Behaviours." *Academy of Management Review* 11, no. 4, pp. 710–25. www.jstor.org/stable/258391

Broad, M., and J. Newstrom. 1992. *Transfer of Training: Strategies to Ensure High Payoff from Training Investment.* Reading, MA: Addison-Wesley.

Clinard, M.B., and R. Quinney. 1973. *Criminal Behavior System: A Typology.* New York: Rinehart & Winston.

Clinard, M.B., and P. Yeager. 1980. *Corporate Crime.* New York: The Free Press.

Cortina, L.M., and V.J. Magley. 2003. "Raising Voice, Risking Retaliation: Events Following Interpersonal Mistreatment in the Workplace." *Journal of Occupational Health Psychology* 8, no. 4, pp. 247–65. doi:10.1037/1076-8998.8.4.247

Crant, J.M. 2000. "Proactive Behavior in Organizations." *Journal of Management* 26, no. 3, pp. 435–62. doi:10.1177/014920630002600304

Department of Defense (USA). 2013. *Annual Report.* http://sec.gov./oig

Devine, T., and T. Maassarani. 2011. *The Corporate Whistleblower's Survival Guide: A Handbook for Committing the Truth.* San Francisco, CA: Berrett-Koehler.

Di Maggio, P.J., and W.W. Powell. 1983. "The Iron Cage Revisited: Institutional Isomorphism and Collective Rationality in Organizational Fields." *American Sociological Review* 48, no. 2, pp. 147–60.

Egan, K. 1985. "Teaching as Story-Telling: A Non-Mechanistic Approach to Planning Teaching." *Journal of Curriculum Studies* 17, no. 4, pp. 397–406. doi:10.1080/0022027850170405

Eichenwald, K. 2001. *The Informant (a True Story).* New York: Broadway Books.

Engwall, L. 2007. "The Anatomy of Management Education." *Scandinavian Journal of Management* 23, no. 1, pp. 4–35. doi:10.1016/j.scaman.2006.12.003

Festinger, L. 1957. *A Theory of Cognitive Dissonance.* Stanford, CA: Stanford University Press.

Foucault, M. 2001. *Fearless Speech.* Los Angeles: Pearson.

Fraschini, G., N. Parisi, D. Rinoldi. 2011. *Il Whistleblowing.* Roma: Bonanno.

French, J.R.P., and B. Raven. 1959. "The Bases of Social Power." In *Studies in Social Power*, ed. D. Cartwright, 150–67. Ann Arbor: University of Michigan Press.

Frese, M., and D. Fay. 2001. "Personal Initiative (PI): The Theoretical Concept and Empirical Findings." In *Research in Organizational Behaviour*, eds. B.M. Stave, and R.M. Sutton, 133–87. Amsterdam: The Netherlands.

Gauthier, S. 2006. "Understanding Internal Control." *Government Finance Review* 22, no. 1, pp. 10–16. doi:10.1016/j.jaccedu.2012.12.001

George, J. 1992. "The Role of Personality in Organizational Life: Issues and Evidence." *Journal of Management* 18, no. 2, pp. 185–213. doi:10.1177/014920639201800201

Goffman, E. 1963. *Stigma: Notes on the Management of Spoiled Identity.* Englewood Cliffs, NJ: Prenctice-Hall.

Green, S.P. 2006. *Lying, Cheating, and Stealin: A Moral Theory of White-Collar Crime.* Oxford: Oxford University Press (It. trans. I crimini dei colletti bianchi, Milano: Egea, 2008).

Gundlach, M.J., S.C. Douglas, and M.J. Martinko. 2003. "The Decision to Blow the Whistle: a Social Information Processing Framework." *Academy*

of Management Review 28, no. 1, pp. 107–23. doi:10.5465/AMR2003.
8925239

Hirschman, A.O. 1970. *Exit, Voice, and Loyalty: Responses to Decline in Firms,
Organizations, and States.* Cambridge, MA: Harvard University Press.

Hoban, J.D., S.R. Lawson, P.E. Mazmanian, A.M. Best, and H.R. Seibel. 2005.
"The Self-Directed Learning Readiness Scale: A Factor Analysis Study." *Medical
Education* 39, no. 4, pp. 370–79. doi:10.1111/j.1365-2929. 2005.02140.x

Hofstede, G. 1980. *Culture's Consequences: International Differences in Work-
Related Values.* Beverly Hills, CA: Sage.

Hovland, C.I., I.L. Janis, and H.H. Kelley. 1953. *Communication and Persuasion:
Psychological Studies of Opinion Change.* New Haven, CT: Yale University
Press.

Johnson, R.A. 2002. *Whistleblowing: When It Works—And Why.* Boulder, CO:
Rienner Publishers.

Jones, J.M., and T.F. Pettigrew. 2005. "Kenneth B. Clark. 1914–2005." *American
Psychologist* 60, no. 6, pp. 649–65. doi:10.1037/0003-066X.60.6.649

Kerr, J., and J.W. Slocum, Jr. 2005. "Managing Corporate Culture Through
Reward System." *Academy of Management Executive* 19, no. 4, pp. 130–38.
doi:10.5465/AME.2005.19417915

Kirkpatrick, D.L. 1996. "Techniques for Evaluating Training Program." *Training
and Development* 50, no. 1, pp. 54–59.

Kirwan, C., and D. Birchall. 2006. "Transfer of Learning from Management
Development Programmes: Testing the Holton Model." *International
Journal of Training and Development* 10, pp. 252–68. doi:10.1111/j.1468-
2419.2006.00259.x

Knowles, M.S. 1975. *Self-Directed Learning: A Guide for Learners and Teachers.*
Englewood Cliffs, NJ: Prentice-Hall.

Kramer, R.C. 1982. "Corporate Crime: An Organizational Perspective." In
White-Collar and Economic Crime, eds. P. Wickman, and T. Dailey, 75–94.
Lexington, MA: Lexington Books.

Lackey, J. 2008. *Learning from Words: Testimony as a Source of Knowledge.* Oxford:
Oxford University Press.

Malem Seña, J.F. 2002. La corrupción: aspectos eticos, económicos, polìticos
y jurídìcos, barcelona: gedisa. (It. trans. Globalizzazione, commercio
internazionale e corruzione, Bologna: Il Mulino, 2004).

Mansbach, A. 2009. "Keeping Democracy Vibrant: Whistleblowing as Truth-
Telling in the Workplace." *Constellations* 16, no. 3, pp. 363–76. doi:10.1111/
j.1467-8675.2009.00547.x

Martin, B., and W. Rifkin. 2004. "The Dynamics of Employee Dissent:
Whistleblowers and Organizational Jiu-Jitsu." *Public Organization Review* 4,
pp. 221–38. doi:10.1023/B:PORJ.0000036869.45076.39

McLean, B., and P. Elkind. 2004. *The Smartest Guys in the Room: the Amazing Rise and Scandalous Fall of Enron*. London: Penguin Books.

Meyer, J., and B. Rowan. 1977. "Institutionalized Organizations: Formal Structure as Myth and Ceremony." *American Journal of Sociology* 83, no. 2, pp. 340–63. www.jstor.org/stable/2778293

Mezirow, J. 1991. *Transformative Dimensions of Adult Learning*. San Francisco: Jossey-Bass. (It. trans. Apprendimento e trasformazione, Milano: Raffaello Cortina, 2003).

Miceli, M.P., J.P. Near, and T.M. Dworkin. 2008. *Whistle-blowing in Organizations*. New York: Routledge.

Miethe, T.D. 1999. "Whistle-Blowing at Work: Tough Choices in Exposing Fraud." *Waste and Abuse on the Job*. 2nd ed. Boulder, CO: Westview Press.

Morrison, E.W., and F.J. Milliken. 2003. "Guest Editor's Introduction: Speaking up, Remaining Silent: The Dynamics of Voice and Silence in Organizations." *Journal of Management Studies* 40, pp. 1353–58. doi:0022-2380

Moscovici, S., and C. Nemeth. 1974. "Minority Influence." In *Social Psychology: Classic and Contemporary Integrations*, ed. C. Nemeth, 217–49. Chicago, IL: Rand McNally.

Near, J.P., J.R. Van Scotter, M.T. Rehg, and M.P. Miceli. 2004. Does Type of Wrongdoing Affect the Whistle-Blowing Process? *Business Ethics Quarterly* 14, no. 2, pp. 219–42. doi:10.5840/beq200414210

Noe, R.A., J.R. Hollenbeck, B. Gerhart, and P.M. Wright. 2010. *Human Resource Management*. 7th ed. Chicago: MacGraw-Hill. (It. trans. Gestione delle risorse umane, Milano: Apogeo, 2012).

Organ, D.W. 1990. The Motivational Basis of Organizational Citizenship Behaviour. In *Research in Organizational Behaviour*, eds. B.M. Stave, and L.L. Cummings, 43–72. Greenwich, CT: JAI Press.

Peters, G.B. 1995. *The Politics of Bureaucracy*. New York: Longman. (It. trans. La pubblica amministrazione. Un'analisi comparata. Bologna: il Mulino, 1999).

Pfeffer, J., and G.R. Salancik. 1978. *The External Control of Organizations*. New York: Harper & Row.

PNA (Piano Nazionale Anticorruzione). 2013. *Anti-Corruption National Plan*. Presidenza Consiglio dei ministri/dipartimento della funzione pubblica (Italy). http://www.anticorruzione.it

Porath, C.L., and C.M. Pearson. 2010. "The Cost of Bad Behavior." *Organizational Dynamics* 39, no. 1, pp. 64–71. doi:10.1016/j.orgdyn.2009.10.006

PwC (PricewaterhouseCoopers). 2014a. *Global Economic Crime Survey*. A Swiss Perspective. http://pwc.com

PwC (PricewaterhouseCoopers). 2014b. *Global Economic Crime Survey/ Addendum Italiano/Executive Summary*. http://pwc.com/it

Public Concern at Work. 2013. *YouGov Survey*. http://pcaw.org.uk

Rehg, M.T., M.P. Miceli, J.P. Near, and J.R. Van Scotter. 2008. "Antecedents and Outcomes of Retaliation Against Whistleblowers: Gender Differences and Power Relationships." *Organization Science* 19, no. 2, pp. 221–40. doi:org/10.1287/orsc.1070.0310

Rivoltella, P.C. 2001. *Media Education.* Roma: Carocci.

Robinson, S.L., and M.S. Kraatz. 1998. "Constructing the Reality of Normative Behavior: The Use of Neutralization Strategies by Organizational Deviants." In *Dysfunctional Behaviour in Organizations*, eds. R.W. Griffin, A. O'Leary-Kelly, and J.M. Collins, 203–20. Stanford, CA: Jai Press.

Rokeach, M. 1973. *The Nature of the Values.* New York: Free Press.

Rothschild, J., and T.D. Miethe. 1994. "Whistleblowing as Resistance in Modern Work Organizations." In *Resistance and Power in Organizations*, eds. J.M. Jermier, D. Knights, and W.R. Nord, 252–73. London: Routledge.

SEC (Securities and Exchange Commission). 2013. *Annual Report to Congress on the Dodd-Frank WhistleBlower Program.* http://sec.gov

Siddiquee, N.A. 2010. "Combating Corruption and Managing Integrity in Malaysia: A Critical Overview of Recent Strategies and Initiatives." *Public Organization Review* 10, no. 2, pp. 153–71. doi:10.1007/s11115-009-0102-y

Sutherland, E.H. 1949. *White Collar Crime.* New York: Holt, Rinehart & Winston.

Transparency International. 2013. *Whistleblowing in Europe. Legal Protections for the Whistleblower in the Europe.* http://transparency.org

Van den Bossche, P., M. Segers, and N. Jansen. 2010. "Transfer of Training: The Role of Feedback in Supportive Social Networks." *International Journal of Training and Development* 14, no. 2, pp. 81–94. doi:10.1111/j.1468-2419.2010.00343.x

Vandekerckhove, W. 2006. *Whistleblowing and Organizational Social Responsibility: A Global Assessment.* Hampshire: Ashgate.

Wankel, C. 2009. "Management Education Using Social Media." *Organization Management Journal* 6, pp. 251–62. doi:10.1057/omj.2009.34

Wickman, P., and T. Dailey eds. 1982. *White-Collar and Economic Crime.* Lexington, MA: Lexington Books.

Windolf, P. 2004. "Corruption, Fraud, and Corporate Governance: A Report on Enron." In *Corporate Governance and Firm Organization: Microfoundations and Structural Forms,* ed. A. Grandori. Oxford: Oxford University Press.

CHAPTER 4

Integrity and Ethics in Higher Education: The Role Played by Teachers and Theories in Forming New Managers

Andrea Tomo, Paolo Canonico, and Stefano Consiglio

Department of Economics, Management, Institutions
University of Naples "Federico II"

Ernesto De Nito

Department of Public Law Organization, Economics and Society
University of Catanzaro Magna Græcia

Lorenzo Mercurio

Department of Business and Economics Studies
University of Naples "Parthenope"

Introduction: The Role of Ethics in Management Education

During the last decade, corporate scandals have involved business education in a wave of criticism as responsible for moral ignorance in the business world and for their failure in educating students with the standards of good conduct (Ivory et al. 2006; Mintzberg and Gosling 2002; Pfeffer and Fong 2004; Pfeffer 2005).[1]

Hence, the new approach of humanistic management seems to play a crucial function in searching for a new ethical role of managerial theories and practices.

By looking at the contents within management education courses, it is possible to consider that several authors (Cavico and Mujtaba 2009; Wankel and Stachowicz-Stanusch 2011) argue that professors and lecturers interpret the several key issues within the managerial domain adopting a short-term perspective that may be prejudicial for the long-term opportunities and relationships (Mitroff 2004, 185).

What looks interesting to underline is the (in)capacity of business schools of imparting useful skills and knowledge, preparing leaders for doing what is right, teaching norms of ethical behavior (Bennis and O'Toole 2005).

For instance, Ghoshal (2005) argues that "business schools have actively freed their students from any sense of moral responsibility" because faculty members teach theories that are ideological in nature (Cavico and Mujtaba 2005, 76).

Another interesting ethical problem in the business schools world is outlined by Anthony (1998). The author uses an oxymoron to describe how managers act nowadays: he has introduced the expression of "barbarian elite," by playing on the contradiction between the moral privilege attributed to the idea of the elite and the use of pure strength of the barbarians.

---

[1] This research was carried out in the frame of Programme STAR (2013, L1 Napoli_call2013_23) and financially supported by UniNA and Compagnia di San Paolo.

By this way, Anthony expresses the opportunity of enforcing the ethical dimension in business schools programs in order to help managers to exert their power in a sustainable way. The concept of humanism has become crucial to understand the broader economic, social, and managerial challenges (Acevedo 2012; Aktouf 1992; Melé 2003, 2012; Spitzeck 2011) brought by the latest financial crisis and the new challenges that management education institutions are facing (Mangia et al. 2012).

Melé evidences that the theoretical perspective of humanistic management may be conceived as an outlook emphasizing the common human needs, and is concerned with human characteristics (2003, 78).

The idea behind the concept of humanism in the managerial domain is related to the consideration that "it is possible to provide an ethical and anthropological foundation for economics and business" (Giovanola 2009, 431).

In particular, the humanistic perspective on management and business relies on the conviction that only an ethical and anthropological underpinning may help us in handling or coping with the most relevant shortcomings of economics and business (Mangia et al. 2012; Giovanola 2009; Stachowicz-Stanusch and Amman 2012).

The particular emphasis put over the theoretical perspective of humanistic management implies that the idea of ethics has to play a crucial role, since it represents the pillar on which to set up a long-lasting community (Acevedo 2012; Giovanola 2009; Wankel and Malleck 2010).

Several authors (Dierksmeier et al. 2011; Dierksmeier 2011) have put the emphasis on the humanistic perspective, underlining that human beings should "change" their role, needing to be:

> [R]einstated in the system of economic interactions as its active subjects. Human beings must hence never be accounted for as mere cost factors or labor suppliers, i.e., secondary factors in an economy geared to primarily quantitative goals. Rather they need to be regarded as the primary qualitative objective of business. (Dierksmeier 2011, 22)

The theoretical reflections carried on by Sen (Sen 1999; Sen 2006; Sen and International Labour Office 1975; Sen and Hawthorn 1987;

Spitzeck et al. 2009) confirm the strong relation between the idea of humanism and the one of dignity. The author rejects the terminology of human capital or human resources: it could sound a bit paradoxical, but this theoretical direction expresses Sen's willingness to recommend to re-conceptualize business around human relations and human capabilities (Boselie 2010).

The concept of dignity is often taken into account to analyze people's ethical behavior.

As highlighted by Dierksmeier (2011), the idea of dignity changes its meaning depending on the theoretical perspective we may adopt: the author shows in his work how the concept of dignity changed over time. Starting from the antiques, when only some humans were seen as worthy of dignity, moving to the Christian religion, where dignity is attributed to all humans as a result of divine creation, going to, finally, the era of modernity, where more emphasis is given to the idea of freedom (Dierksmeier 2011).

Furthermore, the author puts the accent over the relationship between the Kantian ideas of freedom and dignity; stating, "every human being has dignity through being able to be moral–but only those who do, in fact, lead moral lives also deserve the praise of personal ethical value." The consequence is that we should try to make a distinction between human beings who use their dignity appropriately and human beings who use it inappropriately (Dierksmeier 2011).

This theoretical reasoning should be taken into account in many practical implications, even in an eventual new setting up of the management education: this means that every man and woman should always be educated with dignity. In other words, as stated by Dierksmeier (2011) "respect for dignity means, consequently, respect for the capacity of the human being to define its own ends, ideally but not always actually, in the pursuit of a moral life."

Hence, looking to business students' behavior, several authors (Neubam et al. 2009; Cavico and Mujtaba 2009) have shown how business school students are not less ethical than their non-business peers. The authors argue that many of the recent discussions of business schools have centred not on the good their graduates do, but on how the theoretical foundations of business school education may be linked to ethical lapses and scandals involving managers who have been subjected to business school training. (Neubam et al. 2009, 9)

There are also other studies (Ferraro, Pfeffer, and Sutton 2005; Rutherford et al. 2012) that, on the other side, point out a different result by arguing the problem is that business students behave less ethically than their colleagues enrolled in other programs.

The contribution given by Ferraro, Pfeffer, and Sutton (2005) is particularly interesting since the authors point out the nature of economics as a self-fulfilling theory: the concept of self-interested behavior that business and economics students learn in their classes influence their behavior in that direction, becoming true (Ferraro, Pfeffer, and Sutton 2005).

A review over many researches has been conducted by Rutherford et al. (2012) to comprehend how business students behave in critical contexts. The results of this work presents a very sad picture.

For instance, Cadsby and Maynes (1998) and Marwell and Ames (1981) point out how business and economics students are more likely to free-ride; Carter and Irons (1991) put into evidence that these students are more likely to keep more resources for themselves. At the same time, it seems that business students are more corruptible than others (Bauman and Rose 2011; Frank and Schulze 2000).

Nonis and Swift (2001) found that students who engaged in unethical behavior in college were more likely to assume unethical behavior even at work. More recently, Long, Malhotra, and Murnighan (2011) found a positive relationship between economics education and students' attitudes toward greed.

According to these considerations, Long, Malhotra, and Murnighan (2011) argue that even if it could be completely unintentional, "a systematic exposure to economics and business disciplines" may provide students with convenient theoretical frameworks that license greed and other unethical values with concrete effects on the practical behaviors.

The self-interest maximization assumption is definitively pervasive in the field of economics and management, so that other typologies of human motivations may be overlooked (Long, Malhotra, and Murnighan 2011). Economics is assuming a very strong role in business education, and many theoretical models are based on a rationalistic and calculative approach: the economics "thinking" regards the entire society, and it has become a sort of unique true that creates consensus among people; as result, everyone thinks self-interest is the only way to manage a society.

The way business and economics students behave and perceive the external reality depends directly on the way they are considered and described within business schools. Bejou (2005) argues that students within the western management education system are typically inter-preted and approached to as customers, rather than as just students. In the competitive marketplace, business schools must sell courses and other collateral products and services that are devoted to enrich students' life (Bejou 2005).

Furthermore, we should also consider a matter of language: as Acevedo (2012) argues, language is not just a tool to communicate, but it represents also a way to determine reality. Snyder (2007) has pointed out how this language has been deeply influential in the United States, in the UK, and in Europe and Australia.

The 1994 Group states that, "roles of the modern student include: Learner, Citizen, Colleague, Consumer, Scholar, Ambassador; but per-haps the most important role of all is Partner" (The 1994 Group 2007, 2), and that "all students are increasingly being viewed, and viewing them-selves, as consumers" (14).

As underlined by Obermiller, Fleenor, and Raven (2005), Acevedo's statement may be useful to understand the reality referring both to public and to private universities across different countries and disciplines. In other words, we may refer to the Sapir Whorf hypothesis, which states that there is a strong interrelationship between the language and the concrete reality, in the sense that, language discovers truth previously unknown or creates new realities.

As pointed out by many authors (Edmunson 1997; Clayson and Haley 2005; Furedi 2007) the entire society risks to have a generation of managers, politics, and so on, influenced by the negative outcomes of our (western) education system in the business domain, as the following:

- Students with a short-term perspective
- The absence of a strong and sincere sense of accountability
- A general commoditization of education
- The "loss" of academic values, that is, integrity and freedom.

As result of this process, the risk is to have a class of managers who behave in an opportunistic and unethical way.

Recovering and Restoring the Ethical Values

In recent years, defining vision, mission, or core values has become very common not only among entrepreneurs, but also within the higher education system. In fact, numerous higher schools are proud of their core values and present them to their employees, students, and stakeholders by adorning walls in their campuses with placards expressing those core values as well as including them in the first pages of many academic publications. But it seems the role and influence of these core values are restricted to these superficial actions: true core values appear dead and forgotten (Stachowicz-Stanusch 2012; Wankel and Stachowicz-Stanusch 2012).

As noted by Stachowicz-Stanusch (2012), often decisions made by a university's authority do not fit declared core values; by not creating an internal culture of integrity, they foster a culture of cynicism and a lack of trust in interpersonal relations, which may cause the atrophy of organizational bonds and the decrease of social capital inside the university.

Despite this, the current crisis of academic ethos has inspired colleges and universities to be more introspective and to draw lessons from public mistakes; in some cases, they are trying to start a process of redefining their ethos in order to better educate honest and responsible future leaders in the world.

To form ethic-oriented students, a fundamental academic value is truth, because it permeates the three basic spheres of academic activity (Stachowicz-Stanusch 2012): scientific research, education, and social servicing. Along with truth, other important values that are characteristic of academic life are reliability and responsibility.

These values strongly influence the academic activities and are fundamental because they drive the whole society behavior.

Hence, during scientific research, the academic community should search for truth and act in a reliable and responsible way itself, and then educate students in a responsible way.

The Center for Academic Integrity (1999) has individuated as fundamental values at the basis of an ethic-oriented academic community respect, trust, honesty, responsibility, and effort. Actually, what is really important is not to define the set of values, but the process of constructing academic integrity, the process of creating values and their cultivation in an ethical way, by making those values shared and accepted among all the community members.

Core values are also defined as the principles that are permanent, fundamental, and inviolable, but, as an organization develops and transforms itself during its life, its core values may change during time as the external context and the entire society.

This leads to the necessity to understand how these values change over time in order to evaluate if they need to be "updated" or protected by "new unethical" behavior.

As highlighted by Stachowicz-Stanusch (2012),

> Time, success, and other factors blur human memory about the reasons for success. Moreover, the new, unfamiliar values that are identified by higher schools' management or that were considered to be better and more competitive are often imposed on a university's participants. In such a case, in the university there develops a strong and centralized organizational culture that hinders initiatives and innovation—a culture supporting bureaucracy and egocentric behaviors. There are two primary reasons for this:
>
> • First, it is often forgotten that core values are not something that may be "bought or borrowed." Core values are an internal element of an organization, they are those values that are shared by its members in the deepest and strongest way;

- Secondly, core values as a core of culture of integrity have not been passed from one generation of management to following one.

What causes the persistence and development of an organization and is a fundamental of integrity at university is not just awareness of its core values but also a consequent management of them and implementing them into organizational life in a morally positive manner.

Methodology

This study has involved 187 students, coming from the two Universities of Ghent (Belgium) and Naples (Italy). The participants volunteered immediately after the completion of an intermediate-level economics or education class session, on a single basis. The participants had been in college for an average of 2.5 years.

Fifty percent of economics students were male (94) and 50 percent were female (93). The students belonged to a homogenous annual intake of approximately 1,000 students in each university.

The questionnaire was given to:

- Eighty eight Italian students enrolled at the Faculty of Economics "Napoli Federico II," Napoli (Italy)
- Fifty six Belgian students enrolled at the Faculty of Economics "Ghent University," Ghent (Belgium)
- Forty three International students, involved in the Erasmus project, attending courses in the Faculty of Economics of Ghent University at that time

The survey was not completely face-to-face. The interviewer was available to ask questions and to assist the respondent in answering to them, but the respondents answered by using a computer with the interviewer away (to preserve the anonymity and the privacy of the answers). All the students answered within the premises of the universities or in university residences. Data are based solely on the perceptions of the respondents, and thus, may be subject to bias.

The objective of the survey was to gather perceptions about ethics, personal integrity, and the concept of management integrity among students in economics and management science.

The survey was articulated in four sections:

1. Business ethics and moral values assessment
2. Leadership and integrity
3. Teaching ethics and moral values
4. Moral values and performance

In the first section of the questionnaire, the respondents answered two questions about ethical behavior in today's business world and the moral code of conduct in the companies.

In the second section, the students were asked to give their opinion about the relation between management and integrity.

In the third section, the purpose was to have a better understanding of the students' opinions about teaching ethics in schools and universities.

In section four, the goal was to understand the participants' thoughts about the link between integrity and performance and integrity and organizational behavior.

The main aim of this survey is not to find statistical implications, but to raise some interesting discussion points over this important aspect within higher education systems.

According to this, the following section will theoretically discuss the results of the survey, while specific data and results of the survey are shown in the appendix.

Discussion

Several studies have tried to understand the impact of ethical values in higher education: recently, for example, Arfaoui et al. (2015), have tested the effectiveness of an ethics intervention before and after ethics education within a group of accounting students in Tunisia. Their study revealed that unethical behavior has consequences in the long term; this demonstrates the importance of the intervention, and that it may influence the students' decisions and their perceptions of the potential consequences of their decisions.

The participants to our survey have indicated in 59 percent of the cases the role of ethics as strongly relevant in higher education.

Furthermore, asking them if, as managers of a company, they would set up a code of conduct for the employees, more than 85 percent answered yes, confirming a particular interest in the theme of moral and ethical conduct.

The need of such an ethical intervention is also confirmed from what is evidenced by Osiemo (2012) and Natale and Doran (2012).

Osiemo (2012) has pointed out that

> Ignorance and apathy characterize the university life of many a student more than the ideal desire for an intellectual experience that would be expected. Much of this apathy and ignorance can be attributed to a failure to help the students appreciate what the university ought to be and what they can gain from it in their time there. (Osiemo 2012, 131)

Natale and Doran (2012) highlight the problem about "the marketization of education": "Business practices and principles now commonly suffuse the approach and administration of Higher Education in an attempt to make schools both more competitive and 'branded'"(Natale and Doran 2012, 187).

Natale and Doran also evidence that the higher education system has worked for centuries because founded on the belief that education was a process, today's system, instead, views higher education as a product from a perspective of economic value. A university in a consumer-driven culture should stimulate students to participate as informed purchasers in the market economy, then the institution must prepare students by doing more than developing their sense of economic self-interest (Natale and Doran 2012).

On this point, the participants to our survey agree (48 percent) and strongly agree (37 percent) that schools and universities should be more active in seeking to adopt core ethical values like honesty and responsibility, to develop good and respectful characters in students.

According to Osiemo (2012), the first step to do this is that the universities have to offer a system of values that students can emulate, since "they learn more from what they see the institution doing to live up to an ideal of contributing to the society, than what lecturers will try to tell them in the classroom" (135).

The second step is that the universities have to concentrate in bringing out the best in the students and help them to realize their full potential, not just focusing over their performance to improve their ranking.

Other initiatives should be founded on shaping a kind of leader who is people-oriented, realistic, confident, and responsible (Osiemo 2012).

Finally, the universities through their courses and initiatives should demonstrate leadership that is capable of integrating, resourcing, and orchestrating different activities, thus exhibiting a capacity to face complex problems of modern society.

Considering the answers given by the students and some literature contributions cited earlier, it looks clear that an ethical crisis has emerged within education internationally, and an intervention that requires a cultural change involving students, faculty, and administrators in an integrated process is urgently needed.

Conclusions

This work has been centered on the need to restore and transmit ethical values in teaching economics and management in higher education systems.

As mentioned earlier, the crucial role of professors along with taught theories is evidenced by several academic contributions.

Along with a review of the literature on ethics in higher education, we have conducted an analysis by submitting a survey among economics and management students in Italy and Belgium to understand if ethical values matters to them, and to understand their perspective of ethical issues in their present work and in their future as managers.

The results highlight that students perceive the importance of ethical values and behavior, and within organizations, recognize the role played by the CEO.

In particular, students point that the CEO influences the hiring process and the way people act within the organization, thus creating a more or less ethical way to behave.

Participants who do not think that the CEO may influence other people's behavior mainly think that an organization acts within a wider context in which several stakeholders operate that limit the CEO's power to influence ethical behavior.

But, what really looks worrying is that, a part of the students think that business is all about profitability and that there is no place for ethics.

Recent literature evidences the need of ethical intervention in the higher education system, even as an answer to a general apathy surrounding students and to what Natale and Doran (2012) have defined as "the marketization of education."

What looks mainly necessary is to explain the consequences of unethical behavior to students since they are very young: if we want to form ethic-oriented managers, we need to grow up ethic-oriented students.

A possible solution presented by Arfaoui et al. (2015) to arouse and maintain the students' interests is to demonstrate the importance of ethical behavior by involving the use of innovative tools (such as mind maps, quizzes, role-playing, and so on) and by exposing students to the real-world ethical dilemmas that reflect the complexities they should probably face in the future.

In addition, even Osiemo (2012) agrees on the fact that "As definitive institutions of higher learning, universities ought to play a big part in shaping the next generation of leaders" (131).

Furthermore, Osiemo (2012) underlines that, after the fall of large international corporations in the recent past as a result of acts of negligence, what is needed is a corporate culture strongly rooted in ethical and responsible behavior, more than laws and rules restricting what people should or should not do in the workplace.

In brief, the whole educating system is involved in the process of teaching and recovering ethical values, but the real challenge is that of universities as "culmination" of the formative years in the life of students and as important time to develop their life and career aspirations, and to equip them with the necessary knowledge and ethic values to make a positive contribution to the society.

References

Acevedo, A. 2012. "Personalist Business Ethics and Humanistic Management: Insights from Jacques Maritain." *Journal of Business Ethics* 105, no. 2, pp. 197–219.

Aktouf, O. 1992. "Management and Theories of Organizations in the 1990s: Toward a Critical Radical Humanism?" *The Academy of Management Review* 17, no. 3, pp. 407–31.

Anthony, P.D. 1998. "Management Education: Ethics Versus Morality." In *Ethics and Organizations*, ed. M. Parker, 269–81. London: Sage Publications.

Arfaoui, F., S. Damak-Ayadi, R. Ghram, and A. Bouchekoua. April 2015. "Students' Level of Moral Development: Experimental Design in Tunisian Audit Context." *Journal of Business Ethics.* doi:10.1007/s10551-015-2643-z

Bauman, Y., and E. Rose. 2011. "Selection or Indoctrination: Why Do Economics Students Donate Less than the Rest?" *Journal of Economic Behavior andamp; Organization* 79, no. 3, pp. 318–27.

Bejou, D. 2005. "Treating Students Like Customers." *BizEd* 4, no. 3, pp. 44–47.

Bennis, W.R., and J. O'Toole. 2005. "How Business School Lost Their Way." *Harvard Business Review* 83, no. 5, pp. 96–104.

Boselie, P. 2010. *Strategic Human Resource Management: A Balanced Approach.* London: McGraw-Hill Higher Education.

Cadsby, C.B., and E. Maynes. 1998. "Choosing Between a Socially Efficient and Free-Riding Equilibrium: Nurses Versus Economics and Business Students." *Journal of Economic Behavior and Organization* 37, no. 2, pp. 183–92.

Carter, J.R., and M.D. Irons. 1991. "Are Economists Different, and If So, Why?" *Journal of Economic Perspectives* 5, no. 2, pp. 171–77.

Cavico, F.J., and B.J. Mujtaba. 2009. "The State of Business Schools, Business Education, and Business Ethics." *Journal of Academic and Business Ethics* 2, pp. 1–18.

Clayson, D.E., and D.A. Haley. 2005. "Marketing Models in Education: Students as Customers, Products, or Partners." *Marketing Education Review* 15, no. 1, pp. 1–11.

Dierksmeier, C. 2011. *Reorienting Management Education: From the Homo Economicus to Human Dignity.* Ref Type: Unpublished Work.

Dierksmeier, C., W. Amann, E. Von KImakovitz, H. Spitzeck, and M. Pirson. 2011. *Humanistic Ethics in the Age of Globality.* London: Palgrave Macmillan.

Edmunson, M. 1997. "On the Uses of a Liberal Education as Lite Entertainment for Bored College Students." *Harper's Magazine* 295, no. 1768, pp. 39–49.

Ferraro, F., J. Pfeffer, and R.I. Sutton. 2005. "Economics Language and Assumptions: How Theories Can Become Self-Fulfilling." *Academy of Management Review* 30, no. 1, pp. 8–24.

Frank, B., and G.G. Schulze. 2000. "Does Economics Make Citizens Corrupt?" *Journal of Economic Behavior and Organization* 43, no. 1, pp. 101–13.

Furedi, F. 2007. "There's no Added Value in Sales Talk." *Times Higher Education Supplement*, December 14.

Giovanola, B. 2009. "Re-Thinking the Anthropological and Ethical Foundation of Economics and Business: Human Richness and Capabilities Enhancement." *Journal of Business Ethics* 88, no. 3, pp. 431–44.

Ivory, C., P. Miskell, H. Shipton, A. White, K. Moeslein, and A. Neely. 2006. *UK Business Schools: Historical Contexts and Future Scenarios.* London: Advanced Institute of Management.

Long, W., D. Malhotra, and J.K. Murnighan. 2011. "Economics Education and Greed." *Academy of Management Learning and Education* 10, pp. 643–60.

Mangia, G., S. Consiglio, P. Canonico, and E. De Nito. 2012. "The Subterfuge of Business Integrity: Legal Complicity with Criminal Organizations in Italy." In *Integrity in Organizations–Building the Foundations for Humanistic Management*, eds. W. Amann, and A. Stachowicz-Stanusch, 1–32. London: Palgrave MacMillan.

Marwell, G., and R.E. Ames. 1981. "Economists Free Ride, Does Anyone Else?" *Journal of Public Economics* 15, no. 3, pp. 295–310.

Melé, D. 2003. "The Challenge of Humanistic Management." *Journal of Business Ethics* 44, no. 1, pp. 77–88.

Melé, D. 2012. *Management Ethics: Placing Ethics at the Core of Good Management.* Basingstoke: Palgrave Macmillan.

Mintzberg, H., and J. Gosling. 2002. "Educating Managers Beyond Borders." *Academy of Management Learning and Education* 1, no. 1, pp. 64–76.

Mitroff, I.I. 2004. "An Open Letter to the Deans and the Faculties of American Business Schools." *Journal of Business Ethics* 54, no. 2, pp. 185–89.

Natale, S.M., and C. Doran. 2012. "Marketization of Education: An Ethical Dilemma." *Journal of Business Ethics* 105, no. 2, pp. 187–96.

Neubam, D.O., M. Pagell, J. Drexler, F.M. Kee-Ryan, and E. Larson. 2009. "Business Education and Its Relationship to Student Personal Moral Philosophies and Attitudes Toward Profits: An Empirical Response to Critics." *Academy of Management Learning and Education* 8, no. 1, pp. 9–24.

Nonis, S., and C.O. Swift. 2001. "An Examination of the Relationship Between Academic Dishonesty and Workplace Dishonesty: A Multicampus Investigation." *Journal of Education for Business* 77, no. 2, pp. 69–77.

Obermiller, C., P. Fleenor, and P. Raven. 2005. "Students as Customers or Products: Perceptions and Preferences of Faculty and Students." *Marketing Education Review* 15, no. 2, pp. 27–38.

Osiemo, L.B. 2012. "Developing Responsible Leaders: The University at the Service of the Person." *Journal of Business Ethics* 108, no. 2, pp. 131–43.

Pfeffer, J. 2005. "Why Do Bad Management Theories Persist? A Comment on Ghoshal." *Academy of Management Learning and Education* 4, no. 1, pp. 96–100.

Pfeffer, J., and C.T. Fong. 2004. "The Business School 'Business': Some Lessons from the U.S. Experience." *Journal of Management Studies* 41, no. 8, pp. 1501–20.

Rutherford, M.A., L. Parks, D.E. Cavazos, and C.D. White. 2012. "Business Ethics as a Required Course: Investigating the Factors Impacting the Decision to Require Ethics in the Undergraduate Business Core Curriculum." *Academy of Management Learning and Education* 11, no. 2, pp. 174–86.

Sen, A. 1999. *Development as Freedom.* Oxford: Oxford University Press.

Sen, A. 2006. *Identity and Violence the Illusion of Destiny.* New York: W.W. Norton & Co.

Sen, A., and G. Hawthorn. (1985) 1987. *The Standard of Living the Tanner Lectures.* Clare Hall: Cambridge.

Sen, A., and International Labour Office. 1975. *Employment, Technology and Development a Study Prepared for the International Labour Office Within the Framework of the World Employment Programme.* Oxford: Clarendon Press.

Snyder, W. 2007. *Child Language: The Parametric Approach.* Oxford: Oxford University Press.

Spitzeck, H. 2011. "An Integrated Model of Humanistic Management." *Journal of Business Ethics* 99, no. 1, pp. 51–62.

Spitzeck, H., M. Pirson, W. Amann, S. Khan, and E. von Kimakowitz, eds. 2009. *Humanism in Business.* Cambridge: Cambridge University Press.

Stachowicz-Stanusch, A. 2012. *Academic Ethos Management: Building the Foundation for Integrity in Management Education.* New York: Businesss Expert Press.

Stachowicz-Stanusch, A., and W. Amman. 2012. *Integrity in Organizations-Building the Foundations for Humanistic Management.* Basingstoke: Palgrave Macmillan.

The 1994 Group. November 2007. "Enhancing the Student Experience: Policy Statement." http://old.1994group.ac.uk/documents/public/SEPolicy Statement.pdf

The Center for Academic Integrity. 1999. *The Fundamental Values of Academic Integrity.*

Wankel, C., and S. Malleck. 2010. *Emerging Ethical Issues of Life in Virtual Worlds.* Charlotte, NC: Information Age Pub.

Wankel, C., and A. Stachowicz-Stanusch, eds. 2011. *Management Education for Integrity: Ethically Educating Tommorrow's Business Leaders.* Bingley, UK: Emerald Group Publishing.

Wankel, C., and A. Stachowicz-Stanusch. 2012. *Handbook of Research on Teaching Ethics in Business and Management Education.* PA: IGI Global.

Appendix

1 Business Ethics and Moral Values Assessment

"Do you think that ethical behavior is relevant in today's business world?"

Absolutely yes	59%
Sometimes	32%
No	9%
No answer	1%

"If you were a manager of a company, would you provide a moral code of conduct to all of your employees?"

Yes	86%
No	6%
Do not know	9%

Therefore, it emerges a significant appreciation about the issue of managerial ethical behavior and about the statement of a moral code of conduct.

There is no significant gender difference about these perceptions.

In the same section, the respondents were asked the question "What kind of traits should a good leader have?" And, they had to rate each question on a scale 1–4 (where 1 = Not very important; 2 = Moderately important; 3 = Very important; 4 = Extremely important).

Table A.1 resumes the main descriptive statistics of the collected answers.

Dedication received the highest average within all the students (Italians, Belgians, and Internationals) involved in the survey. After dedication, we found integrity. The results show that integrity matters, and it is one of the most important traits that a leader should have.

According to the Italian students, dedication is the main trait of a leader, followed by creativity and integrity (which has a score very similar to the score in the preceding table).

Dedication was also chosen by Belgian students as the principal feature of leadership. For those students, fairness comes before integrity, and

Table A.1 Descriptive overall statistics of the question "What kind of traits should a good leader have?"

	Mean	**Dev**	**Var**	**SD**
Openness	3.2995	95.2299	0.5093	0.7136
Humility	2.8449	136.503	0.73	0.8544
Magnanimity	2.4278	119.775	0.6405	0.8003
Integrity	3.4064	83.1123	0.4445	0.6667
Dedication	3.5455	70.3636	0.3763	0.6134
Assertiveness	3.2487	121.312	0.6419	0.8012
Fairness	3.2727	111.091	0.5941	0.7708
Sense of humor	2.4439	136.16	0.7281	0.8533
Creativity	3.3369	115.775	0.6191	0.7868

furthermore, we can notice that creativity (rated as second trait for Italians) comes fifth for Belgians.

International students place integrity at the top, while creativity comes immediately after.

Belgian students assess dedication, fairness, and integrity as the main three traits. For them, creativity is not in the top four positions. Italian and Erasmus students put creativity in the top three.

Italian students do not consider fairness as one of the most important traits of a leader as Belgian and Erasmus do.

Humility, magnanimity, and sense of humor take the last positions for Italians and Belgian and Erasmus. For Belgian students, assertiveness matters much more than to Italians and Erasmus.

After that, we asked students to assess their own moral values (results are shown in Table A.2). The purpose was to find out what was their dominant value in their personal lives that is different than work life.

The question was: "Assess your own moral values. 1 = Not very important; 2 = Moderately important; 3 = Very important; 4 = Extremely important."

As a matter of fact, students indicate respect as their most important moral value and then truth and responsibility.

Table A.2 Descriptive overall statistics of the question "Assess your own moral values"

	Mean	Dev	Var	SD
Fairness	3.2781	117.54	0.6286	0.7928
Humility	3.1551	104.503	0.5588	0.7476
Reverence for life	3.0894	90.5698	0.506	0.7113
Tolerance	3.0321	105.807	0.5658	0.7522
Preservation of nature	2.9949	124.995	0.6377	0.7986
Responsibility	3.4064	89.1123	0.4765	0.6903
Freedom	3.3529	90.7059	0.4851	0.6965
Devotion	2.9412	110.353	0.5901	0.7682
Respect	3.6898	50.0107	0.2674	0.5171
Compassion	2.6738	123.102	0.6583	0.8114
Honor	2.9144	144.631	0.7734	0.8794
Truth	3.4118	85.2941	0.4561	0.6754
Social harmony	3.2299	107.112	0.5728	0.7568
Generosity	2.8877	116.642	0.6238	0.7898

2 Leadership and Integrity

"In your opinion, do the ethics of a CEO play a meaningful role in the way an organization is run?"

- *Eighty percent of the participants responded YES.*
  Students were also asked to justify their answers, choosing one answer from four choices:
  Thirty-three percent said that the ethics of a CEO play a meaningful role because it has an influence on people in the organization both in terms of hiring who works in the organization and also on how those people act.

  According to those, the CEO has an enormously important role in setting, joining, leading, and responding to breaches of organizational ethics. If the CEO does not care, it is demoralizing and anxiety-producing for all others associated. When the CEO cares and acts consistently and speaks of ethics, others are heartened and encouraged, and held accountable, and all involved feel proud of and identify with their organizations.

Thirty-one percent think that ethics of a CEO are important because leadership starts at the top, so leaders must lead by example. Great leaders inspire by example. The behavior of ethical CEO's trickles all the way down into an organization. Leading by example sets the pace for the rest of the organization and the competitors as well. As the old saying goes, "if you do not stand for something, you will fall for anything."

Fourteen percent declared that the CEO represents the brand/reputation of the company. He/she is the "face of the company." That's why his/her ethics play a meaningful role in the organization. If leaders misinform their people, make false claims to justify their actions, and base their actions on the convenient point of view that the "ends justify the means," they will lose the credibility and ultimately the ability to lead.

The answer good ethics can save you money collected only 2 percent of responses among the people who think that ethics of the CEO plays a meaningful role. Ethics are always an individual thing. The need for ethics exists from a utility perspective. It pays off to display ethical behavior. However, this is not the reason one should be ethical. The CEO should be ethical because ethics helps him/her to pass from a competitive approach to a creative approach. It also allows him/her to focus on his own abilities rather than the strengths of others.

- *Twenty percent of participants answered NO.*
  Only 1 percent said that the ethics are not important. These students believe that there are many CEOs in the business world who do not have the integrity or ethics necessary to manage their corporations properly.

  The answer CEO does not impact front line employees gathered 3 percent of the responses. One person and his or her ethics do not affect the way business gets done. There are too many stakeholders who drive a corporation—CEOs who rock the boat in one direction or another tend to be weeded out very quickly. This 3 percent of the respondents do not believe that a CEO alone has the power to enforce a strong sense of ethics when the system is entrenched in rewarding the lack thereof.

Nine percent said that the importance of the ethics of the CEO depends on the context. For example, they think that in a smaller company, ethics can play a larger role than in a larger company. They also believe that the ethics of the CEO depend on the industry and who your peers are.

Seven percent of the students believe that business is all about profitability, not ethics. In major companies, the only ethic is profit, and boards reward even failure by huge payouts to failed CEOs. One student, during the survey, told me that "there are ethics and then there are ethics" implying that the ends justify only when ends equal large sums of money. Short-term profit sales drive the strategy and also CEOs are paid based on profitability only.

After that, students were also asked to assess a leader's integrity capability (see Table A.3 for results). We gave 15 different choices and they had to rate each question on a scale 1–4 (where 1 = Not very important; 2 = Moderately important; 3 = Very important; 4 = Extremely important).

The table shows that the leader's prime capability is to "show personal courage and take responsibility," followed by to "establish and maintain successful business relationships and partnerships." In the last position, we found "effectively deal with one's own and others' emotions." Comparing the three groups observed, we found that:

Erasmus students are the only ones who put the answer "demonstrate strong values, ethical standards, and personal integrity" as first. For them, this capability comes before "show personal courage …." While Belgian students do not believe that "use intuition and make sound judgment" is one of the most important leader's capability; Italians and Erasmus put it respectively in the fourth and third place. Delivering value to stakeholders is slightly more important for Erasmus students than for Italians and Belgium. While display personal drive, confidence, and resilience comes second for Belgians, for Italians and Erasmus, it comes tenth.

Table A.3 Descriptive overall statistics of the question "Assess a leader's integrity capability"

	Mean	Dev	Var	SD
Demonstrate strong values	3.315508	86.38503	0.461952	0.679671
Show personal courage and take responsibility	3.438503	72.04278	0.385256	0.62069
Display personal drive, confidence, and resilience	3.005348	70.99465	0.379651	0.616158
Effectively deal with one's own and others' emotions	2.679144	94.4866	0.506677	0.711813
Commit to professional and personal development and excellence	3.010695	91.97861	0.491864	0.70133
Demonstrate self-awareness and understanding of others	3.058824	98.35294	0.525952	0.725225
Use intuition and make sound judgment	2.962567	92.73797	0.495925	0.704219
Manage own workload and competing priorities	2.839572	95.18717	0.509022	0.713458
Establish and maintain successful business relationships and partnerships	3.145946	89.05946	0.481402	0.693832
Facilitate cooperation and partnerships	3.181818	81.81818	0.43753	0.661461
Nurture the positive internal and external relationships and professional networks	3.122995	98.17112	0.524979	0.724555
Consider yourself to be customer-focused	2.84492	106.5027	0.569533	0.754674
Deliver value to a stakeholder	2.914439	112.631	0.602305	0.776083
Demonstrate political sensitivity and organizational awareness	2.791444	114.8663	0.614258	0.783746
Create and promote team identity and professionalism	3.144385	119.1016	0.636907	0.798065

3 Teaching Ethics and Moral Values

Here, our purpose was to have a better understanding of the students' opinions about teaching ethics in schools and universities.

"Can ethics and moral values be taught?"

Eighty-six percent students answered YES, with no substantial difference between male and female students.

"Is that important to teach ethics in universities?"

Only 5 percent of students said that teaching ethics in universities is not very important. There were also 31 percent participants answering that having an ethics course in universities is extremely important.

"Schools and universities should be more active in seeking to adopt core ethical values like honesty, responsibility, respect, and developing good character in children and students?"

Strongly agree	37%
Agree	48%
Neither agree nor disagree	12%
Disagree	3%
Strongly disagree	1%

"In your opinion, does integrity require moral goodness?"

Yes	70%
No	15%
Do not know	15%

A striking majority of the respondents are convinced that integrity is internally related to a host of virtues, which includes goodness.

4 Moral Values and Performance

"How far do you agree with the statement: There is a strong connection between ethical values, performance, and success?"

Strongly agree	17%
Agree	44%
Neither agree nor disagree	23%
Disagree	14%
Strongly disagree	2%

Once again, the majority (61 percent) believes that performance and success are linked with each other. They think that the more a company is ethical, the higher the performance is, at least the long-term one.

"How far do you agree with this following statement: Setting up a culture of business integrity and ethical values in a organization could deduct from performance?"

Strongly agree	3%
Agree	40%
Neither agree nor disagree	37%
Disagree	18%
Strongly disagree	2%

In this case, the uncertainty of the participants is evident. A significant number of them is unable to decide whether a culture of business integrity can worsen the performance.

"How far do you agree with this statement: An organization's success depends on the integrity of its employees?"

Strongly agree	16%
Agree	45%
Neither agree nor disagree	29%
Disagree	9%
Strongly disagree	1%

"Do you think that legal conduct and ethical behavior are identical?"

Always	3%
Most of the time	29%
Sometimes	62%
Never occurs	6%

The responses show that students still confuse legal conduct with ethical behavior. Most societies also have legal rules that govern behavior, but ethical norms tend to be broader and more informal than laws.

PART III

Light and Darkness in Higher Education Management

The Dark Side of the Transformational Leadership Paradigm: Why Leadership Education Curricula Need to Be Reconsidered

Fabiola Gerpott

Jacobs University Bremen and VU University Amsterdam

Sven C. Voelpel

Jacobs University Bremen

Introduction

Leaders can improve individual, team, and organizational performance (Gang et al. 2011), and have been shown to significantly affect followers, for example, with regard to their state of health (Franke, Felfe, and Pundt 2014), creativity (Dong, Hui, and Loi 2012), commitment (Tyssen, Wald, and Heidenreich 2014), as well as their work engagement and voice behavior (Cheng et al. 2014). Given how influential leaders are as role models in organizations, their education and development is pivotal for shaping the firms' corporate culture and social responsibility (Jones Christensen, Mackey, and Whetten 2014). However, a number of counterproductive leader behaviors has recently caused ethical scandals, companies' bankruptcy, and irresponsible practices (Pearce, Wassenaar, and Manz 2014). Nevertheless, most researchers and practitioners still stick to functional leadership approaches that concentrate primarily on uncovering and teaching leadership skills and competencies (Crossan et al. 2013). In particular, the concept of transformational leadership has received considerable attention as the "one-and-only" solution to becoming an effective leader (Tourish, Craig, and Amernic 2010; van Knippenberg and Sitkin 2013; Yukl 2012). While a variety of other leadership styles, for example, instrumental leadership (Rowold 2014), dominant, and prestige-based leadership (Cheng, Tracy, and Henrich 2010) or coercive and authoritative leadership (Schneider and Schröder 2012), have also raised the scholars' and teachers' interest, this chapter focuses on transformational leadership since it has been the most popular leadership model in business education over the last few decades (McCleskey 2014; Tourish, Craig, and Amernic 2010), and is exemplary of the functionalist assumptions inherent in most other "traditional" leadership concepts.

In this chapter, we criticize the narrowed transformational leadership curricula in business schools and universities by pointing out that the approach has a number of limitations, and inhibits the implementation of more balanced leader-development programs. Our chapter is structured into three parts. First, we describe the constituting elements and the rise of the transformational paradigm. Given the prevalence of the concept in research, education, media, and organizations, we argue that it has developed into an ideology that is no longer questioned. Second, we outline three major areas of leadership that fall short when focusing solely on the transformational leadership concept, namely (1) a lack of follower orientation and interpersonal skills development, (2) an under-emphasis of ethical and reflective aspects, and (3) a functionalist rather than holistic perspective implying a neglect of organizational tensions and paradoxes as a source of high performance. We do not only portray and criticize the transformational approach, but also offer a way forward by reviewing alternative approaches to designing curricula for leadership education. In order to structure the field and give an overview of alternative paths to leadership education, we systematically reviewed the last three years (2012–2014) of literature on new teaching methods published in the journal *Academy of Management Learning & Education* (AMLE). We conclude that, although some promising avenues have been explored, we need highly innovative concepts that not merely regard leadership as an "add-on" topic to general management education, but that integrate human resource management into other disciplines.

The Rise of the Transformational Leadership Paradigm

Since the 1980s, the leadership concept has been steered away from its original emphasis on the day-to-day, operational task of aligning the employees' actions to reach a common goal toward a focus on the leader's transformational power (van Knippenberg and Sitkin 2013). Common to this new, visionary focus is the assumption that leaders can transform their subordinates into highly motivated followers, and thus influence a company's destiny: "Leaders exist to 'change things.' They render organizations as something different. They help organizations to transform for the better—to find heretofore unknown meaning, to articulate and advance common goals, and to effect (allegedly) outstanding performance" (Tourish, Craig, and Amernic 2010, S41). In order to achieve these extraordinary outcomes, most transformational approaches embrace that leaders must possess charisma (Bass 1990; House and Shamir 1993; Shamir, House, and Arthur 1993). Dating back to Weber (1947, 329), this indispensable ingredient of transformational leaders describes "a certain quality of an individual personality by virtue of which he is set apart from ordinary men and treated as endowed with supernatural, superhuman, or at least specifically exceptional qualities." Furthermore, a number of other admirable skills have been added to the transformational concept, for example, the communication of an inspiring vision, intellectual stimulation, and individualized consideration of the followers' different needs (Bass 1985; Bass and Avolio 1995).

Considering these extraordinary attributes, it is not surprising that this emotional and miraculous approach to leadership has drawn both the social scientists' and practitioners' attention. On the one hand, researchers have extensively explored the impacts of transformational leadership on a number of organizational outcomes (for meta-analytic reviews, see DeRue et al. 2011; Gang et al. 2011; Judge and Piccolo 2004; Lowe, Kroeck, and Sivasubramaniam 1996). On the other hand, almost all business schools have adapted their curricula to teach transformational skills to their students, for example, by using case studies of extraordinary managers (Tourish, Craig, and Amernic 2010) or by prompting instructors to become transformational educators (Balwant, Birdi, and Stephan 2014). Business journalists have also jumped on the bandwagon, publishing numerous bestsellers praising charismatic-transformational leaders, like Steve Jobs (Blumenthal 2012; Elliot and Simon 2011; Isaacson 2011) or Jack Welch (Krames 2003; Slater 1993, 1994), thus further supporting the societal heroization of managers as "corporate saviors" (Hegele and Kieser 2001; Khurana 2003).

Given the popularity of the transformational leadership paradigm, we argue that it has become an unquestioned ideology in western industrialized countries. An ideology is commonly defined as a social group's system of ideas characterized by a shared mental value-knowledge system that is immune to doubts, and the fulfillment of a functional role for its adherers (Eagleton 1991; Nienhueser 2011; Van Dijk 1998).

First, an ideology is a shared set of ideas, values, and knowledge that individuals, who follow it, consider superior to other concepts. The adherers support a "body of statements, which suggests truth but is at the same time difficult to falsify and even immunize themselves to falsification" (Nienhueser 2011, 373). Fulfilling this criterion, "there is a widely shared consensus that charismatic-transformational leadership is a particularly effective form of leadership," and thus is defended against skeptics (van Knippenberg and Sitkin 2013, 1). Critics arguing that the impact of company leaders on firm performance is limited (Hawawini, Subramanian, and Verdin 2003; Lieberson and O'Connor 1972; Wernerfelt and Montgomery 1988) have received little attention. Instead, enormous faith is placed in the power of charismatic leaders (Fanelli and Grasselli 2005): Environmental and other influencing factors are neglected when linking the positive outcomes to transformational supervisors (Tourish 2013). Many of the researchers who follow the transformational leadership paradigm have used the Multifactor Leadership Questionnaire (Bass and Avolio 1995)—an instrument criticized by a number of scholars for poor measurement properties (Lievens, Van Geit, and Coetsier 1997; Rafferty and Griffin 2004)—to generate evidence that "seems to again and again confirm its [transformational leadership's] effectiveness" (van Knippenberg and Sitkin 2013, 48). Yet, these authors not only largely ignore the absence of appropriate measurement methods, but their conceptualization of transformational leadership also lacks a definition independent of its effects and a theoretically grounded configurational model explaining the relationship between the different dimensions of transformational leadership (van Knippenberg and Sitkin 2013; Yukl 1999). However, appreciating these problems inherent in the transformational approach would jeopardize the perpetuation of the ideology—a threat that supporters try to avoid. Individuals prefer simple explanations for complex outcomes, like organizational performance, and thus are likely to overestimate the influence of human actors and to underestimate situational factors—a tendency known as "fundamental attribution error" (Ross 1977; Tetlock 1985).

These human preferences lead to the second constituting element of ideologies, namely their functional role. Ideologies serve a purpose and help explain phenomena in organizational life (Weick 1995), contributing to an increase in the social groups' or institutions' power. Transferring this functional aspect into the transformational approach, a number of stakeholders profit from the pervasiveness of the charismatic leadership paradigm.

First, the concept provides a promising basis for researchers to publish studies on the ingredients of leadership effectiveness in high-tier journals, as they can build on widespread scientific acceptance and calls for further research in this area. Furthermore, by offering an appealing framework, which attracts the attention of various social groups beyond the scientific community, the approach has helped increase the status of leadership scholars over the last decades. The introduction of the transformational concept

> created such a sense of excitement that new researchers were brought into the field and management practitioners became convinced that scholars were now beginning to capture the real essence of leadership. This whole movement then sharply accelerated the development of the field. (Hunt 1999, 138)

Second, business schools and universities prefer easily teachable and plausible leadership concepts that attract a large number of (MBA) students (Antonacopoulou 2010). The transformational approach can be used to support the achievement of this target because it is straightforward and appeals to (future) managers, since it promises that, owing to their personality, extraordinary talents, and virtues, they will be able to make a difference at their employers (Peterson et al. 2003). Thus, the paradigm can increase the learners' self-confidence and create the impression that their tuition fees will pay off, as it promises to provide them with the necessary skills to become influential at their future employers—a central motivation for numerous MBA students (Mintzberg 2005).

Third, individuals who occupy higher echelon positions within corporations are keen to maintain their status as firm saviors, who are able to convert disengaged employees into highly motivated followers. This heroic image of the leader not only brings about considerable tangible financial benefits, but also a number of emotional rewards, such as social recognition and appreciation. Thus, in order for managers to preserve their power and sustain their self-image as charismatic visionaries, it is crucial for them to defend the leaders' pivotal role in ensuring organizational success. The transformational approach serves to achieve these goals by seeking "to position the CEO as the fount of all wisdom and certainly as the final arbiter of anything resembling an important decision" (Tourish 2013, 38).

Given the positive functionality outlined earlier, it becomes obvious why the transformational approach has enjoyed an extraordinarily positive reception in the Western world. Nevertheless, as discussed in the following section, this leadership style has a number of shortcomings that may bring about considerable negative side-effects for organizations in the long term.

Shortcomings of the Transformational Paradigm and Future Alternatives

We acknowledge that the transformational approach has contributed significantly to teaching business students and (future) managers the importance of communicating a convincing vision and providing inspirational motivation, individual consideration, and intellectual stimulation to followers. However, we agree with van Knippenberg and Sitkin (2013) that the transformational paradigm needs to be reconsidered: "In a spirit of 'creative destruction,' we actually need to take a good thing [i.e., the transformational approach] apart in order to make it better." We argue that this step is necessary not only due to the approach's conceptual problems (Gerpott and Voelpel 2014; van Knippenberg and Sitkin 2013), but also because its underlying hierarchical logic inhibits a more balanced understanding of leadership. Specifically, we identify three limitations that future leadership education should tackle.

First, the transformational paradigm-induced heroization of leadership can prevent sustainable organizational learning, foster group thinking, and suppress the followers' voice. Second, the neglect of moral responsibility and critical thinking within the transformational approach can contribute to the emergence of questionable ethical practices by distorting business students and future leaders "into critters with lopsided brains, icy hearts, and shrunken souls" (Leavitt 1989, 39). Third, the concentration on an "either-or" approach to leadership and the search for unambiguous solutions to complex managerial problems negate the dualistic character of most organizational challenges, and prevents leaders from appreciating tensions between the soft, relations-oriented, and hard, business-oriented side of leadership as a source of inspiration (Lewis, Andriopoulos, and Smith 2014). Taking a proactive approach, we elucidate these weaknesses in the following to derive suggestions for alternative skill sets desirable for future leaders (Figure 5.1).

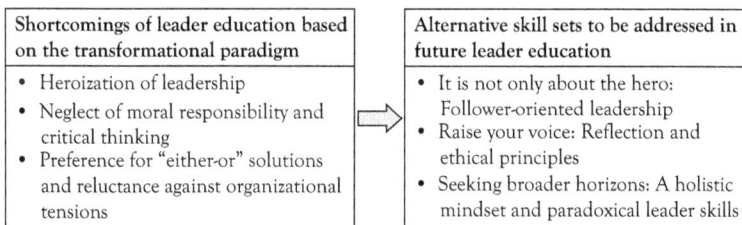

Shortcomings of leader education based on the transformational paradigm	Alternative skill sets to be addressed in future leader education
• Heroization of leadership • Neglect of moral responsibility and critical thinking • Preference for "either-or" solutions and reluctance against organizational tensions	• It is not only about the hero: Follower-oriented leadership • Raise your voice: Reflection and ethical principles • Seeking broader horizons: A holistic mindset and paradoxical leader skills

Figure 5.1 Shortcomings of transformational leadership education and future alternatives

It Is Not Only About the Hero: Follower-Oriented Leadership

The transformational paradigm constitutes a concept clearly emphasizing the leader's pivotal role as a change agent who instills a purely economic logic into followers, that is, the idea that "corporate profitability [is] the core of effective management" (Antonacopoulou 2010, S10). Implicitly, it is proposed that employees, too, consider the economic logic worthwhile, and that they should, thus, be motivated to contribute to achieving this goal (Hay and Hodgkinson 2006). Simultaneously, the approach assumes a hierarchical, mostly unidirectional relationship between leaders and followers: The supervisor has the power to transform subordinates into highly engaged employees, to reward and punish them, and to fulfill or neglect their needs (Tourish 2013). Quotes of highly famous transformational leaders reflect this attitude: "My job is not to be easy on people. My job is to take these great people we have and to push them and make them even better" (Steve Jobs, co-founder of Apple, cited from *Forbes* 2013).

This top-down approach to leadership has entered into business school curricula (Doh 2003; Tourish, Craig, and Amernic 2010) and substantially influences leadership practices. The personification of success provides a fertile ground for producing overconfident leaders who underestimate risks and overestimate positive outcomes (Shipman and Mumford 2011; Tourish and Vatcha 2005) or identify so heavily with their vision that they make considerable errors (Conger 1990). Since these highly self-confident leaders are very convinced of their opinions, they are likely to suppress the followers' valuable feedback and inhibit sustainable organizational learning by precluding employees to speak up (Tourish 2013). Related to this phenomenon is the threat of group thinking, that is, a tendency toward conformity within the team, frequently resulting in poor decision-making (Baron 2005). Transformational leaders, who tend to restrict negative and emphasize positive information, tend to invoke group thinking (Conger 1990; Whyman and Ginnet 2005). As Conger (1990) points out in his reflection of the dark sides of leadership, self-convinced leaders may substitute organizational leadership with personal goals, overlook problems, and market opportunities, create an illusion of control through affirming information, and ignore the costs of strategy implementation. Thus, the visionary qualities that distinguish the transformational leader from the gray-suited manager also contain the ingredients of disaster and great failure.

The controlling and leader-focused nature of the transformational paradigm inhibits a constructive dialog about the (partly invisible) organizational reality, which is characterized, for example, by the employees' disagreement, unproductive behavior, or disengagement (Tourish, Craig, and Amernic 2010). To develop future leaders, who do not see themselves as the center of the universe, but are open to a more nuanced understanding of the leader-follower relationship, leadership should be discussed as a co-constructed phenomenon in leadership education. Business school curricula need to include a wider variety of leadership styles and support the critical reflection on approaches that are more follower-oriented, like shared leadership (Pearce, Manz, and Akanno 2013, Pearce, Wassenaar, and Manz 2014) or discursive leadership (Clifton 2012; Fairhurst 2007, 2008). These alternative models have in common that they imply a "fundamental change in the way formal leaders understand their practice and the way they view their leadership role" (Harris 2013, 546): Leadership is understood as a dynamic give-and-take relationship (Pearce, Wassenaar, and Manz 2014). Shared leadership researchers acknowledge that all leadership is, to a certain degree, shared. Whether or not shared leadership is treated as a notable concept depends on the degree to which the organizational members are involved in the process of leading one another (Pearce, Conger, and Locke 2008). Pearce, Manz, and Sims (2014) identify four distinct forms of shared leadership, which depend on the amount of responsibility sharing, namely rotated, integrated, distributed, and comprehensive shared leadership. In contrast to this position-oriented approach, the discursive concept takes a social constructionist perspective, and assumes that leadership is dialogically developed in interactions (Clifton 2012). Those company members who are able to influence the management of meaning in organizations emerge as leaders "in the eyes of the beholders" (Meindl 1993, 1995)—a role that may be shifted and distributed among several leadership actors (Fairhurst 2008; Gronn 2002).

Summarizing these follower-oriented approaches to leadership, we find that keeping the egos of (future) managers in check is one of the main challenges of distributing leadership more equally between supervisors and subordinates. It is necessary to continuously engage individuals with formal authority to implement co-constructed leadership (Pearce,

Wassenaar, and Manz 2014; Waldman 2014). (Future) leaders should be sensitized to the finding that allowing different individuals, depending on the prevailing contextual conditions or project phase, to adopt a leadership role can increase performance and innovativeness (Gerpott, Jordanis, Lehmann-Willenbrock, and Voelpel 2014). Paying more attention to the development of social, interpersonal, and communicative skills could, thus, be a promising path for leadership education.

Raise Your Voice: Reflection and Ethical Principles

The transformational concept assumes that leaders motivate followers by changing how followers see themselves: Instead of purely executing instructions, employees should identify with the leader's goal, working toward it on their own volition. Tourish (2013) notably describes how this process of "coercive persuasion" encourages followers to internalize dominant organizational norms as their own. In this manner, leaders link "surveillance with intense indoctrination" (Tourish 2013, 41)—once employees internalize the leader's belief system, minimal control is required to ensure their followership. Combined with the low relevance of accountability and responsibility issues in business school education and organizational practice (Datar, Garvin, and Cullen 2010), this convergence-oriented aspect of transformational leadership bears the threat of not sufficiently considering ethical liabilities, like the moral evaluation of business practices, civic commitment, and responsibility toward society. Accordingly, the transformational style has been linked to unethical behaviors, like corruption, elicited by "the charismatic leaders' ability to create façades and influence followers to participate in, enable, or hide wrongdoing" (DeCelles and Pfarrer 2004, 67).

To overcome these shortcomings, a focus on the moral aspects and reflections (of oneself and of the organizational environment) is urgently needed in leadership education and managerial practice. Recently, the concept of ethical leadership, that is, a leader's use of social influence to promote ethical conduct (Brown and Treviño 2002), has gained increased attention. Yet, the complexity of findings regarding positive (Marinova and Park 2014; Mayer et al. 2012) or negative effects (Yang 2014) and ethical leader's impact within and across hierarchies (Schaubroeck et al. 2012) indicate that profound discussions in leadership education are necessary to successfully tackle the challenge of considering both economic and social aspects in managerial practice. Thus, to develop responsible leaders, business schools should not only formally teach knowledge about topics such as ethical leadership, but also put much more emphasis on the reflection and critical questioning of established theories and procedures (Antonacopoulou 2010). Recalling the assumptions of ancient Greek scholars (Aristotle 1999), business teachers need to accept that a person's character does not mature on its own, but depends on habits, that is, on the consistent application of values over the course of an individual's (manger's) life (Crossan et al. 2013). Thus, curricula that focus on not only equipping students with testable, short-term knowledge, but on growing character in the long-term can contribute to furthering management education.

Seeking Broader Horizons: A Holistic Mindset and Paradoxical Leader Skills

Leadership education following the transformational framework tends to support the "either-or" mentality of management: Tensions (e.g., between leaders and followers or within teams) should be reduced, so that work may progress swiftly without time-consuming disruptions. An alternative stream of organizational research sheds a different light on tensions and emphasizes the potential of organizational paradoxes, that is, "contradictory yet interrelated elements that exist simultaneously and persist over time" (Smith and Lewis 2011, 382, cf. also Lewis 2000). Lewis, Andriopoulos, and Smith (2014) argue that the competing demands of the modern, fast-paced management-world (e.g., stability versus flexibility, commitment versus change, established routines versus novel approaches) can only be mastered by using paradoxical leadership, a leadership style that proactively identifies and raises tensions, appreciates paradoxes as a source of innovativeness, and consistently communicates both and vision. The authors point out that each element of a paradox can be detrimental if treated without considering the other side:

Excessive strategic planning raises the danger of inertia, as competitive advantages become entrenched, inhibiting responsiveness. Likewise, single-minded attention to change can frustrate the development of core capabilities that provide the foundation for adaptation and learning. Leaders must have the skills to recognize and engage these tensions. Yet, such inconsistencies create ambiguity and uncertainty, often sparking anxiety and defensiveness. (Lewis, Andriopoulos, and Smith 2014, 59)

Summarizing this statement, the authors highlight the performance-related positive effects of discussing tensions and broach the psychological side of dealing with paradoxes. It has become evident that accepting uncertainties, rather than trying to solve them contradicts the individuals' preferences for unambiguousness. Hence, leaders need to develop a psychological skill named "ambiguity tolerance" (Frenkel-Brunswik 1949; Shullman and White 2012), that is, a neutral or open way to address uncertain situations.

From this, we conclude that leadership education curricula should be modified in such a way that they prepare future managers to lead followers and make decisions in hypercomplex, interdependent, and largely unpredictable environments. Certainly, the academic silos (an educational strategy in which academic diversity is limited) of the universities' different functional departments (Porter and McKibbin 1988) that manifest in a coexistence, rather than integration of different teaching modules do not contribute to the development of reflective and holistic managers (Mintzberg 2005). A re-examination of the practices, methods, and tangible outcomes of leadership education is certainly necessary to be able to develop new forms of leadership education that not only focus on the teaching of testable knowledge, but having an understanding of the "bigger picture," also seek to develop leadership personalities (Crossan et al. 2013).

Where to Go From Here: Alternative Approaches to Leadership Education

A number of scholars and practitioners, in addition to merely criticizing business school education, has proactively developed alternative approaches to training (future) leaders. However, until now, although many of these different concepts reflect comparable pedagogical approaches and educational goals, they have somehow remained unrelated to each other. In order to structure the field and give an overview of alternative paths to leadership education, we systematically reviewed the last three years (2012–2014) of literature on new teaching methods published in the journal *Academy of Management Learning & Education*. We chose this journal because it is the most often-cited magazine in our area of interest (Currie and Pandher 2013) and because the editors emphasize their aim to contribute to the development of innovative leadership training, stating that they are interested in "a wide variety of provocative manuscripts on current and future issues and trends in teaching, learning, and management education" (Academy of Management 2014).

We conducted our review by first scanning the AMLE issues for relevant articles, that is, contributions that provide an educational concept for developing leadership skills in the areas of follower-oriented/interpersonal, ethical/reflexive or holistic/paradoxical leadership. Our search strategy involved reading the abstracts of all articles published in AMLE between 2012 and 2014 and including every piece of work fulfilling these criteria. Following Rubin and Dierdorff's (2013) review procedure, we included only publications of knowledge creation rather than knowledge dissemination. Thus, we did not analyze contributions from the journal's "Book and Resource Reviews," interviews, or the editors' and associate editors' introductions. This procedure resulted in a set of 27 articles. Second, we read the selected articles in their entirety to gain a thorough understanding of their general topic, learning goal/content, and teaching method. Since the focus of some scholarly work only became clear in this phase of deeper elaboration, we eliminated six articles that turned out not to discuss our topic of interest. Thus, we finally based our analysis on 21 publications. Table 5.1 summarizes the identified articles, their topics, learning goals/content and teaching approaches, as well as which of the three suggested skill sets for future leaders they suggest: (follower-oriented/interpersonal, ethical/reflexive and holistic/paradoxical skills.

Table 5.1 *Overview of alternative approaches to leadership education published in AMLE (2012–2014)*

Author(s)	General topic	Learning goals/content	Teaching approach	Leader skills		
				Follower-oriented and interpersonal	Ethical and reflective	Holistic and paradoxical
Briner and Walshe (2014)	Teaching review skills to students to effectively implement evidence-based management*	Students should understand the concept of evidence-based management and develop systematic review skills to search for and reflect on (scientific) evidence.	Embedded in one academic course; alteration between lectures, working on reviews individually with faculty, participating in workshops designed to teach the skills.		X	
Baden (2014)	Explores how positive and negative role models of business affect the students' attitudes, expectations, and ethical behavioral intentions	Increasing the students' intention to act in an ethically responsible way through role models; the authors find that positive role models lead to increased intentions to engage in ethical business practices and negative role models lead to intentions to avoid unethical behavior, but also increased cynicism.	Embedded in one academic course; exposing students to positive and negative role models of business and inviting them to reflect upon the business examples presented. After 10 weeks: Survey that asks for their views regarding the effect of positive and negative examples of business practices.		X	

			X
Bedwell, Fiore, and Salas (2014)	Review of teaching tools to develop the student's interpersonal skills in regular university courses	Students should develop (1) effective communication skills (active listening, oral/writing/assertive/nonverbal communication) and (2) relationship-building skills (cooperation and coordination, trust, intercultural sensitivity, service orientation, self-presentation, social influence, conflict resolution, and negotiation).	Conceptual paper; the authors provide a number of teaching techniques based on the IDPD framework (information, demonstration, practice, and feedback): development of learning objectives (I), lectures (I), watching and reflecting on films (D), making short films (P), mock press conference (P), experiential exercises (D), feedback questionnaires (F), behavioral observation scales (F), qualitative feedback (F).	X
Varela and Gatlin-Watts (2014)	Improvement of cultural intelligence (CQ; components: metacognitive, cognitive, motivational, and behavioral dimensions) through a stay abroad	Increase the students' CQ through a stay abroad; the authors find that, while the cognitive-based components of the participants' CQ developed; studying abroad was ineffectual in advancing the participants' motivational and behavioral CQ.	Send business students in groups of three or four to either a summer or a short academic semester abroad in a hosting university of their choice. From their findings, the authors suggest to not only focus on international exchanges with in-class	X

Table 5.1 (Continued)

Author(s)	General topic	Learning goals/content	Teaching approach	Leader skills		
				Follower-oriented and interpersonal	Ethical and reflective	Holistic and paradoxical
			lectures, but to aim for deep-level learning through programs combining educational features (e.g., role-play orientations and full-immersion exchanges) purposely designed to generate holistic developments of multicultural competence.			
Berkovich (2014)	Dialogical pedagogy in authentic leadership development	Students should develop eight leadership skills (self-exposure, open mindedness, empathy, care, respect, critical thinking, contact, and mutuality) in their exchanges with others and supported by dialogical pedagogy.	Conceptual paper; the author suggests four pillars of dialogical pedagogy (candor, inclusion, confirmation, and presentness) and recommends two teaching methods, namely mentoring and encounter groups ("T-groups").	X	X	

Eisenberg et al. (2013)	Improvement of CQ (CQ; components: metacognitive, cognitive, motivational, and behavioral dimensions) through an academic cross-cultural management course	Increase the students' CQ through a cross-cultural management course; the authors find that the cross-cultural management courses have stronger effects on metacognitive and cognitive CQ than on motivational and behavioral CQ.	Embedded in one academic course, content: 60 percent academic-based activities, such as lectures on cultural dimensions and definitions of culture, and 40 percent experiential content, such as simulation games, interaction with nationals from the target culture, and cultural self-awareness exercises; compared to a control group in which students worked in multicultural settings without a structured course, the course had higher effects on the students' CQ.	X
Mendenhall, Arnardottir, Oddou, and Burke (2013)	Developing cross-cultural competencies in management education by using methods from the cognitive behavioral theory	Students should develop cross-cultural management competencies in the traditional classroom settings without requiring significant geographic relocation or additional financial resources.	Conceptual paper; the authors propose a four-phased pedagogical framework based on the principles of cognitive behavior therapy: (1) conceptualizing the problem, (2) moving from "knowing" to "doing" via personal development	X

Table 5.1 (Continued)

Author(s)	General topic	Learning goals/content	Teaching approach	Leader skills		
				Follower-oriented and interpersonal	Ethical and reflective	Holistic and paradoxical
			planning, (3) strengthening commitment by enhancing accountability, and (4) celebrating and cementing gains via self-reflection.			
Erez et al. (2013)	Improvement of CQ	Increase the students' CQ and global identity through a constructivist, collaborative experiential learning approach; the authors find positive effects of these two variables, but not on local identity (i.e., an individual sense of belongingness to the local context).	Online, four-week virtual multicultural team project with MBA and graduate students from 17 universities in 12 countries. Use of experience-based cycles of acquiring new knowledge, experimenting, and reflecting upon the process.	X		
Rosenblatt, Worthley, and MacNab (2013)	Improvement of CQ and the role of expectancy disconfirmation	Investigates impeding factors of the students' CQ development; the authors find that the positive	Embedded in one academic course; students were exposed to one CQ education intervention	X		

		relationship between the participants' perception of optimal cross-cultural contact and CQ development is mediated by the experience of expectancy disconfirmation.		encompassing cross-cultural contact (e.g., interactions with culturally different religious groups, participation in culture-specific sport and wellness activities).
Taras et al. (2013)	Improvement of CQ	Increase the students' CQ through experiential learning relevant to international collaboration; the authors find changes in several types of attitudes and perceptions relevant to international collaboration.	X	Embedded in one academic course; students from 80 universities in 43 countries worked in global virtual teams for 2 months. Task: Develop a business proposal for a company of the team's choice.
Mor, Morris, and Joh (2013)	Improvement of CQ	To improve intercultural collaboration, students should learn cultural perspective taking, that is, the ability to consider how others' cultural backgrounds shape their behavior in a given context.	X	Interventions that ask the US students to take the perspective of another culture in a prisoner's dilemma task; participants who were asked to think about their counterpart's culture before making their decision showed increased cooperation with the foreign counterpart, thus providing evidence

Table 5.1 (Continued)

Author(s)	General topic	Learning goals/ content	Teaching approach	Leader skills		
				Follower-oriented and interpersonal	Ethical and reflective	Holistic and paradoxical
			for the effectiveness of including cultural perspective taking in business school curricula.			
Grossman et al. (2013)	Using instructional features to enhance demonstration-based training in management education	Increase learning of managerial skills through demonstrations (e.g., videos) combined with the students' active discussion of the content.	Conceptual paper; the authors suggest 17 guidelines (e.g., discussions, perspective taking, imagery exercises, and goal setting) on how to effectively integrate demonstrations into academic courses.		X	(X)
Waddock and Lozano (2013)	Developing more holistic management education	Raising the students' self-awareness and self-development in the context of MBA education; improvement of (1) reflective practices that develop awareness, the will to	One-year program consisting of 24 afternoon sessions and three weekend-long sessions. Content: three interrelated thematic blocks (techno-economic block, sociopolitical block, culture,	X	X	X

				X
	manage, and what some call "heart and soul;" (2) systems thinking, integration, and understanding of how to work effectively in today's globalized world; (3) application of these attributes to understanding and implementing the broad responsibilities, purposes, and (ethical) values associated with businesses and other organizations.	and values block). Pedagogical approaches: reflective practice (through journaling, in dialog with speakers and other participants), engaged learning (interaction and dialog with other participants, speakers, and faculty; speaking from personal experience/ awareness as well as reading assignments, work-based action-learning project, service to other and civic commitment), technology (web-based platform to access course materials and communicate, serving as a space for dialog).		
Crossan et al. (2013)	Developing leadership character in business programs	Encourage and enable leadership character development in business education to increase the students' character strength, that is, the chosen or voluntary processes or mechanisms	The authors implemented an elective course designed for building character; however, they suggest this purpose should be included in all managerial courses. Teaching methods like role-	

Table 5.1 (Continued)

Author(s)	General topic	Learning goals/ content	Teaching approach	Leader skills		
				Follower-oriented and interpersonal	Ethical and reflective	Holistic and paradoxical
		by which virtues (wisdom, courage, humanity, justice, temperance, and transcen-dence) are expressed.	plays, collaborative learning techniques, service-learning opportunities, training in ethical decision-making skills, experiential methods that challenge implicit cognitive biases, reflection exercises designed to surface dissonance between the type of person one is and the type of person one might wish to become, and mentoring can affect character development.			
Rasche, Gilbert, and Schedel (2013)	Cross-disciplinary exam-ination of ethics educa-tion in MBA programs	Review of ethics education in MBA programs; the authors build the argu-ment that business schools increasingly risk creating a	Conceptual paper; the authors claim that effective ethics education requires structural changes to the curriculum, particularly		X	

Giacalone and Promislo (2013)	Ethics education against the background that many students are socialized with destructive thinking toward ethic and virtue ("stigmatization of goodness")	Improve ethical behavior of students who have been exposed all their life to two distinct ideologically driven languages building on a materialistic world view, namely (1) the econophonic language in which money is used to dictate and justify all actions, and (2) the potensiphonic language, emphasizing power and supremacy as appropriate instruments to manage people and societies.	gap between their upbeat rhetoric around ethics education and their actual MBA curriculum. / more mandatory ethics courses and a stronger integration of ethics-related debates into other disciplines (e.g., finance, and accounting).	X	Conceptual paper; the educators should be aware of the students' past socialization and try to improve the students' ethical decision-making by focusing on three goals: (1) Teach critical thinking skills and teach students that acting in ethical ways may imply paying a price, (2) use the power of those students who do not carry the baggage of negative thinking about ethical issues, and (3) exemplify interactional justice.

Table 5.1 (Continued)

Author(s)	General topic	Learning goals/ content	Teaching approach	Leader skills		
				Follower-oriented and interpersonal	Ethical and reflective	Holistic and paradoxical
Li, Mobley, and Kelley (2013)	Improvement of CQ	Understand the influence of learning style in CQ development; the authors find that the positive relationship between the length of an overseas experience and CQ is strengthened when individuals have a divergent learning style (i.e., a style emphasizing concrete experience and reflective observation), not when they have an assimilative, convergent, or accommodative learning style.	When sending leaders abroad, it should be assured that their learning style matches the work design in the foreign country; the findings imply that cultural intelligence does not develop overnight–the longer one is immersed in a different culture, the higher the level of CQ one may develop.	X		
Dufresne and Offstein (2012)	Holistic and intentional character development	Develop the students' character (moral sensitivity, moral judgment, moral motivation, and moral courage); the authors	Methods used to develop responsible and ethical behavior: Academic curriculum, co-curriculum (e.g., respect program),		X	

				X			
	extracurricular activities (athletics), leadership development (students hold rotational leadership positions in the cadet chain of command), selection and training of educational staff, mentoring and advising, physical structures (e.g., naming of buildings) to remind students of role models.	investigate a program at the United States Military Academy at West Point to inform how business schools may learn from this model.					
Kwong, Thompson, and Cheung (2012)	Effectiveness of social business plan competitions in developing social and civic awareness and participation	Increase the students' social awareness through the discussion of case studies or through the development of a social business plan for the students' own ideas.	Embedded in one academic course on social entrepreneurship; application and comparison of using the case study method (CSM) versus business plan teaching (BPT). Advantages of CSM: The development of national and international perspective. Advantages of BPT: Increases local awareness and civic matters, gain a deep managerial and technical understanding of how to manage organizations.				

Table 5.1 (Continued)

Author(s)	General topic	Learning goals/ content	Teaching approach	Leader skills		
				Follower-oriented and interpersonal	Ethical and reflective	Holistic and paradoxical
Smith et al. (2012)	Managing conflicting demands arising from dual commitments to improving social welfare and achieving commercial viability in the context of social entrepreneurship	(Future) social entrepreneurs should develop three interrelated leadership meta-skills to embrace conflicting social and economic demands, namely accepting (viewing both financial and social goals as demands as simultaneously possible), differentiating (recognizing the unique contribution of each demand), and integrating the competing demands (bringing financial and social goals together such that the conflict between them becomes productive).	Investigation of two programs: (1) highly interactive, experiential and dynamic classroom course, including reflection and exploration tasks (e.g., gratitude exercise, instructor role modeling, reflection on biographies, and narratives), (2) learning on the job (e.g., through collaborations with other organizations to reflect on one's own work) at Digital Divide Data, a social enterprise with offices around South-East Asia, seeking to employ and educate disadvantaged people in a for-profit information technology business.			X

Nelson, Poms, and Wolf (2012)	Develop efficacy beliefs for ethics and diversity management	Improve the students' ability to deal with ethics and diversity issues in organizational life.	Embedded in one academic course; students had to complete a written assignment in which they had to assume the role of a consultant charged either with improving the employees' ethical behavior or with improving the management of diversity within an organization. This task increased self-efficacy beliefs on the chosen topic (diversity or ethics management) beyond that accounted for by course content.		X

* With regard to the recent trend of evidence-based management, that is, the utilization of scientific evidence as a starting point for managers to make decisions (van Aken and Romme 2012), a vast number of articles in this area broach the issue of teaching students to critically reflect on the scientific evidence that should be applied to managerial practice. To avoid duplicates, we included the comprehensive study of Briner and Walshe (2014) to represent other studies (e.g., Kepes, Bennett, and McDaniel 2014) mentioning the necessity to critically reflect on the findings used in evidence-based management.

With regard to the development of our first suggested future leadership skill, that is, follower-orientation and interpersonal intelligence, we find a clear tendency to focus on the sub-facet of intercultural intelligence. Eight studies, accounting for 38 percent of all articles included in our review, deal with the topic of how to improve the students' intercultural intelligence. Although we appreciate that the ongoing internationalization justifies an emphasis of this topic in separate and specifically designed courses, it is a pity that so few teaching approaches integrate intercultural skills development into other disciplines. Furthermore, we notice that no visible attention has been given to including the follower's role in creating leadership in business school curricula. This creates an urgent need to (1) integrate and diversify, rather than separate interpersonal skills development, and (2) sensitize students toward the benefits of follower-oriented leadership in future business education. Going forward, the different approaches to interpersonal skills development could provide useful starting points to transfer teaching methods from this area to the topic of follower-oriented leader development concepts. For instance, Mor, Morris, and Joh (2013) have shown that requesting individuals to adopt another culture's perspectives can improve cooperation in multicultural negotiation tasks. Thus, using case studies, vignettes, and role-playing games that require students to change their perspective when making and understanding leadership decisions might be a fruitful way to advance business school programs.

Taking a closer look at the field of ethical and reflexive approaches, it becomes evident that there has been tremendous progress in including ethical aspects into managerial practice and business education (Giacalone and Promislo 2013). A number of approaches have focused not only on the students' reflections of their own experiences, but also on the need to proactively question organizational realities and managerial assumptions, for example, with regard to the distribution of power relations and democracy in organizations (Arbaugh, Dearmond, and Rau 2013). While some researchers have raised concerns about ethics education not being integrated more deeply into other disciplines (Rasche, Gilbert, and Schedel 2013), we conclude from our review that a number of promising approaches are on the way. It seems as if business schools have understood the (societal) expectations of increasing their ethical responsibility, and at least try to integrate reflexive elements into students' education. There is certainly still much room for improvement; however, owing to the current awareness related to ethical and reflexive approaches, we are optimistic that ongoing progress will be made in this area.

By contrast, the area we find most concerning is the development of holistic managers, who possess paradoxical leadership skills. Accepting tensions between, for example, leaders and followers implies withstanding the inherent feelings of anxiety—a skill not at all addressed in the current management education. This inertia of leadership education stands in stark contrast to the vast amount of management literature pointing out the new challenges of leaders in the VUCA world, that is, a volatile, uncertain, complex, and ambiguous context (Horney, Pasmore, and O'Shea 2010). It would be presumptuous to assume that individuals in positions of authority develop the skills to deal with such hyper-complex environments by themselves. Instead, inertia and resistance toward decision making and changes are likely to occur (Lewis, Andriopoulous, and Smith 2014). Although few conceptual papers (Grossman et al. 2013) provide ideas for re-evaluating and adapting common educational techniques to improve the students' ability to deal with complex managerial tasks, very few scholarly works describe the application of such forms. An example is the publication on the Vicens Vives program (Waddock and Lozano 2013), a comprehensive teaching approach to bridge the gap between the professional and personal dimensions of managing/leading, to develop new attitudes toward personal engagement, to affect professional changes and new commitments, and to enhance the future leaders' ability to master complex managerial tasks. This one-year program tackles all three skill sets we suggest for future leaders and can serve as an inspiring example for other business schools.

In summary, given the underdevelopment of this area of leadership education, we strongly encourage researchers to go beyond purely describing the characteristics of the changing business environment, and start developing approaches prompting students to work through tensions occurring in organizational reality. Educators could, for example, borrow pedagogical concepts from other areas, such as leadership education in the military (Dufresne and Offstein 2012), the development of social entrepreneurs (Smith et al. 2012) or creativity enhancement in arts programs

(Baker and Baker 2012). As part of paradoxical leader development, it is important that students not only learn about the positive potentials of appreciating tensions, but also become aware of the coping strategies they may need to develop in order to manage feelings of uncertainty, anxiety, and bewildering emotional reactions (Dean and Jolly 2012). It is our hope that more efforts will be devoted to investigating teaching methods that will help increase future leaders' "capacity to intuitively grasp salient features of ambiguous situations and to constitute a 'landscape' of possible paths of response" (Shotter and Tsoukas 2014, 224). Business schools will continue to maintain their legitimacy in the long term only if the leader development curricula are adapted to the changing environment, and include completely new forms of leadership education.

Going forward, given that structured methods (e.g., based on cognitive behavioral theory, see Mendenhall et al. 2013) are likely not sufficient to develop leaders in a boundary-less world, unstructured teaching approaches provide a promising avenue in managerial education. For instance, educators at Harvard Business School have developed the Field Immersion Experiences for Leadership Development (FIELD), which should encourage students to think and act like leaders (Harvard Business School 2014). Covering one academic year, students work in a self-directed manner on a real-world, complex, and unstructured project to develop new products and services for global partner companies located in emerging markets. Course participants travel to their global partner's location to understand the firm-specific peculiarities, and finally, present their results to the company's managers. Thus, similarly to the Vicens Vives program (Waddock and Lozano 2013), the course takes a much more holistic and realistic approach that confronts students with the hassles and tensions of project work in an international context. We look forward to seeing whether new isolated programs and universities following alternative educational approaches will be founded and attract highly skilled students.

In conclusion, this chapter argues that the transformational leadership paradigm has become an ideology in the western business world. Currently, the concept is taught as the most effective form of leadership in almost all leader development programs. However, we claim that, to achieve sustainable outcomes in a complex business environment, future leaders should possess a set of skills beyond the transformational paradigm, one that focuses on followers and interpersonal skills, the ethical and reflective aspects of managerial practice, and the ability to utilize the potentials of paradoxical tensions.

References

Academy of Management. 2014. "Academy of Management Learning and Education: Information for contributors." Retrieved October 21, 2014 from http://aom.org/Publications/AMLE/Information-for-Contributors.aspx

Antonacopoulou, E.P. 2010. "Making the Business School More 'Critical': Reflexive Critique Based on Phronesis as a Foundation for Impact." *British Journal of Management* 21, no. s1, pp. 6–25. doi:10.1111/j.1467-8551.2009.00679.x

Arbaugh, J.B., S. Dearmond, and B.L. Rau. 2013. "New Uses for Existing Tools? A Call to Study On-line Management Instruction and Instructors." *Academy of Management Learning and Education* 12, no. 4, pp. 635–55. doi:10.5465/amle.2011.0018A

Aristotle. 1999. *Nicomachean Ethics*. Indianapolis, IN: Hacket Publishing. doi:10.1111/j.1467-8551.2009.00679.x

Baden, D. 2014. "Look on the Bright Side: A Comparison of Positive and Negative Role Models in Business Ethics Education." *Academy of Management Learning & Education* 13, no. 2, pp. 154–70. doi:10.5465/amle.2012.0251

Baker, D.F., and S.J. Baker. 2012. "To 'Catch the Sparkling Glow': A Canvas for Creativity in the Management Classroom." *Academy of Management Learning & Education* 11, no. 4, pp. 704–21. doi:10.5465/amle.2010.0003

Balwant, P.T., K. Birdi, and U. Stephan. 2014. "Practice What You Preach: Instructors as Transformational Leaders in Higher Education Classrooms." *Academy of Management Annual Meeting Proceedings* no. 1, pp. 1685–90. doi:10.5465/AMBPP.2014.57

Baron, R.S. 2005. "So Right It's Wrong: Groupthink and the Ubiquitous Nature of Polarized Group Decision Making." In *Advances in Experimental Social Psychology*, ed. M.P. Zanna, 219–53. Vol. 37. San Diego, CA: Elsevier Academic Press.

Bass, B.M. 1985. *Leadership and Performance Beyond Expectations*. New York: Free Press.

Bass, B.M. 1990. "From Transactional to Transformational Leadership: Learning to Share the Vision." *Organizational Dynamics* 18, no. 3, pp. 19–31. doi:10.1016/0090-2616(90)90061-S

Bass, B.M., and B.J. Avolio. 1995. *Manual for the Multifactor Leadership Questionnaire: Rater form (5X short)*. Palo Alto, CA: Mind Garden.

Bedwell, W.L., S.M. Fiore, and E. Salas. 2014. "Developing the Future Workforce: An Approach for Integrating Interpersonal Skills into the MBA Classroom." *Academy Of Management Learning & Education* 13, no. 2, pp. 171–86. doi:10.5465/amle.2011.0138

Berkovich, I. 2014. "Between Person and Person: Dialogical Pedagogy in Authentic Leadership Development." *Academy of Management Learning & Education* 13, no. 2, pp. 245–64. doi:10.5465/amle.2012.0367

Blumenthal, K. 2012. *Steve Jobs: The Man Who Thought Different*. New York: Square Fish.

Briner, R.B., and N.D. Walshe. 2014. "From Passively Received Wisdom to Actively Constructed Knowledge: Teaching Systematic Review Skills As a Foundation of Evidence-Based Management." *Academy of Management Learning & Education* 13, no. 3, pp. 415–32. http://dx.doi.org/10.5465/amle.2013.0222

Brown, M., and L. Treviño. 2002. "Conceptualizing and Measuring Ethical Leadership: Development of an Instrument." *Academy of Management Proceedings & Membership Directory*, no. 1, pp. D1–D6. doi:10.5465/APBPP.2002.7519501

Cheng, J., S. Chang, J. Kuo, and Y. Cheung. 2014. "Ethical Leadership, Work Engagement, and Voice Behavior." *Industrial Management & Data Systems* 114, no. 5, pp. 817–31. doi:10.1108/IMDS-10-2013-0429

Cheng, J.T., J.L. Tracy, and J. Henrich. 2010. "Pride, Personality, and the Evolutionary Foundations of Human Social Status." *Evolution and Human Behavior* 31, no. 5, pp. 334–47. doi:10.1016/j.evolhumbehav.2010.02.004

Clifton, J. 2012. "A Discursive Approach to Leadership: Doing Assessments and Managing Organizational Meanings." *Journal of Business Communication* 49, no. 2, pp. 148–68. doi:10.1177/0021943612437762

Conger, J.A. 1990. "The Dark Side of Leadership." *Organizational Dynamics* 19, no. 2, pp. 44–55. doi:10.1016/0090-2616(90)90070-6

Crossan, M., D. Mazutis, G. Seijts, and J. Gandz. 2013. "Developing Leadership Character in Business Programs." *Academy of Management Learning & Education* 12, no. 2, pp. 285–305. doi:10.5465/amle.2011.0024A

Currie, R.R., and G. Pandher. 2013. "Management Education Journals' Rank and Tier by Active Scholars." *Academy of Management Learning & Education* 12, no. 2, pp. 194–218. doi:10.5465/amle.2010.0184

Datar, S.M., D.A. Garvin, and P.G. Cullen. 2010. *Rethinking the MBA: Business Education at a Crossroads*. Boston: Harvard Business School Press.

DeCelles, K.A., and M.D. Pfarrer. 2004. "Heroes or Villains? Corruption and the Charismatic Leader." *Journal of Leadership & Organizational Studies* 11, no. 1, pp. 67–77. doi:10.1177/107179190401100108

DeRue, D., J.D. Nahrgang, N. Wellman, and S.E. Humphrey. 2011. "Trait and Behavioral Theories of Leadership: An Integration and Meta-Analytic Test of Their Relative Validity." *Personnel Psychology* 64, no. 1, pp. 7–52. doi:10.1111/j.1744-6570.2010.01201.x

Doh, J.P. 2003. "Can Leadership Be Taught? Perspectives from Management Educators." *Academy of Management Learning & Education* 2, no. 1, pp. 54–67. doi:10.5465/AMLE.2003.9324025

Dong, L., L. Hui, and R. Loi. 2012. "The Dark side of Leadership: A Three-Level Investigation of the Cascading Effect of Abusive Supervision on Employee Creativity." *Academy of Management Journal* 55, no. 5, pp. 1187–1212. doi:10.5465/amj.2010.0400

Dufresne, R.L., and E.H. Offstein. 2012. "Holistic and Intentional Student Character Development Process: Learning from West Point." *Academy of Management Learning & Education* 11, no. 4, pp. 570–90. doi:10.5465/amle.2010.0023

Eagleton, T. 1991. *Ideology: An Introduction.* London: Verso.

Eisenberg, J., H. Lee, F. Bruck, and R. Bell. 2013. "Can Business Schools Make Students Culturally Competent? Effects of Cross-Cultural Management Courses on Cultural Intelligence." *Academy Of Management Learning & Education* 12, no. 4, pp. 603–21.

Elliot, J., and W.L. Simon. 2011. *The Steve Jobs Way: Leadership for a New Generation.* New York: Vanguard Press.

Erez, M., A. Lisak, R. Harush, E. Glikson, R. Nouri, and E. Shokef. 2013. "Going Global: Developing Management Students' Cultural Intelligence and Global Identity in Culturally Diverse Virtual Teams." *Academy of Management Learning and Education* 12, no. 3, pp. 330–55.

Fairhurst, G.T. 2007. *Discursive Leadership: In Conversation with Leadership Psychology.* Thousand Oaks, CA: Sage.

Fairhurst, G.T. 2008. "Discursive Leadership: A Communication Alternative to Leadership Psychology." *Management Communication Quarterly* 21, no. 4, pp. 510–21. doi:10.1177/0893318907313714

Fanelli, A., and N. Grasselli. 2006. "Defeating the Minotaur: The Construction of CEO Charisma on the US Stock Market." *Organization Studies* 27, no. 6, pp. 811–32. doi:10.1177/0170840606061070

Forbes. 2013. "50 Heavyweight Leadership Quotes." Retrieved from www.forbes.com/sites/ekaterinawalter/2013/09/30/50-heavyweight-leadership-quotes (accessed October 21, 2014).

Franke, F., J. Felfe, and A. Pundt. 2014. "The Impact of Health-Oriented Leadership on Follower Health: Development and Test of a New Instrument Measuring Health-Promoting Leadership." *Zeitschrift für Personalforschung*

(German Journal of Research in Human Resource Management) 28, nos. 1/2, pp. 139–61. doi:10.1688/ZfP-2014-01-Franke

Frenkel-Brunswik, E. 1949. "Intolerance of Ambiguity as an Emotional and Perceptual Personality Variable." *Journal of Personality* 18, no. 1, pp. 108–43. doi:10.1111/1467-6494.ep8930758

Gang, W., O. In-Sue, S.H. Courtright, and A.E. Colbert. 2011. "Transformational Leadership and Performance Across Criteria and Levels: A Meta-Analytic Review of 25 Years of Research." *Group & Organization Management* 36, no. 2, pp. 223–70. doi:10.1177/1059601111401017

Gerpott, F., and S.C. Voelpel. 2014. "Zurück auf Los! Warum ein Überdenken des transformationalen Führungsstils notwendig ist (Back to the Drawing Board: Why we Need to Rethink Transformational Leadership)." *PersonalFührung* 47, no. 4, pp. 17–21.

Gerpott, F., L. Jordano-Kudalis, N. Lehmann-Willenbrock, and S.C. Voelpel. 2014. "Reden Sie noch oder führen Sie schon? Wie Sie durch gezielte Kommunikation zur Führungskraft werden (Still Talking or Leading Already? How specific Communication Creates Leadership)." *Personalführung* 47, no. 8, pp. 70–75.

Giacalone, R.A., and M.D. Promislo. 2013. "Broken When Entering: The Stigmatization of Goodness and Business Ethics Education." *Academy of Management Learning & Education* 12, no. 1, pp. 86–101. doi:10.5485/amle.2011.0005

Gronn, P. 2002. "Distributed Leadership as a Unit of Analysis." *Leadership Quarterly* 13, no. 4, pp. 423–51. doi:10.1016/S1048-9843(02)00120-0

Grossman, R., E. Salas, D. Pavlas, and M.A. Rosen. 2013. "Using Instructional Features to Enhance Demonstration-Based Training in Management Education." *Academy of Management Learning & Education* 12, no. 2, pp. 219–43. doi:10.5465/amle.2011.0527

Harris, A. 2013. "Distributed Leadership: Friend or Foe?" *Educational Management Administration & Leadership* 41, no. 5, pp. 545–54. doi:10.1177/1741143213497635

Harvard Business School. 2014. "Field Overview and Video." Retrieved October 21, 2014 from www.hbs.edu/mba/academic-experience/FIELD/Pages/default.aspx

Hawawini, G., V. Subramanian, and P. Verdin. 2003. "Is Performance Driven by Industry- or Firm-Specific Factors? A New Look at the Evidence." *Strategic Management Journal* 24, no. 1, pp. 1–16. doi:10.1002/smj.278

Hay, A., and M. Hodgkinson. 2006. "Rethinking Leadership: A Way Forward for Teaching Leadership?" *Leadership & Organization Development Journal* 27, no. 2, pp. 144–58. doi:10.1108/01437730610646642

Hegele, C., and A. Kieser. 2001. "Control the Construction of Your Legend or Someone Else Will: An Analysis of Texts on Jack Welch." *Journal of Management Inquiry* 10, no. 4, pp. 298–309. doi:10.1177/1056492601104003

Horney, N., T. Pasmore, and O. Shea. 2010. "Leadership Agility: A Business Imperative for a VUCA World." *People & Strategy* 33, no. 4, pp. 32–38.

House, R.J., and B. Shamir. 1993. "Toward the Integration of Transformational, Charismatic, and Visionary Theories." In *Leadership Theory and Research*, eds. M.M. Chemers, and R. Ayman, 81–107. San Diego, CA: Academic Press.

Hunt, J.G. 1999. "Transformational/Charismatic Leadership's Transformation of the Field: An Historical Essay." *Leadership Quarterly* 10, no. 2, pp. 129–44. doi:10.1016/S1048-9843(99)00015-6

Isaacson, W. 2011. *Steve Jobs*. New York: Simon & Schuster.

Jones Christensen, L., A. Mackey, and D. Whetten. 2014. "Taking Responsibility for Corporate Social Responsibility: The Role of Leaders in Creating, Implementing, Sustaining, or Avoiding Socially Responsible Firm Behaviors." *Academy of Management Perspectives* 28, no. 2, pp. 164–78. doi:10.5465/amp.2012.0047

Judge, T.A., and R.F. Piccolo. 2004. "Transformational and Transactional Leadership: A Meta-Analytic Test of Their Relative Validity." *Journal of Applied Psychology* 89, no. 5, pp. 755–68. doi:10.1037/0021-9010.89.5.755

Kepes, S., A. Bennett, and M.A. McDaniel. 2014. "Evidence-Based Management and the Trustworthiness of Our Cumulative Scientific Knowledge: Implications for Research, Teaching and Practice." *Academy of Management Learning & Education* 13, no. 3, pp. 446–66.

Khurana, R. 2003. *Searching for a Corporate Savior: The Irrational Quest for Charismatic CEOs*. Princeton, NJ: Princeton University Press.

Krames, J.A. 2003. *The Welch Way: 24 Lessons from the World's Greatest CEO*. New York: McGraw Hill.

Kwong, C.C.Y., P. Thompson, and C.W.M. Cheung. 2012. "The Effectiveness of Social Business Plan Competitions in Developing Social and Civic Awareness and Participation." *Academy of Management Learning and Education* 11, no. 3, pp. 324–48. doi:10.5465/amle.2011.0007A

Leavitt, H.J. 1989. "Educating our MBAs: On Teaching What We Haven't Taught." *California Management Review* 31, no. 3, pp. 38–50.

Lewis, M.W. 2000. "Exploring Paradox: Toward a More Comprehensive Guide." *Academy of Management Review* 25, no. 4, pp. 760–76. doi:10.5465/AMR.2000.3707712

Lewis, M.W., C. Andriopoulos, and W.K. Smith. 2014. "Paradoxical Leadership to Enable Strategic Agility." *California Management Review* 56, no. 3, pp. 58–77. doi:10.1525/cmr.2014.56.3.58

Li, M., W.H. Mobley, and A. Kelly. 2013. "When do Global Leaders Learn Best to Develop Cultural Intelligence? An Investigation of the Moderating Role of Experiential Learning Style." *Academy of Management Learning and Education* 12, no. 1, pp. 32–50.

Lieberson, S., and J.F. O'Connor. 1972. "Leadership and Organizational Performance: A Study of Large Corporations." *American Sociological Review* 37, no. 2, pp. 117–30. doi:10.2307/2094020

Lievens, F., P. Van Geit, and P. Coetsier. 1997. "Identification of Transformational Leadership Qualities: An Examination of Potential Biases." *European Journal of Work and Organizational Psychology* 6, no. 4, pp. 415–30. doi:10.1080/135943297399015

Lowe, K.B., K.G. Kroeck, and N. Sivasubramaniam. 1996. "Effectiveness Correlates of Transformational Leadership and Transactional Leadership: A Meta-Analytic Review of the MLQ Literature." *Leadership Quarterly* 7, no. 3, pp. 385–425. doi:10.1016/S1048-9843(96)90027-2

Lund Dean, K., and J.P. Jolly. 2012. "Student Identity, Disengagement, and Learning." *Academy of Management Learning & Education* 11, no. 2, pp. 228–43. doi:0.5465/amle.2009.0081

Marinova, S.V., and H. Park. 2014. "Does It Matter If Leadership Is About Us? A Meta-Analysis of Other-Oriented Leadership." *Academy of Management Annual Meeting Proceedings*, no. 1, pp. 1082–87. doi:10.5465/AMBPP.2014.267

Mayer, D.M., K. Aquino, R.L. Greenbaum, and M. Kuenzi. 2012. "Who Displays Ethical Leadership, and Why Does It Matter? An Examination of Antecedents and Consequences of Ethical Leadership." *Academy of Management Journal* 55, no. 1, pp. 151–71. doi:10.5465/amj.2008.0276

McCleskey, J. 2014. "Situational, Transformational, and Transactional Leadership and Leadership Development." *Journal of Business Studies Quarterly* 5, no. 4, pp. 117–30.

Meindl, J.R. 1993. "Reinventing Leadership: A Radical, Social Psychological Approach." In *Social Psychology in Organizations: Advances in Theory and Research*, ed. J.K. Munighan, 89–118. Englewood Cliffs, NJ: Prentice Hall.

Meindl, J.R. 1995. "The Romance of Leadership as a Follower-Centric Theory: A Social Constructionist Approach." *Leadership Quarterly* 6, no. 3, pp. 329–41. doi:10.1016/1048-9843(95)90012-8

Mendenhall, M.E., A. Arnardottir, G.R. Oddou, and L.A. Burke. 2013. "Developing Cross-Cultural Competencies in Management Education via Cognitive-Behavior Therapy." *Academy of Management Learning & Education* 12, no. 3, pp. 436–51. doi:10.5465/amle.2012.0237

Mintzberg, H. 2005. *Managers Not MBAs*. San Francisco, CA: Berrett-Koehler.

Mor, S., M. Morris, and J. Joh. 2013. "Identifying and Training Adaptive Cross-Cultural Management Skills: The Crucial Role of Cultural Metacognition."

Academy of Management Learning & Education 12, no. 3, pp. 453–75. doi:10.5465/amle.2012.0202

Nelson, J., L. Wheeler Poms, and P.P. Wolf. 2012. "Developing Efficacy Beliefs for Ethics and Diversity Management." *Academy of Management Learning and Education* 11, no. 1, pp. 49–68. doi:10.5465/amle.2009.0115

Nienhueser, W. 2011. "Empirical Research on Human Resource Management as a Production of Ideology." *Management Revue* 22, no. 4, pp. 367–93. doi:10.1688/1861-9908

Pearce, C.L., J.A. Conger, and E.A. Locke. 2008. "Shared Leadership Theory." *Leadership Quarterly* 19, no. 5, pp. 622–28. doi:10.1016/j.leaqua.2008.07.005

Pearce, C.L., C.C. Manz, and S. Akanno. 2013. "Searching for the Holy Grail of Management Development and Sustainability: Is Shared Leadership Development the Answer?" *Journal of Management Development* 32, no. 3, pp. 247–57. doi:10.1108/02621711311318274

Pearce, C.L., C.C. Manz, and H.P. Sims. 2014. *Share, Don't Take the Lead.* Charlotte, NC: Information Age.

Pearce, C.L., C.L. Wassenaar, and C.C. Manz. 2014. "Is Shared Leadership the Key to Responsible Leadership?" *Academy of Management Perspectives* 28, no. 3, pp. 275–88. doi:10.5465/amp.2014.0017

Peterson, R.S., P.V. Martorana, D. Smith, and P.D. Owens. 2003. "The Impact of Chief Executive Officer Personality on Top Management Team Dynamics: One Mechanism by Which Leadership Affects Organizational Performance." *Journal of Applied Psychology* 88, no. 5, pp. 795–808. doi:10.1037/0021-9010.88.5.795

Porter, L.W., and L.E. McKibbin. 1988. *Management Education and Development: Drift or Thrust into the 21st Century?* New York: McGraw-Hill.

Rafferty, A.E., and M.A. Griffin. 2004. "Dimensions of Transformational Leadership: Conceptual and Empirical Extensions." *Leadership Quarterly* 15, no. 3, pp. 329–54. doi:10.1016/j.leaqua.2004.02.009

Rasche, A., D. Gilbert, and I. Schedel. 2013. "Cross-Disciplinary Ethics Education in MBA Programs: Rhetoric or Reality?" *Academy of Management Learning & Education* 12, no. 1, pp. 71–85. doi:10.5485/amle.2011.0016A

Rosenblatt, V., R. Worthley, and B. MacNab. 2013. "From Contact to Development in Experiential Cultural Intelligence Education: The Mediating Influence of Expectancy Disconfirmation." *Academy of Management Learning & Education* 12, no. 3, pp. 356–79.

Ross, L. 1977. "The Intuitive Psychologist and His Shortcomings: Distortions in the Attribution Process." In *Advances in Experimental Social Psychology,* ed. L. Berkowitz, 173–220. New York: Academic Press.

Rowold, J. 2014. "Instrumental Leadership: Extending the Transformational-Transactional Leadership Paradigm." *Zeitschrift Für Personalforschung* 28, no. 3, pp. 367–90. doi:10.1688/ZfP-2014-03-Rowold

Rubin, R.S., and E.C. Dierdorff. 2013. "Building a Better MBA: From a Decade of Critique Toward a Decennium of Creation." *Academy of Management Learning & Education* 12, pp. 125–41. doi:10.5465/amle.2012.0217

Schaubroeck, J.M., S.T. Hannah, B.J. Avolio, S.W. Kozlowski, R.G. Lord, L.K. Trevinño, N. Dimotakis, and A.C. Peng. 2012. "Embedding Ethical Leadership Within and Across Organization Levels." *Academy of Management Journal* 55, no. 5, pp. 1053–78. doi:10.5465/amj.2011.0064

Schneider, A., and T. Schröder. 2012. "Ideal Types of Leadership as Patterns of Affective Meaning: A Cross-Cultural and Over-Time Perspective." *Social Psychology Quarterly* 75, no. 3, pp. 268–87. doi:10.1177/0190272512446755

Shamir, B., R.J. House, and M.B. Arthur. 1993. "The Motivational Effects of Charismatic Leadership: A Self-Concept Based Theory." *Organization Science* 4, no. 4, pp. 577–94. doi:10.1287/orsc.4.4.577

Shipman, A.S., and M.D. Mumford. 2011. "When Confidence Is Detrimental: Influence of Overconfidence on Leadership Effectiveness." *Leadership Quarterly* 22, no. 4, pp. 649–65. doi:10.1016/j.leaqua.2011.05.006

Shotter, J., and H. Tsoukas. 2014. "In Search of Phronesis: Leadership and the Art of Judgment." *Academy of Management Learning & Education* 13, no. 2, pp. 224–43. doi:10.5465/amle.2013.0201

Shullman, S.L., and R.P. White. 2012. "Build Leadership's Tolerance for Ambiguity." *Chief Learning Officer* 11, no. 10, pp. 30–33.

Slater, R. 1993. *The New GE: How Jack Welch Revived an American Institution.* Homewood, IL: Irwin.

Slater, R. 1994. *Get Better or Get Beaten! 31 Leadership Secrets from GE's Jack Welch.* New York: McGraw-Hill.

Smith, W.K., M.L. Besharov, A.K. Wessels, and M. Chertok. 2012. "A Paradoxical Leadership Model for Social entrepreneurs: Challenges, Leadership Skills, and Pedagogical Tools for Managing Social and Commercial Demands." *Academy of Management Learning & Education* 11, no. 3, pp. 463–78. doi:5465/amle.2011.0021

Smith, W.K., and M.W. Lewis. 2011. "Toward a Theory of Paradox: A Dynamic Equilibrium Model of Organizing." *Academy of Management Review* 36, no. 2, pp. 381–403. doi:10.5465/AMR.2011.59330958

Taras, V., D.V. Caprar, D. Rottig, and V. Zengyu Huang. 2013. "A Global Classroom? Evaluating the Effectiveness of Global Virtual Collaboration as a Teaching Tool in Management Education." *Academy of Management Learning and Education* 12, no. 3, pp. 414–35. doi:10.5465/amle.2012.0195

Tetlock, P.E. 1985. "Accountability: A Social Check on the Fundamental Attribution Error." *Social Psychology Quarterly* 48, pp. 227–36. doi:10.2307/3033683

Tourish, D. 2013. *The Dark Side of Transformational Leaders.* New York: Routledge.

Tourish, D., and N. Vatcha. 2005. "Charismatic Leadership and Corporate Cultism at Enron: The Elimination of Dissent, the Promotion of Conformity and Organizational Collapse." *Leadership* 1, no. 4, pp. 455–80. doi:10.1177/1742715005057671

Tourish, D., R. Craig, and J. Amernic. 2010. "Transformational Leadership Education and Agency Perspectives in Business School Pedagogy: A Marriage of Inconvenience?" *British Journal of Management* 21, pp. 40–59. doi:10.1111/j.1467-8551.2009.00682.x

Tyssen, A.K., A. Wald, and S. Heidenreich. 2014. "Leadership in the Context of Temporary Organizations: A Study on the Effects of Transactional and Transformational Leadership on Followers' Commitment in Projects." *Journal of Leadership & Organizational Studies* 21, no. 4, pp. 376–93. doi:10.1177/1548051813502086

van Aken, J.E., and A.G.L. Romme. 2012. "A Design Science Approach to Evidence-Based Management." In *The Oxford Handbook of Evidence-based Management*, ed. D.M. Rousseau. New York: Oxford University Press.

van Dijk, T.A. 1998. *Ideology. A Multidisciplinary Approach.* London: Sage.

van Knippenberg, D., and S.B. Sitkin. 2013. "A Critical Assessment of Charismatic-Transformational Leadership Research: Back to the Drawing Board?" *Academy of Management Annals* 7, no. 1, pp. 1–60. doi:10.1080/19 416520.2013.759433

Varela, O.E., and R. Gatlin-Watts. 2014. "The Development of the Global Manager: an Empirical Study on the Role of Academic International Sojourns." *Academy of Management Learning & Education* 13, no. 2, pp. 187–207.

Waddock, S., and J.M. Lozano. 2013. "Developing More Holistic Management Education: Lessons Learned from Two Programs." *Academy of Management Learning & Education* 12, pp. 265–84. doi:10.5465/amle.2012.0002

Waldman, D.A. 2014. "Bridging the Domains for Leadership and Corporate Social Responsible." In *Handbook of Leadership and Organizations*, ed. D. Day, 541–57. New York: Oxford University Press.

Weber, M. 1947. *The Theory of Social and Economic Organization*, translated by A.M. Henderson, and T. Parsons. New York: Free Press.

Weick, K. 1995. *Sense Making in Organizations.* London: Sage.

Wernerfelt, B., and C.A. Montgomery. 1988. "Tobin's q and the Importance of Focus in Firm Performance." *American Economic Review* 78, no. 1, pp. 246–50.

Whyman, W., and R. Ginnett. 2005. "A Question of Leadership: What Can Leaders Do to Avoid Groupthink?" *Leadership in Action* 25, no. 2, pp. 13–14. doi:10.1002/lia.1110

Yang, C. 2014. "Does Ethical Leadership Lead to Happy Workers? A Study on the Impact of Ethical Leadership, Subjective Well-Being, and Life Happiness in the Chinese Culture." *Journal of Business Ethics* 123, no. 3, pp. 513–25. doi:10.1007/s10551-013-1852-6

Yukl, G. 1999. "An Evaluation of Conceptual Weaknesses in Transformational and Charismatic Leadership Theories." *Leadership Quarterly* 10, no. 2, pp. 285–305. doi:10.1016/S1048-9843(99)00013-2

Yukl, G. 2012. "Effective Leadership Behavior: What We Know and What Questions Need More Attention." *Academy of Management Perspectives* 26, pp. 66–85. doi:10.5465/amp.2012.008

CHAPTER 6

Bullying and Single Cases of Harassment in Higher Education Organizations: Managerial Solutions to Eliminate the Problem

Jolita Vveinhardt

Lithuanian Sports University (Lithuania) and
Vytautas Magnus University (Lithuania)

Introduction

Relevance of the research. Education is the sphere in which the occurrence of bullying is one of the most intense form of harassment (Vveinhardt 2009). Although bullying and harassment are often analyzed in the psychological aspect, it is also a management problem, the decision of which is a complex part of personnel and human resource management system. Normally, psychologists can offer victims of bullying a few options as the solution: treatment or leaving the organization, as without the intervention of the management of the organization, it is difficult to define real help to the victim. The withdrawal from the organization is one of the solutions to the assaulted victim, but not to the organization, as it does not help to solve the problem of destructive employee relationships. Bullying and harassment signalize that the organizational culture is going through a crisis, which is determined by a variety of factors of different types— value, structural, psychological, communication factors, and so on.

This research contributes to the analysis of the phenomenon, revealing latent actions of bullying in higher education organizations. Not all of the previous studies highlight the same actions. This is influenced by the fact that researchers in different countries use different diagnostic tools and have different research aims. In this part, bullying is analyzed only in the case of individual higher education institutions of Lithuania, highlighting the problem aspects; however, it is not generalization of the whole situation in the system of higher education. In future, the research could be expanded by comparison with other countries.

The educational institution must take into account the variety of relationships: relationships between pupils, relationships between pupils and teachers, relationships between students, relationships between students and teachers, and relationships between the administration and educational staff. The problems of pupils who experience bullying receive a lot of publicity, but the problem of bullying among employees of educational organizations is not less relevant. It is evident that a person's psychological, educational features, and character traits in organizations are revealed in critical situations related to keeping income, workplace, status, and under other circumstances. Thus, the causes of occurrence of bullying and harassment within an organization are influenced by both internal and external factors.

Therefore, the *problem of the research* is formulated by the questions: what is the occurrence of bullying in employee relations in educational organizations, and how after distinguishing the most frequent methods of pressure in higher education organizations, to form managerial solutions to eliminate the problem?

Aim of the research. To analyze the occurrence of bullying in relationships between the employees of educational organizations, distinguishing the most frequent methods of pressure in higher education organizations and forming managerial solutions to eliminate the problem.

To achieve the aim, the following *research objectives* are set:

1. To discuss bullying, single cases of harassment, and methods of pressure in the theoretical aspect.
2. To compare the results of empirical studies of 2008 through 2014, analyzing the occurrence of bullying in employee relations of educational organizations.

3. To distinguish the most frequent methods of pressure in higher education organizations.

4. To develop managerial solutions to eliminate the problem.

Methods of the research. The first, theoretical part is based on analysis, synthesis, deduction, induction, and generalization of scientific literature. The second, empirical part of the research is prepared by using a comparative analysis of the results of the empirical studies carried out by the author in 2008 to 2014. In the research presented in the third part, the methods of the interview, text transcription, and qualitative content analysis were used. The fourth part is prepared on the basis of the findings on the results of quantitative and qualitative theoretical and empirical studies, the modeling method is used.

Bullying and Single Cases of Harassment in Higher Education Organizations: Theoretical Insights

Definition of Workplace Bullying

The notions with the same meaning are often defined differently in various countries. This is influenced by the terminology, recommended by language specialists in each country. In Lithuania, the following notions are attributed to the term "bullying": nagging, harassment, oppression, and so on that brings in a considerable amount of discussion and confusion. A variety of terms are used in different authors' works to name the attack on the victim in the workplace, for example *employee abuse, workplace terrorism, mobbing, bullying,* and so on. Sometimes, the terms *mobbing* and *bullying* in general context are used as synonyms as well (e.g., Baillien, Neyens, and De Witte 2011; Leon-Perez et al. 2013). However, does the use of two terms really mean completely different concepts?

Historically, the term "mobbing" has been formed from the research of animals' behavior (attacking the victim excluded from a group) (Lorenz 1966); later it was used by Heinemann (1972) to define terrorization of students and by Leymann (1990) to name specific attack on the victim used by coworkers in the workplace. A German and Swedish scientist Leymann (1996) defined mobbing as social interaction through which one individual (seldom more) is attacked by one or more (seldom more than four) individuals almost on a daily basis and for periods of many months, bringing the person into an almost helpless position with potentially high-risk of expulsion. The scientific literature still follows the provision, formulated by him that mobbing is the attack, when hostile actions are repeated at least once a week and last for at least six months (Leymann 1990, 1993; Leymann and Gustaffson 1996). Most authors follow the definition that has become classical (Duffy and Sperry 2007; Vveinhardt and Žukauskas 2012). The term "mobbing" is defined as antagonistic behaviors with unethical communication directed systematically at one individual by one or more individuals in the workplace (Yildirim, Yildirim, and Timucin 2007). In other words, the phenomenon of mobbing is distinguished by the high intensity of attack and long duration of the attack. However, it can be argued that because of the fact that the phenomenon was started to research relatively recently, one can notice that aspects of the content of attack itself can be interpreted in different ways. For example, Leymann (1996) attributed sexual harassment to mobbing. Later, Duffy and Sperry (2007) argued that mobbing is harassment of nonsexual nature, used by one person or a group of people to remove the victim from the organization. However, subsequent studies included not only humiliating and unfavorable communication, verbal threats, and physical attacks, but also verbal or behavioral sexual attacks (Somunoğlu et al. 2013). Actually, speaking about physical violence, Leymann (1996) himself identified the threat to use force or the use of minor force as one of the mobbing actions against the victim.

It can be noted that the term *mobbing* is more common in the literature of German-speaking countries, as well as in Sweden, Italy, Austria, and in the French literature, mobbing is identified as *harcèlement moral* (psychological harassment, persecution, and torture) (Lohro and Hilp 2001). The term bullying is also used in English-speaking countries to describe the phenomenon of mobbing (Kolodej 2005; Melia and Becerrill 2007; Messinger and Rüdenberg 1977; Lohro and Hilp 2001). The more so as the formula of frequency and duration of attack used by Leymann to describe mobbing is also used in the analysis of cases of bullying in the workplace (Salin 2008; Baillien, Neyens, and De Witte 2011). Thus, the use of terms "mobbing" and "bullying" can be regarded as not different terms, but a certain tradition of the use, established in different scientific communities in respect of the country.

On the other hand, the word *bullying* is used in a much broader sense, for example, *customer bullying* (Bishop and Hoel 2008), *school bullying* (Moon and Jang 2014), not necessarily with emphasis on the relationships between colleagues. Although the term *bullying* is more commonly used in the United States, it does not capture the particular grievousness of mobbing that refers to a group attack on a worker, rather than an attack by a single individual, which is described as bullying (Duffy and Sperry 2007, 398).

The concept of workplace mobbing, with the exception of some aforementioned interpretations, is solid. The same characteristics are usually distinguished in definitions of workplace mobbing: the phenomenon is defined as negative, unethical course of action, which causes psychological pain to the victim distinguished from the rest of the coworkers, there is an intention to displace him or her in the division or organization (Leymann 1993; Einarsen and Skogstad 1996; Zapf 2002). The *psychological* aspect of impact of workplace mobbing on the victim is basically highlighted, irrespective of the nature of the selected actions, which are described by Leymann—through social relationships, the victim's reputation, work tasks, and health. Both in early and later studies, the same approach is followed, but the authors extend the concept of mobbing and supplement it with new aspects. We should also consider the fact that during more than three last decades, since the beginning of the studies carried out by Leymann, some new technical opportunities to reach and attack the victim, to harm its reputation not only in the eyes of employees, but also in the community outside the workplace, thereby reinforcing the negative effects, have appeared. A variety of communication technologies and social networks are used for that purpose. Bartlett and Bartlett (2011) note the fact that the use of technologies is not widely discussed in the literature. They state that research is needed to examine the impacts of cyber bullying in the workplace.

The authors who researched mobbing (Vartia-Vaananen 1996; Zapf, Knorz, and Kulla 1996; Resch 1997; Rayner, Hoel, and Cooper 2002; Meschkutat, Stackelbeck, and Lagengoff 2002; Premper 2002; Vartia-Vaananen 2003; Heames and Harvey 2006; Baillien, Neyens, and De Witte 2011.) have found the connection of workplace mobbing with poor, contentious organizational climate. Mobbing exists in the working environment, which is characterized by a high level of role conflict and a poor social climate (Einarsen 2000), with intense negative relationship dynamics (Duffy and Sperry 2007), and hostility between the employees has a negative impact on work satisfaction and well-being of the victim (Ashforth 1997; Einarsen and Raknes 1997; Mikkelsen and Einarsen 2002; Salin 2005; Tepper 2000.). As a result of the high frequency of attacks and long-term hostile behavior, an employee experiences psychological, social suffering, stress, and psychosomatic disorders (Leymann 1993; Zuschlag 1994; Prosch 1995; Niedl 1996; Lewis 2004). Zapf (1999) defined mobbing as a long-term strong social stressor; moreover, there is empirical evidence that the co-occurrence of emotional work and organizational problems lead to high levels of burnout (Zapf 2002). "Isolated incidents or unique cases of conflict should not be considered as bullying cases, but if they are repeated, in time, these incidents become bullying situations" (Chirila and Constantin 2013, 1178).

Therefore, the term *bullying* used in this part of the book is defined as a certain form of discrimination in relations between colleagues, revealing the dysfunctional aspects of interpersonal relationships based on intensive and long-term oppression of the victim (Vveinhardt 2009). *Single cases of harassment* are negative actions creating an intimidating environment, directed against a person, abusive, insulting verbal and nonverbal behavior, which causes discomfort, stress, psychological pain to the victim, affects the dignity of the person, and can adversely affect health (Vveinhardt and Žukauskas 2012). *Methods of pressure (or harassment, bullying)* are psychological violence directed to the restriction of freedom of social action of a person, performed as complex, systematic offensive actions, by one person or involving a group, excluding the victim from others, making it feel emotional, social discomfort in the work environment (Žukauskas and Vveinhardt 2013).

Bullying in Educational Institutions

Research on bullying in educational organizations can be grouped into two large parts: bullying among pupils (Rigby 2004) and bullying among the staff of educational institutions (Blase and Blase 2002). Only a few researches cover a broader context, systematically discussing the relationships of students, teachers, and the wider community, and the influence on the spread of the phenomenon (Lee 2009; Richard, Schneider, and Mallet 2011). The employee, the organization, and the society constitute a triangle, where each component interacts with another one. Although it may be analyzed separately, only systemic understanding of the problem may lay the foundation for its solutions (Vveinhardt and Žukauskas 2012, 371). In addition, a paradoxical situation is highlighted during the analysis of bullying research in the international academic literature: the problem is analyzed by the academic community; however, the research of the phenomenon in higher education institutions is not abundant. Although, as we will see later, the problem is really relevant in this area, and its solution is related not only to the issues of academic ethics, but also to the scientific activity, its quality, and scientists' motivation in both areas of research and training of young researchers.

Bullying is characterized by intensive dynamics of interpersonal relationships (Parzefall and Salin 2010; Duffy and Sperry 2012); however, these relationships have two main directions (or their combinations). Usually, bullying in organizations is divided into horizontal (among employees of the same rank) and vertical (among employees of different subordination) (Zapf et al. 2003; Katrinli et al. 2010; Vveinhardt and Žukauskas 2012). The studies carried out in the educational organizations, which also focus on individual and organizational factors, can be grouped according to these directions.

According to Samier and Atkins (2010, 579), the positions of power and influence provide motive and opportunity for the damaging character of this personality disorder to negatively affect the work life of colleagues and sabotage organizational effectiveness, ranging in degree from mild annoyance to extreme disabling. Cemaloğlu (2011) has found that there is a positive relationship between the transformational leadership acts of principles and organizational health, and a negative relationship between the transformational leadership acts of principles and workplace bullying. While a reverse relationship between the organizational health and workplace bullying is identified, there is a relationship between the transactional leadership acts of principles and organizational health. No relationship between the transactional leadership acts of principles and workplace bullying is found (495).

During the research carried out in Australia, it was found that 99.6 percent of the respondents had experienced some form of bullying during their employment. Half of the respondents experienced 32 or more of the 44 listed survey items, while their health was adversely affected by persistent and frequent bullying (Riley, Duncan, and Edwards 2011, 7). According to Harvey et al. (2006, 2), bullies can have a significant impact on the daily task-specific abilities of the employees. Also, ambitious employees, those employees who go the extra mile for the firm, may have their generous behavior crushed. Blase and Blase (2002) found that the

> Effects of such mistreatment are extremely harmful to teachers' professional and personal lives; like many thousands of workers represented in the extant literature—a number that has been extrapolated to be multimillions of workers—abused teachers experienced the same devastating effects. (p. 714)

A lot of studies analyze the situation in primary (Tam 2013) and secondary schools (DeSouza and Ribeira 2005; Casimir et al. 2012); however, the problem is not less relevant in higher education institutions (Thomas 2005; Yildirim, Yildirim, and Timucin 2007; Casimir et al. 2012; Vickers 2013). The situation is illustrated by Thomas' (2005) research. A total of 42 employees responded, 19 reporting experiencing one or more forms of bullying in the previous two years, while 17 had witnessed colleagues being bullied. The top four bullying tactics ranked in terms of frequency of reporting were undue pressure to produce work, undermining of ability, shouting abuse, and withholding necessary information (Thomas 2005, 273). Another research shows that the academic staff, who had been exposed to mobbing behaviors experienced various physiological, emotional, and social reactions. They frequently "worked harder and [were] more organized" and "worked very carefully to avoid criticism" to avoid mobbing (Yildirim, Yildirim, and Timucin 2007, 447).

Bullying in higher education institutions is a complicated ethical problem that is not always effectively solved (Westhues 2006). And, as Casimir et al. (2012) state, downward bullying reduces employee effectiveness because the ensuing negative affect and physical symptoms hamper the employees from performing optimally. Furthermore, targets may adopt avoidance strategies, such as absenteeism and turnover, to avoid being bullied (411). On the other hand, bullying often occurs as a consequence in organizations with tense competitive environment, where important changes are implemented (Vveinhardt 2009; Vveinhardt and Žukauskas 2012). The higher education institutions in many states are going through the years of significant changes. As Zabrodska et al. (2011, 709) noted, the reformed neoliberal universities, with their micromanagement of ever-increasing productivity, competitiveness, and individualization, have recently been described as unhealthy institutions, creating conditions that incite incivility, workplace bullying, and other forms of employee abuse.

Bullying is of particular relevance, as not always the leaders of the organizations tend to admit the existing problems of bullying and single cases of harassment (Brown, Aalsma, and Ott 2012; Vveinhardt and Žukauskas 2012), so they remain unsolved, or they are dealt with an insufficiently efficient way. Some important points should be noted. *First*, this is the level of competence of the head of the educational institution, which allows or hinders understanding of the harm caused by bullying and single cases of harassment, and the ability to organize the system that would eliminate them. *Second*, the legal requirements identify the managers as persons responsible for the employees' welfare. While "workplace bullying has been a subject of increasing study in recent years, particularly in the UK, Scandinavia" (Thomas 2005, 273), a few European countries still have no antibullying actions at a national level (Ananiadou and Smith 2002, 471). And, this situation has little changed for over a decade. As regards the international legal provisions dealing with prevention of bullying, it needs to be pointed out that, notwithstanding legislation of individual states in this field, the international community has not adopted any special obligatory or purely recommendatory legal acts. However, this does not mean that the problem of bullying is absolutely ignored at the international level and no discussions are held concerning this phenomenon (Petrylaitė 2011, 124).

No unambiguous answers to why the work in educational institutions is related to a higher risk of experiencing bullying have been submitted yet. For example, how much influence does higher education have on the frequency of bullying, and how much does education help identify bullying and consider it inappropriate form of interpersonal relationships? Some studies show that even employees of the same professional field, education, identify and evaluate bullying diversely. Comparing the reactions of education systems employees, the major difference has been found—respondents from Australia reacted to bullying in a more sensitive way than their colleagues from Uganda (Africa) (Casimir et al. 2012). The term *bullying* in the workplace and the origins of its content are related to the research of bullying in children's relationships carried out by Heinemann (1972, as cited in Olweus 1999); however, this phenomenon is usually analyzed separately. Bullying in relationships of employees of educational institutions is not an exception. However, some studies of bullying in students' relationships may be particularly useful when analyzing the negative aspects of the phenomenon in work environment, and can help both in understanding the dynamics of negative relations and when trying to stop the assault or helping to avoid it. In this aspect, the research of the phenomenon with regard to social ecology is of major importance. For example, Lee (2009) looked at bullying in students' relationships in the aspect of social ecology, highlighting the role of psychological climate, social relationships inside and outside school. In this case, the influence of the relationships between adults on the students' relationships as the overall psychosocial background has been revealed. However, there is a great lack of such studies of relationships between employees of educational institutions; therefore, it raises the task to prepare the theoretical base for future research. We also need to answer the questions that arise regarding the particularly frequent identification of the phenomenon in educational institutions.

Most studies of bullying as harsh treatment in interpersonal relationships in the workplace are focused on a social, immoral behavior of an individual during a conflict, on conditions of organization of work, underestimating the history of the formation of such a model of behavior, and the broader context beyond the boundaries of the organization. A situation of bullying in educational organizations is also specific because of the fact that the influence of deeply ingrained bullying in relationships between teachers on students' relationships remains underestimated. It can be assumed that the narrow analysis of the spectrum of reasons or dissociation of relations between students and teachers is one of the factors impeding a more efficient solution of the problem of bullying at school, which, as the accompanying phenomenon, moves into the workplace and affects the further professional career of the former student.

Generalizing and systematizing the experience of the studies of negative relations in educational organizations (among students and among staff), it is possible to find answers to why the problem of violence in the work environment continues to be quite intimidating and hard to overcome despite the efforts.

Prevalence of Bullying in Employee Relations in Educational Organizations: A Comparative Analysis

In this section, we will present the prevalence of bullying in employee relations in the educational organizations based on the results of a survey conducted in Lithuania.

Research methodology. The issue of prevalence of bullying in relationships between the employees of educational organizations is raised in the *problem of the research*. One of the parts of the *aim of this research* is to *analyze the prevalence of bullying in relationships between employees of educational organizations*. On the basis of the problem, the aim of the research and the analysis of theory, the following theoretical assumptions were set up:

1. Some of the most emphasized actions when analyzing bullying are both actions of verbal and nonverbal communication or noncommunication. The authors who researched bullying in the context of communication (Leymann 1990, 121; Zapf 1999, 82; Cemaloglu 2011, 507) argue that verbal and nonverbal behavior, reduced communication, absence of communication, and deliberate miscommunication are the strategies of bullying, which increases hostility and isolation of the victim. According to the authors who analyzed the links between noncommunication or isolation and mobbing (Leymann 1990, 121; Zapf 1999, 71; Einarsen 1999, 18; Ayoko, Callan, and Härtel 2003, 292), the victim experiences a strong negative impact of social isolation, and these efforts are quite intense.

2. Another particularly sensitive focus is the formation of a negative opinion about the victim in the workplace by giving the victims various work tasks that discredit them. The authors researching bullying in the aspect of debasement of authority (Leymann 1990, 121; Blase, Blase, and Du 2008, 275; Vickers 2009, 261, 265) note that when giving malicious tasks, the victim's professional status is diminished, and self-confidence is reduced. The nature of the work tasks is elaborated by Leymann (1990, 1993), Einarsen (1999), and Riley et al. (2011).

3. Finally, the analysis of scientific research related to psychical and physical well-being of the victims of bullying (Leymann 1990, 122; Zapf 1999, 79) inevitably touches the issue of material and other damage (Einarsen 1999, 17; Carnero, Martinez, and Sanchez-Mangas 2012, 335).

On the basis of the fore mentioned assumptions, the dimensions have been identified. The characteristics of the dimensions are presented as follows: communication interference in relationships between employees; formation of a negative opinion and the nature of work; employee physical, psychological well-being, and consequences.

1. Characteristics of the dimension of *communication interference in relationships between employees*: this dimension is properly described in such practices as avoiding contact with the victim, the use of intrusive gestures, glances, verbal and physical assault, speaking in a raised voice, unsound criticism, hindering from expressing an opinion, and so on. The actions that socially exclude the victim from the group, like avoidance of communication or banning communication, ignoring, moving the place of work further away from the coworkers, and so on are included.

2. The characteristics of the dimension of *formation of a negative opinion and the nature of work* include actions by which a negative opinion about the victim is formed, such as dissemination of unfaithful information, verbal assault and battery, mockery and abasement of physical features, social origin, and beliefs of the victim. Work reputation and professional authority of the victim are harmed; they

are debased by the wrong assessment of work, challenging solutions, deliberately giving the tasks the victim is not obliged to carry out or cannot perform properly, while being aware of it in advance and anticipating it.

3. The characteristics of the dimension of *employee physical, psychological well-being, and consequences* cover the actions that foster the occurrence of physical, psychological, and material damage to the victim. Tasks harmful for health, the threats to use power, and the use of it are included, victims are forced to experience the sense of fear, and the situations where material losses incurred are created.

Following the analysis of the characteristics of the dimensions, the following criteria were attributed to them:

1. The criteria of the dimension of communication interference in relationships between employees: *communication* and *isolation*.
2. The criteria of the dimension of formation of a negative opinion and the nature of work: *reputation* and *tasks*.
3. The criteria of the dimension of employee physical, psychological well-being, and consequences: *health* and *damage*.

In the *first phase* of the strategy of research methodology, the results of the quantitative research are presented: grouping of research results (the results of written surveys using questionnaires), the comparative analysis of the results of the research, and the interpretation of the research results.

Organization of the research. To carry out the research Vveinhardt's questionnaires "Mobbing as discrimination in relations between employees in the context of organizational climate" (2008 and 2009) and "Harassment and mobbing in relations between employees" (2010 through 2014) were used. The surveys were carried out annually from 2008 through 2014, in order to identify the occurrence of bullying in Lithuanian organizations.

Sample of the survey. The sample size was selected for the research using a simple random sampling method (reliable, random sampling method). Simple random sampling is a method in which each part of the general population has equal probability of being selected to participate in the survey, unequal to zero. The probability to be selected is equal to n/N, where n is the sample size, and N is the general population size.

Results of the research. Table 6.1 provides the percentage of five most vulnerable areas of professional activity in respect of bullying. The employees of organizations of 21 (average) areas of professional activities that have been distinguished in accordance with the Lithuanian Classification of Economic Activities were surveyed during the empirical researches. As we can see, every year the area of education falls within the top five most vulnerable areas of professional activities.

Some cases of activation of bullying and single cases of harassment in certain years can be explained by the reform that took place in the area of education in the country. As one can see from the results of the research, the area of professional activities of education took the first place among the most vulnerable areas for three consecutive years (2009, 2010, and 2011). The seven-year average is 16.1 percent. However, the year 2010, when 22.5 percent was recorded, can be considered a peak. In 2013 and 2014, the intensification of bullying in relationships between employees is observed again. The research carried out by the Ministry of Education and Science of the Republic of Lithuania (Damskis et al. 2012, 32) concludes that "the number of pupils is rapidly declining, funding of education is uneven. Teachers' salaries and jobs in Lithuania depend on the number of pupils directly." Bubelienė and Merkys (2012, 107) argue that "it is the social factors are most often thematized, emotionally strongly coloured, moreover, they are subjectively perceived by participants in the discourse as factors that are the most painful and most traumatizing to the teacher."

The studies that would analyze the relationship of bullying with the changed external and internal environments of organizations are not abundant. But, the surveyed professionals offering psychological assistance (Vveinhardt 2009, 107–09; Vveinhardt and Žukauskas 2012, 262–69) who worked with the victims of negative relationships at work, pointed out that the economic crisis, the increased risk of unemployment, insecurity, and reduced income influenced the increase of conflict. The reforms of education and relationship with students cause the most stress to employees of higher education institutions (Bulotaitė, Pociūtė, and Bliumas 2008, 118). Lazutka and Skučienė (2009, 152) who have carried

Table 6.1 *Five of the most vulnerable areas of professional activity with respect to bullying*

Year	2008	2009	2010	2011	2012	2013	2014
Sample	N = 351	N = 1,379	N = 1,015	N = 1,477	N = 1,086	N = 2,405	N = 856
Areas*	20	22	20	20	22	24	22
Place							
1	Publishing, 15.5%	Education, 10.9%	Education, 22.5%	Education, 21.9%	Administrative activities, 27.0%	Administrative activities, 19.5%	Education, 20.9%
2	Education, 13.8%	Healthcare and social work, 10.3%	Administrative activities, 17.5%	Administrative activities, 12.3%	Trade, 18.4%	Education, 14.6%	Trade, 16.1%
3	Recreational, cultural, and sporting activities, 12.1%	Trade, 9.1%	Information and communications, 8.5%	Healthcare and social work, 11.8%	Public administration and defense, 10.1%	Trade, 12.4%	Healthcare and social work, 11.8%
4	Healthcare and social work, 10.3%	Transport, 8.5%	Healthcare and social work, 8.1%	Information and communication, 8.0%	Education, 7.9%	Healthcare and social work, 7.6%	Administrative activities, 10.4%
5	Transport, 8.6%	Public administration and defense, 7.9%	Financial and insurance activities, 7.5%	Financial and insurance activities, 7.3%	Recreational, cultural, and sporting activities, 7.0%	Public administration and defense, 7.5%	Information and communication, 6.2%

* The number of areas of professional activity.

out the research among professionals of higher schools also stated that the system of social guarantees and employment on the whole raises tension and stress. Other studies (Vveinhardt 2011) show that the educational organizations pay little attention to the management of bullying.

The Most Common Methods of Pressure in Relationships Between Employees in Higher Education Organizations

In this section, we will present the most common methods of pressure in relationships between employees in higher education organizations based on the results of a survey conducted in Lithuania.

Research methodology. The issue of *the most common methods of pressure in relationships between employees of higher education organizations* is highlighted in the *problem of the research*. One of the parts of the *aim of this research* is *to distinguish the most common methods of pressure in relationships between employees of higher education organizations*. On the basis of the problem, the aim of the research and the analysis of theory, the following theoretical assumptions, providing the basis for the formation of the qualitative survey instrument have been set up.

The authors who researched bullying in higher education institutions (Yildirim, Yildirim, and Timucin 2007, 452–53) claim that the most common methods of pressure are causing isolation from work, attack on professional status, attack on personality, and direct negative behaviors. The characteristics distinguished by the authors partly correspond to the general characteristics distinguished in Leymann's (1996, 170) dimensions (effects on the victims' possibilities to communicate adequately; "effects on the victims' possibilities to maintain their social contacts"; "effects on the victims' possibilities to maintain their personal reputation"; "effects on the victims' occupational situation"; and "effects on the victims' physical health"). However, in Yildirim, Yildirim, and Timucin. (2007) study, physical violence was not a statistically significant factor. Duffy and Sperry (2007, 399–40) included the organizational dynamics and personality dynamics. Zabrodska et al. (2011, 718) pointed out that the changes in universities, increasing productivity, and individualism are connected with the risk of mobbing in unethical relations. In addition, it is necessary to evaluate such general factors, common to mob-bing and bullying as a high level of the role conflict, bad social climate, the nature of relationships (Einarsen 2000; Duffy and Sperry 2007), uncertainty (Zapf 1999), organizational culture (Liefooghe and Olafsson 1999), and inappropriate behavior of the management (Blase and Blase 2003; Cemaloglu 2011; Riley, Duncan, and Edwards 2011). Therefore, it should be assumed that the attack related to unethical communication, work tasks, and scientific and educational activities is possible in higher education institutions.

On the basis of the assumptions, the dimensions were identified. The characteristics of the dimensions are listed as follows:

1. The characteristics of the dimension of work with the scientific research: individual scientific research activities and realization of scientific research activities (production).
2. The characteristics of the dimension of work with students: educa-tional activities and their quality and students' or doctoral students' work.

Following the analysis of the characteristics of the dimensions, the following criteria were attributed to them:

1. The criteria of the dimension of *work with scientific research*: *criticism, exploitation, stopping, and interference.*
2. The criteria of the dimension of work with the students: *subjects taught* and *supervision of students' papers.*

In the *second phase* of the strategy of research methodology, the qual-itative research is carried out: data collection (interviews), data analysis (qualitative content analysis), and interpretation of the results.

Sample of the survey. In order to determine the methods of pressure (or harassment, bullying) in relationships between employees in higher education organizations, the victims of bullying were surveyed in 2014, using the method of structured interview. Earlier, the victims of bullying applied for advice on bullying and single cases of harassment at work by email, visited the website mobingas. lt (author's note: this website provides consultations on issues related to bullying). Following the analysis of the content of messages, 17 potential participants of the research were selected. The informants were selected so that every new informant could provide additional information. Eight possible informants refused to participate in the research, though anonymity was guaranteed, ensuring that only the generalized results of the research will be published, and the audio recording will be deleted after the analysis. The final number of the informants willing to participate in the research was nine, but during the seventh, eighth, and ninth interviews, data saturation occurred; therefore, it was decided to analyze responses of six informants.

The study involved teachers of Lithuanian higher schools. Table 6.2 identifies the main characteristics of the informants (abbreviation I).

It was aimed that the informants would be distributed evenly according to the academic degree and academic title: three Professors and three Associate Professors. Distribution by position similarly corresponds to the academic title, that is, three Professors and three Associate Professors. A comparison of the distribution of the informants by institution shows that five of them work at universities and one at the institute. The difference between the university and the institute is that those who work at the institute focus on scientific research. The distribution of informants by the length of service in the current workplace is quite uneven, as well as the distribution by the age. By gender, the study involved three females and three males.

Organization of the research. With the consent of informants, the interviews were recorded using the voice recorder. After each interview, the recording was downloaded as computer files, the data were transcribed, and then analyzed. The interview was conducted in the Lithuanian language, later it was translated into English. Back translation from English to the Lithuanian language was made by a philologist of the English language. After comparison of both translations, some concepts were specified to correspond the original concept.

Results of the research. The combined results of the interview are presented in Table 6.3. Attention is drawn to the fact that the results of the interview presented as follows, distinguishing only the most frequent methods of pressure in higher education organizations, which are then elaborated when transcribing the text.

Table 6.2 Characteristics of informants

Informants	Academic degree, academic title	Position	Institution	Length of service in the current workplace	Age	Gender
I1	Prof. Dr. Habil.	Professor	University	30	56	Male
I2	Prof. Dr. Habil.	Professor	University	32	60	Male
I3	Prof. Dr. Habil.	Professor	2 universities	22	54	Female
I4	Assoc. Prof. Dr.	Associate professor	Institute, university	9	38	Female
I5	Assoc. Prof. Dr.	Associate professor	University	14	45	Female
I6	Assoc. Prof. Dr.	Associate professor	University	26	51	Male

Table 6.3 *The most common methods of pressure in higher education: scientific research work*

Dimensions	Criteria	Informants					
		1I	2I	3I	4I	5I	6I
Scientific research work	Criticism	–	–	Negative reviews	Debasement of output efficiency	Publication criticized	–
	Exploitation	The abuse of position using pressure in pursuit of personal gain	–	–	Forced sharing of outcomes	–	Pressure to add a surname as a coauthor
	Interference	Procrastination of time	Book publishing is not financed	Delayed reviews	Was not admitted to develop a collective monograph	An attempt to withdraw articles as an outcome	–

Scientific Research Work

Scientific research work is one of the areas in which moral pressure and bullying are experienced. Scientific research activities, in other words, the scientific output, determine the income and career of the higher school teacher.

1I: <<… I was preparing to participate in the competition to a higher position all year long. One of requirements of the competition was that there had to be at least a few scientific articles published in ISI Web of Science journals, or at least certificates that prove the acceptance of the paper for publication had to be presented. My two manuscripts were sent to one journal, whose editor was also preparing to participate in the competition for same position, but there were two positions. So I kind of wouldn't have to suffer any pressure. However, sending the reviews of my manuscript was procrastinated in a variety of methods. To my appeal by e-mail I received responses with promises and deadlines, but the editor didn't keep the promises. Once I "caught" the editor lying that he was abroad, so he couldn't send me the reviews, etc. <…> I had hard feelings and had concern that I lost time, because I could have published my papers in another journal. <…> We both have won the competition; we both have received promotions. After the competition, I received positive reviews for both of my manuscripts (practically without any comments). <…> Later, I found out that this "campaign" against me was helped to arrange by the person who is constantly intriguing against me at work and tries to "get rid of" me because I had refused to prepare a joint publication with him. He persuaded other colleagues to participate in the competition, so that I would have more competitors …>>.

In the case of the first informant, the abuse of position has occurred. The named competitor has no direct institutional power, but has an opportunity to harm by impeding the publishing of the research results and making participation in the competition, in which the results are significant, more difficult. The informant has suffered moral damage because of emotional experience and tension before the competition; by unethical behavior, it was attempted to cause material damage in case the competition to the higher position would not be won. In this case, the pressure was incurred from two sources, which can be regarded as related. Unfair behavior of the competitor has strengthened another lasting assault from the working environment close to the informant. Informant 3I notes another similar case, although competition, as a reason, was not named directly.

3I: <<... I have been sending manuscripts of my researches to the journal published by our university, even by our faculty for several consecutive years. I manage to be published there very rarely (only one my article was published in 5 last years); I am steadily getting negative reviews of my manuscripts. It is also worth to mention that I wait for reviews of my articles several times longer than the others do. Sometimes the process of peer-reviewing is "delayed" so that I worry that the data of my research will become obsolete and irrelevant. The journal is ordinary, it is refereed in several not special databases. Taking a detached view, practically all colleagues, even with their students, get to it. First, I thought that my studies were unworthy of attention, later I decided to make an "experiment": as soon as the local journal rejects my manuscript (this journal is published twice a year, and I send articles it to each issue of it), I am immediately sending it to a foreign journal. To my surprise, all manuscripts rejected by the journal published by our faculty were successfully published in foreign journals. <...> One article even got to the ISI Web of Science Journal! Without a doubt, this attitude against me (and maybe against my research papers?) really frustrates me psychologically. There are some moments when I no longer want to do anything, but I am trying with every last ounce of strength ...>>.

Putting obstacles to the publication of researches causes material damage in addition to nonmaterial damage. Talking of possible causes, it is significant to focus on the data about the conflict situation provided by informant 4I. The results of a more talented, more hard-working colleague draw attention to the smaller achievements of colleagues.

4I: <<... they call me a very productive employee in the scientific sense, because I carry out quite a lot of studies and publish them. In my unit, I am leading in respect of scientific output, and I "earn" a lot of points to my unit. However, regardless of the fact that I am useful to the unit where I work, they started to reduce my workload in every possible way, that is, they let me give fewer lectures. Once the head of my unit told me, "you are too strong to work with this team. You make a huge competition that causes disbalance in working atmosphere. Many would like to climb up a career ladder, but you 'come out' everywhere with your results. Not everyone is so successful, after all" ...>>.

Better results are interpreted as the employee's drawback that "worsens the atmosphere." On the other hand, attack with *undercurrent* is related to the desire to use the results of the work of a coworker, who is put under pressure. Offensive actions occur at several levels simultaneously, creating psychological pressure and making material damage, that is, limiting the victim's ability to earn a higher salary. In this case, the aim may be dual—to supplant the employee in the organization, in which his or her performance causes discomfort or force to share the results.

4I: <<... no one says directly, but I realized that I'd be more tolerated, if I accepted colleagues as co-authors. To accept as a co-author means to work alone and share the results with everyone. <...> I would also like to mention one case where my colleagues were writing a collective monograph. <...> I have prepared my part as well, but the reviews of my part were dreadful and despite a lot of corrections I did in that part, I wasn't accepted as a co-author of the collective monograph. When I saw the published monograph I realized that I wasn't accepted as a co-author of the monograph certainly not because of "poor quality" of my paper. <...> I think that this may be related with competition. My colleagues think that I am trying so hard because I pretend to the position of the head of the department. I emphasized several times that I wasn't interested, but nobody believes me ...>>.

Although 2I did not indicate the reason why his possibilities to self-actualize are limited materially (not providing funds to publishing his papers), it is obvious that the informant is characterized by active scientific and publishing activity, to which his colleagues react negatively. In this case, it can be assumed that the pressure is made not only horizontally (verbal taunting by the colleagues), but also vertically (by the management, not providing funds). Although the informant indicated the formal reason expressed by the management ("there is no money"), the allocation of funding to other colleagues shows that there is a reason not named to the informant.

2I: <<... they tell me that the university lacks funds, so it can't budget for publishing my book. <...> I have published several monographs, scientific studies, textbooks, study books. My colleagues often laugh at me that I am rather a writer than a professor. <…> In fact, I devote a lot of time to writing books, and, strange to say, certainly not for a higher coefficient, but because I want to leave something in this world. I don't have children, so at least I'll leave my papers to students. I write down all my ideas, original thoughts and larger texts, and finally books are born from them. <…> Now, after several years of trying, I don't even go and ask any more, although I see that there is money for publishing other colleagues' books. <…> I have hard feelings <…>. I am looking for sponsors, write applications to funds …>>.

There is an unhealthy, unethical, informal evaluation system of collaborators, and if an employee disagrees with the system, the employee is not tolerated; they aim at eliminating him.

5I: <<… I am quite active in preparing publications with the students (I have teamed up an informal group of young researchers). Colleagues sneer that I use students' work and exploit them. Certainly I do not. We prepare researches together (at the same time I teach them to do it), we process the results together, and sitting together we analyze and write interpretations. On the basis of the jointly prepared researches the papers are published. <…> I don't see anything wrong here, the more as the others don't put a finger to the articles which are published with the students, they just add their name and that's all. Time and again I have found plagiarised texts in such articles, because students sometimes do not avoid doing it in their papers. <…> My problem is that I said it out loud, and other colleagues heard this. <…> Basically, the fault finding to my publications started from the moment, when I told about the incorrect behavior of the colleagues in respect of other fellow colleagues. One year, when providing an annual report on scientific output, they even wanted to nullify all my articles published with the students. I had to argue inviting the student I worked with which part was written by me and which by the student. It was a huge humiliation that they wanted to nullify my publications, rather than those who have published the "plagiarised" texts …>>.

The illegal system of impact on the victims is used to exploit the victims financially. Unethical behavior is tolerated by those who have to take decisions, those who use their institutional power and authority as leverage or sanction in pursuit of personal goals. These sanctions are humiliating the victim's reputation (formation of opinion about "bad teacher," criticism of work) and causing material damage (not allowing teaching) (see 6I).

6I: <<… for several years in a row, I am forced to add the names of colleagues with senior positions to my research. Just the tradition already exists, that in order to have a teaching load, I have to be useful to the head of the department, directors of the study programme, sometimes to the dean of the faculty. <…> I experience a special pressure from the head of the department, who has told me directly that if I wanted to get I had to give. <…> So, I should understand, if I want to get a load, I have to add her surname to my publications as a co-author. I did this for a long time, then I lost my patience and started to publish my studies alone. My load instantly declined, and the arguments of the heads were that the head of the department had reported that students were dissatisfied with my lecturing. Now I add the name of the head of the department as a co-author again, and students are satisfied with the quality of my lectures again …>>.

So the pressure with undercurrent was implemented in this case—the informant 6I was forced to share the results with the people holding authority. Pressure with financial undercurrent, when it is made by a person holding authority, directly or indirectly encouraging rewarding for favorable decisions or forcing to reward in indirect financial expression, can be named the abuse and corruption. The victim is also forced to make moral compromises.

Summarizing the informants' answers about the specifics of the methods of pressure regarding publication used against them, we can say that the used measures are targeted against scientific reputation of a colleague (subordinate) and the competition on certain material resources, which are related to scientific output and the positions, is implemented. It has been revealed that the attack takes place with material undercurrent as well, in order to benefit from the achievements of a colleague.

Table 6.4 contains the second part of the combined interview results to substantiate the dimension of work with students.

Table 6.4 *The most common methods of pressure in higher education: work with students*

Dimensions	Criteria	Informants					
		1I	2I	3I	4I	5I	6I
Work with students	Subjects taught	Ignoring the freely elective subject taught	–	–	Criticism of subjects taught	–	Withdrawal of the subject taught from the study program
	Supervision of students' works	–	Unfair struggle for postgraduate students	Supervision of doctoral dissertations is criticized	–	Criticism of supervised bachelors' papers	Unethical interference in the work of the student supervised by a colleague

Work with Students

1I: <<… I teach a very popular and favourite among students freely elective subject of general university education at the university. I try hard to engage students, because this subject is almost the greatest part of my workload. To be fair, I move heaven and earth so that it would remain so popular every year. Every year this subject is included in the lists, from which students choose the subject they want to study during the next semester. The freely elective subject I teach was not included in the list …>>.

When specifying the provided information, informant 1I pointed out that dealing with a technical employee, who was responsible for the publication of the lists, he was under the impression that this person feels uncomfortable; he mentioned he was unable to do anything, and strongly suggested to contact the person who confirms the lists. The situation basically matches the group of bullying actions, associated with the work tasks, more specifically, not providing them, described by Leymann (1993, 1996). The situation when the victim suffers material loss at work is also created artificially. In the absence of clear responsibility for nonfulfillment of a certain function, such a situation may be called unintentional, the more so because it was corrected formally, but when the damage has already been done. They explained that a mistake has occurred, but it has not been corrected. <<… My requests were simply ignored, almost until the last week, when most of the students have already selected the subjects …>>. The informant pointed out that he did not address the management, although he has saved the email correspondence. He explained that <<… *the search for truth is difficult, because everyone are related here and protect each other* …>>, <<… *here they don't like the truth seekers, and I need to keep a job* …>>. The fact that 1I justified his decision not to address the higher management not by objective arguments, but rather by the general provision *"everyone are related and protect each other"* is significant. The existence (support) of such common attitudes creates illusory power for the one abusing the power he or she has; on the other hand, it gives signals about the problems of the organizational culture related to transparency and publicity of relations and decisions.

6I presents a similar situation: <<… *It has already become the system, which lasts for almost a year. Firstly, withdrawal of the subject I teach from the study programme. Secondly, I advised a student for two years, and before the defence another lecturer, who is a specialist in another field of science, was appointed as his scientific advisor. They explained me that the student's written request was lost, but the student swore he did not write a new written request and did not choose another lecturer. Exactly the same was with another student's course paper.* <…> *That was done by the person with whom I fell out* …>> The informant was not able to name the specific reason of the conflict, related it to the work relationships: <<… *during the meeting I made some well-meant remarks to the study program prepared by the team led by that person, but people take remarks as a personal criticism* …>> as well as provisions: <<… *they treat me as a stranger. I don't attend parties, I don't contribute to collection of money to congratulate someone, because I think that it is more sincere to congratulate personally* …>> As in the case of 1I, 6I was afraid to write an official report or talk to a higher official <<… *I don't think that anything would change, because this has happened not only to me.* <…> *That person has a strong backing and does what he wants* …>> When asked to specify what was meant by *backing*, the informant indicated the close friendship ties with the management. In other words, in this case, the defensive actions of the victim were restricted by nepotic relationships of the abusing person.

The data provided by the informants about the reasons that might have led to attack are significant. One of the main reasons is the internal competition. For example, 2I: <<… *There is constant competition for postgraduates, who are the most prospective pretenders to the doctoral studies. The number of postgraduates in our faculty is very low. Students like me very much, I teach postgraduates several subjects, so very often they choose me as their master's thesis advisor. The malady is that after the master's studies there is a direct way to doctoral studies. When I notice gifted students, I always offer them such a possibility, i.e., to continue their research during doctoral studies* …>> and 4I: <<… *However, my methods are not acceptable for senior colleagues. They criticize me and claim that what I am doing during the lectures are children's games. During the meeting, one colleague even expressed doubts in my expertise and offered that this subject should be taught by another lecturer. It disturbs me, as the assessments of student's knowledge are always very good. The subject has been taught, the students are satisfied … I think that only the colleagues who fail to interest their students in their subject taught are unhappy …>>* Thus, the logical sequence becomes apparent: *exclusiveness* of a colleague determines the *popularity* among students, and in the short or long term means higher *income.* It can be assumed that some colleagues subjectively feel a certain threat posed by a colleague's competitiveness. The sense of tension caused by the threats is reduced not in the way of professional development, but by attacking their reputation. In this case, several methods are used. First, by indirectly (with underlying message) and directly limiting the opportunity to receive work tasks (e.g., 2I: <<… *Before choosing a master's paper advisor my students were set against me on repeated occasions, the administration offered to choose other master's paper advisors (as I found out by hearsay, the staff of the administration were instructed to do so "from above") …>>*). Second, frequently criticizing the results of work directly and indirectly: the direct attack takes place when criticizing the victim's work, indirect attack takes place when criticizing the work of young researchers advised (3I: <<… *the range of problems of the dissertations prepared by my doctoral students is constantly criticized. For a number of years every my advised doctoral student got an earful when presenting the dissertation, although till now there are no students who wouldn't defend their thesis. First of all, I as the advisor have to listen to humiliating colleagues' reproaches in the presence of my and other doctoral students. It is bad if the dissertation topic is interdisciplinary. It is also bad if it is not interdisciplinary. The consequence is that students no longer want me to advise them, because the information "from mouth to mouth" is spreading very quickly. They talk about me as about the advisor whose students never please the head of the department and other colleagues, and this minimizes the students' possibility to defend the thesis on time. On colleagues' initiative, my doctoral students have already been twice "asked" to take an academic leave by open vote, for allegedly poor preparation of the dissertation. The interesting thing is that I work in two universities, and there are no such problems in another university. If the same situation was in another university, I would really start to doubt my competence …>>.* In this case, the principle of unfair competition and moral and material damage to the victim (supervisor) are revealed, as part of the income is lost because of a communicative attack by using unethical actions.

A certain conflict between those who are distinguished for their activities (seeking to be distinguished) and those who use the old methods is highlighted. It is shown by the information provided by 4I and 5I, indicating unconstructive criticism from the colleagues. 4I: <<… *the criticism of the subjects I taught went beyond all limits. During the lectures, I use a variety of methods to engage students in my subject. During seminars I encourage them to present the material prepared to the audience as much resourcefully as possible by performing creative tasks related to the topic of the seminar, in which all the group of students would be able to participate. Certain "competitions" among the students who perform the task best are organised, various incentives are awarded. Students like this kind of lectures very much. They say that in this way they understand "dry" theoretical material better. After a semester, the administration carries out anonymous student surveys, in which the students evaluate the course I teach by very high marks* …>>. And 5I: <<… *every year I have to supervise a large number of students who prepare Bachelors' papers. I always try to help the students choose as much diverse, interesting and "fresh" topics as possible (in our unit everyone develop Bachelor's papers on career or motivation). However, my efforts are not only underestimated, they also receive strong criticism from colleagues. They say there is no need to experiment; you have to give the students more traditional topics, because they themselves do not understand what they write about. It is obvious that my students understand what they write about, I do a very intense work with them, explain, consult, and often help to find necessary material. I prepare the students for public defence of Bachelor's thesis so that they feel strong in their topic and during discussions. However, during the public defence, the colleagues who are the members of the defence committee manage not to ask questions on the topic of the Bachelor's paper; this is not very correct and unethical. Then students are often taken aback, don't know what to answer, the braver students make a defence. Often students have to defend not only their papers, but also the supervisor of their papers* …>>. The problem of the lack of support is significant. 5I: <<… *There are a few colleagues who support me and say that it is time to move that "stagnant water"* …>>. On request to clarify the circumstances of "support" 5I said that the support is provided "*in private conversations,*" not publicly. This is explained by the unwillingness to oppose "*the senior,*" "*authoritative*" colleagues. In other words, those individuals can partly be identified as informal leaders, whose opinions are significant to the team, who have the power. The informant 5I has named "moral satisfaction" and career as a motive of his efforts: <<... *I don't think that I'll work here for all my life, and while being invisible, I won't find a job elsewhere* ...>>. The informant 4I reasoned the efforts by *"personal perfectionism."*

Summarizing the informants' answers about the particularity of the methods of pressure used against them in the context of working with students, it can be argued that the victims find themselves in the epicenter of the attack because of the professional activity and efforts made for it, which make the victims exceptional. In this case, the discriminatory mechanism is working, when an individual is discriminated because of certain features (professional activity), and therefore is treated wrongly, in a discriminatory way. The specifics of activity result in the fact that the attack takes place not only directly (criticizing a colleague's work), but also indirectly, by putting pressure on the students. In addition, the authority of those involved in the assault outweighs the ethical principles.

The informants have also mentioned other methods of pressure during the interview. Since these are less common methods of pressure, they could not be grouped. Single cases are presented in Table 6.5.

During the analysis of the less common methods of pressure in relationships between employees in higher education organizations, informant 5I has mentioned that very rarely he has an opportunity of going to work under the Erasmus program to teach foreign students. He claims that <<... *the other go abroad over and over again, getting into different countries, and not only to get some experience, but to recreate and relax, for example, in warm countries during the winter. Competitions for Erasmus visits are organized in my workplace, so I very rarely win them, but certainly*

Table 6.5 Less common methods of pressure in relations of the employees of higher education organizations

Methods	Informants					
	1I	2I	3I	4I	5I	6I
Less common methods of pressure	–	Nonfunded business trips	–	–	Visits to foreign countries under the Erasmus program	–

not because of my incompetence ...>> When specifying in what ways the *other* persons are different, 5I stated conformance and nepotism *loyalty to the superior and friendly relations* as the reasons.

The Model of Managerial Solutions to Eliminate the Problem of Bullying and Single Cases of Harassment in Higher Education Organizations

In this section, we will present the model of managerial solutions to eliminate the problem of bullying and single cases of harassment in higher education organizations.

The issue *of the development of managerial solutions to eliminate the analyzed problem* is raised in the *problem of the research*. One of the parts of the *aim of the research* is to *develop managerial solutions to eliminate the analyzed problem*. The following theoretical assumptions for the formation of the model of managerial solutions are raised on the basis of analysis of the problem and the aim of the research, analysis of scientific literature, comparative analysis of the results of quantitative researches, and the analysis of the results of the qualitative research:

1. The analysis of the scientific literature on *bullying and single cases of harassment in higher education organizations* enables to make an assumption that the individual cases of bullying and single cases of harassment are determined by the organizational system, which allows to escalate destruction in relationships. This is confirmed by the results of the quantitative and qualitative researches.

2. After the *comparative analysis of the prevalence of bullying in relations between employees of educational organizations*, one more assumption that people working in this area of professional activity particularly suffer from the destructive mutual relationships and do not get effective help should be made.

3. Following the identification of *the most frequent methods of pressure in the relationships with the employees of the higher education organizations*, it should be assumed that academic ethics and the ethics of work relationships are not sufficiently effective measures to deal with destructive relationships, if the problems of organizational system (management) had not been solved.

4. In order to develop *the model of managerial solutions to eliminate the problem of bullying and single cases of harassment in higher education institutions*, it is accentuated that solutions are focused on the development of personal competence, improvement of organizational system, and participation of stakeholders.

In *the third phase* of the research methodology strategy, the formulation of managerial solutions to eliminate the problem of bullying and single cases of harassment is carried out.

The model of managerial solutions to eliminate the problem of bullying and single cases of harassment in higher education organizations is the interventional model. When developing this model, the system of prevention and intervention of bullying and harassment is consistently organized. The organization can choose between the traditional way of vertical administrative decisions or the second way—to include stakeholders and decentralize the decision-making process. *The first way* is the traditional structure of higher education institutions, which may be quite functional in administrative sense, organizing activities, oriented toward certain academic goals, but insufficient to be used in order to avoid and deal with sophisticated conflicts in the academic community. *The second way* is to revise the organizational structure, to include organized structures of stakeholders as equal partners in making decisions on the basis of consensus. When choosing this way, the first thing is to admit (by assuming) that the organizational system may not be functional enough to solve interpersonal conflicts (zero stage). At this stage, the resources available for the organization are estimated, raising the following questions:

- What is the state of the climate on the levels of the organization and units?
- Are the functions of lower level managers and subordinates defined precisely and known, and is the responsibility defined clearly?
- What is the level of competence of managerial staff?
- What are the personal moral values of the organization and managerial staff?

- Are the systems of documents and internal communication functional?
- Are the transparency and openness of decision-making ensured?
- What is the prevalence of internal corruption and what are the possibilities to allow it to spread?
- How effective is the system of complaints and appeals hearing?
- Are stakeholders (the structures representing them) involved in the organizational processes?
- What determines the motivation of stakeholders?
- What are the opportunities to realize the available instruments (e.g., codes of ethics, institutes of ethics maintenance, collective agreements, industrial dispute councils, and commissions)?

Many of these questions focus on the keeping and raising the level of the organizational management culture. At this stage, it is necessary to define the stakeholders and involve them: trade unions, scientists' organizations, students, and other internal communities. At this stage, it is defined what is considered to be harassment, unethical behavior, and what is its extreme form, bullying, and the operational team is formed. The objectives set for the team are: (1) to evaluate the organizational system and (2) to create (or improve) the system for prevention and intervention of single cases of harassment and bullying. Higher education institutions usually have accumulated a high-level of intellectual potential that can be flexibly used at this and other stages.

In Figure 6.1, the five phases are presented: monitoring, surveys or in other words, the research phase, data analysis stage, the stage of decisions, and the stage of changes or the implementation of formulated managerial solutions. The model of managerial solutions demonstrates the process, which consists of the preparation for decision making on two levels, taking into account the threats posed by harassment and bullying in the organization.

At the first stage, the monitoring of the system is carried out, addressing the objectives set and in response to the questions formulated on the stage conditionally called the zero stage on two levels: bullying and

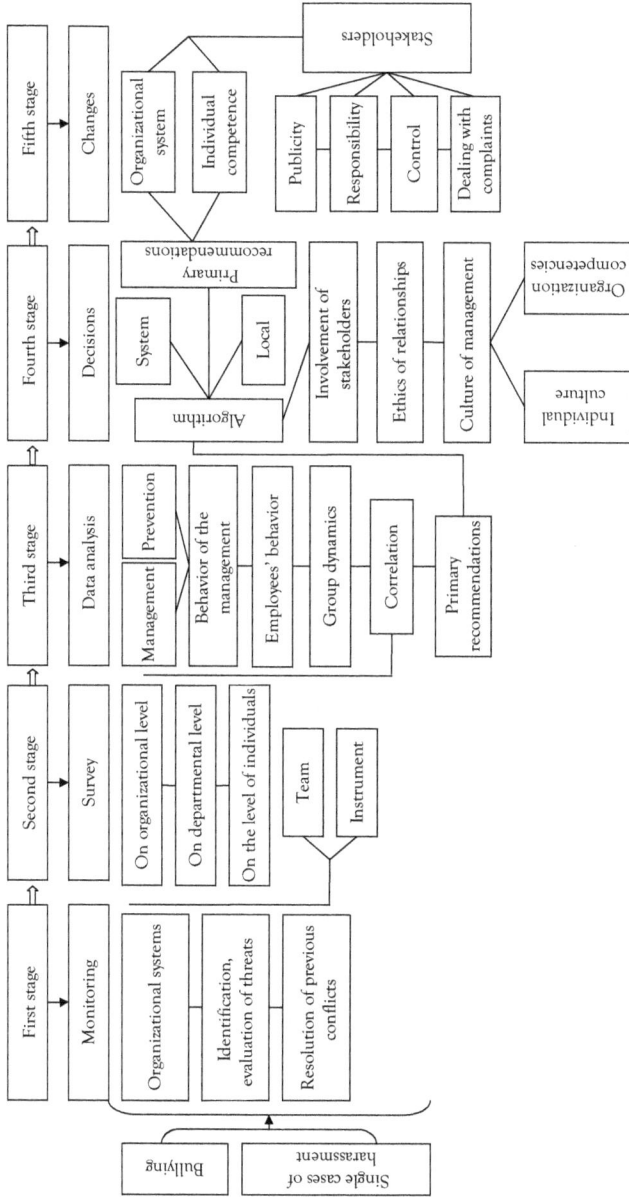

Figure 6.1 The model of managerial solutions to eliminate the problem of bullying and single cases of harassment in higher education organizations

single cases of harassment. The impartial monitoring of the processes and analysis of documents that regulate the performance of the system, complaints, conflicts, and their solutions are carried out. In this case, the basic information on the organizational structure and distribution of functions are collected; as a lack of certainty, duplication of functions can become the basis of conflict situations and the abuse of formal (government) and informal powers. In addition, other threats arising on organizational level, such as workloads, organizational change, competition, transparency and publicity policies, channels of internal communication and feedback, and so on, are evaluated.

The second stage is the stage of in-depth research. At this stage, qualitative and quantitative researches are carried out by external researchers. The quantitative survey of employees of the organization is carried out using the existing or specially developed instrument, but in the latter case, it is necessary to evaluate the time factor that is relevant to the development and testing of the research instrument. At this stage, the complex research consisting of two parts is carried out: (1) diagnostics of organizational climate and (2) diagnostics of bullying and harassment on the levels of departments and the organization. The psychosocial climate is an important factor that indicates whether the conditions for bullying and single cases of harassment to thrive exist or not in the organization. In addition, formal and informal communication, behavior and leadership style of different levels of the management, the nature of the relationships between the employees, the effectiveness of the existing institutions in the organization (actions of the management, professional organizations, workers confidence in the management, and other institutes that govern ethical and working relationships), actions in dealing with interpersonal conflicts and in order to "forestall them," and so on are evaluated. In other words, the research highlights, the strengths and weaknesses of the organizational system; it can show how the systems of prevention and intervention of bullying and single cases of harassment have to be developed. Moreover, even if bullying is not highlighted, it provides the knowledge necessary to make decisions that improve the sociopsychological climate of the organization.

At the third stage, the data obtained during the second stage is analyzed, it is summarized, construed, and submitted to the decision makers.

The process is conducted in two levels: bullying and harassment, which can be both single cases and form some system; however, not turning into bullying. The group dynamics, management behavior, and effectiveness of the institutes of prevention and intervention are analyzed. The correlation of the individual factors with displays of bullying and harassment on the levels of the organization and its departments are analyzed as well. The analysis allows identifying vulnerable "points" of the organization, creating the map of the organization, highlighting both positive and negative factors and the processes. For example, support of the group for the victims of bullying or efforts made by the management of the organization to resolve conflicts effectively should be seen as a positive factor. Developing the support jointly with others, you can expect positive results. If bullying is not diagnosed, systematicness of harassment should be noted. For example, Leymann's definition shows that the process of harassment is already ingrained. However, if harassment is not occasional, but there are repetitive conflicts between employees that last for a longer period of time, or if the intensely attacked employee generally has been working for less than six months, this suggests that the process of bullying may have already started, although according to the mentioned definition, it shouldn't be considered to be bullying.

Organizations have the opportunity to introduce certain organizational measures recommended for the prevention of bullying. However, the analysis of information makes it possible to choose the levers that can effectively change the situation, at lower costs. A certain algorithm that would help the organization to choose purposeful decisions may be made to make decisions at the fourth stage that results from the third stage. It is based on the investigated dimensions or factors of the organizational system (e.g., the aforementioned communication system, actions of the management, and relationships). First, if bullying and harassment have not been found (although there are no ideal organizations, where conflicts of one of another kind do not exist), decisions that improve the functionality of the individual processes are made. Second, when bullying or single cases of harassment have been found, the actions are taken in several organizational and individual aspects: the organizational causes leading to bullying and harassment are removed, the system of prevention and intervention of bullying is improved or developed; the decisions to develop employees' social competence are taken. Bullying and harassment on the levels of the organization and the individual departments can show both the shortcomings (mistakes) of the general organizational system and individual problems of management in particular departments. For example, in the case of Lithuania, many of the higher education institutions have individual codes of ethics, generally accepted ethical standards of international academic community require certain behavior in activities related to scientific situations. However, in the absence of effective supervision and control system, some of the principles may remain unrealized (in more detail in discussing the fifth stage).

It is impossible (or only partly possible) to solve the problem of bullying, if only single cases of harassment are solved. When dealing with the problem of bullying systematically, single cases of harassment are dealt with as well, not allowing them to evolve into bullying. When shaping the system of prevention and intervention of bullying and single cases of harassment, institutionalization of the phenomenon in the documents of the organization and the system of receiving and processing the employees' complaints with the participation of representatives of the employees and students should be addressed. At the first level of the system, the complaints are dealt with and recommendations to the management are provided by the persons appointed by the staff, students, and the management whose competence in the area of bullying and single cases of harassment must be constantly maintained and improved. At the second level, decisions are made by the management. Not only clear moral responsibility, but also disciplinary responsibility in case of misuse or terrorization of subordinates and colleagues is necessary. The research has highlighted the problem of competences of individuals who experience assault in dealing with conflicts; therefore, an important task of the higher education institutions is to develop the employees' competencies in social relations, without letting this issue take its course.

For implementation of decisions (the fifth stage): (a) publicity both in organizational decision making and in dealing with the cases of bullying; (b) participation of stakeholders (representatives of staff and students); and (c) system of control must be ensured. Restriction of possibilities of internal corruption (nepotism, protection, misuse of power, etc.), which emerged as one of the sources of bullying, is associated with clear and high ethical standards in the management of the organization and transparency, formalization of decisions and orders. In addressing these objectives, the opportunities offered by the latest information systems and document management systems should be noted. In other words, the development of the management culture of higher education institutions as a component of the corporate culture can dramatically reduce the possibilities of destructive relationships between the employees and facilitate the implementation of solutions on the intervention (active prevention) of bullying.

Every community has written and unwritten principles of self-regulation. It is required (or at least expected) from the academic community that these principles are based on high moral criteria, logic, and objectivity. In addition, the instruments that would make the activities of the organizations in the sphere of human resources more efficient are expected from the higher education institutions operating in the field of Social Sciences. However, can this requirement be satisfied enough without addressing the issues of the functionality of the relationships between the researchers? This is just a rhetorical question.

The results of the research presented in the previous chapter have shown that the higher education institutions themselves are going through greater or lesser crises of the development of the potential of intellectual capital, which restrict the individuals' academic and scientific activities. The study does not go into social competencies of the academic staff. It looks only at the organizational and managerial conditions under which the development of social competencies emerges.

Figure 6.2 provides the structure of the problem highlighted during the qualitative research.

The dotted lines and the arrows show the range within which the organizations, the norms of academic and personal ethics meet and interact. The points of intersection of arrows indicate a conflict. These are the conflicts of individuals of different degrees (capacities) of an organization. They can be spontaneous, when the weakest link (an individual) is affected and bullying is found, or rational, solved by the generally accepted rules at the level of the organization and social groups.

None of the three factors (individual, organization, and society) is an unchangeable constant, but the speed of their change is different. The

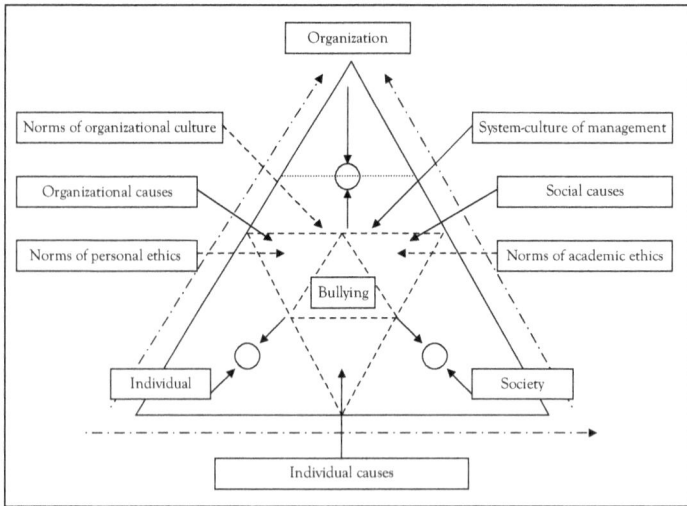

Figure 6.2 The structure of the problem of bullying

individual adapts most flexibly; the organization changes in response to the expectations of the individual and society; however, the vector of changes is never unidirectional. The norms of academic ethics are formulated in accordance with universal moral principles, and this is not a specific norm, which, for example, could be equated to the clerical community. However, it considers the circumstances that are relevant to the objectivity of the obtained outcome of the scientific activities. Objectively, bullying is a natural phenomenon, which, speaking in images, can affect the organism of social relations in the same way as cancer cell metastases.

An organization can never be certain that bullying or single cases of harassment would not arise naturally in one or another level of relationships, but it is (should be) interested in maintaining the balance in the relationships, as with the misbalance the destructive processes begin. This model is based on an agreement between individuals, which is realized under the principles of individual, professional ethics and the organization of relationships between individuals, monitoring and adjustments in the organizational entity to which the individuals delegate the rights to regulate relationships, and refusing a certain degree of sovereignty for the sake of the common good.

Both the empirical studies aforementioned and the latter qualitative study highlighted the problems relevant for many organizations. They can be divided into four large groups: culture of management (the executives' competence in dealing with the conflicts of bullying and harassment, in ensuring the functionality of the system), ethics of relations between the different levels of employees, involvement of employees and their professional organizations and the absence of a preventive system or its ineffectiveness.

Conclusions

1. The scientific literature analyzing the ways of pressure on employees evidences differences between bullying and single cases of harassment, distinguishing the dangerousness of bullying and significantly more difficult consequences to the victim and the organization and the specific method of impact, based on the long-term and intensive harassment. Bad organizational environment (system of work organization), management mistakes, and misuse by the managers create conditions for such intensive and prolonged harassment. Although the problem of bullying in the workplace has been raised and analyzed for more than three decades, there is still the lack of significant progress in dealing with it. The studies indicate that the solution of the problems of bullying, single cases of harassment, and pressure on employees in higher education institutions purely by ethical means is not sufficient. Therefore, it is necessary to fix the system of management and correct mistakes in an integrated way. In the states, national labor codes of which do not define bullying and responsibility for it, the main workload in development of the system of protection from this phenomenon falls on the leaders of the organizations. A special responsibility falls on the higher education institutions, in which, on the one hand, the scientific potential is affected because of the destructive relationships between the employees or researchers, and on the other hand, in preparation of professionals, they cannot effectively ensure the progress in improving the management culture in the organizations of the country.

2. Comparing the results of the empirical research from 2008 through 2014, the analysis of the prevalence of bullying in relations among the educational staff has found the trend of percentage growth and dynamism of changes. The situation in the external environment related to the reforms and the number of pupils influences the relationships between employees within the organizations, increases the tension, the sense of insecurity, and leads to the growth of conflict.

3. The assault experienced by the victims of bullying goes beyond the relationships between the employees (horizontal and vertical) and involves third parties, that is, clients or students of a higher education institution. On the one hand, victims who have found themselves on the vector of the attack, suffer damage, and the quality of educational and academic activities can be affected. On the other hand, undermining the reputation of the victim together affects the business reputation of the organization. The abuse of formal and informal power in the aspects of management (tasks), transparency of decision making, and internal communication disturbance was highlighted. High moral imperatives of victims that appeal to adequate peer behavior, but are not responded, should be noted as well. It turned out that informal, illusory power of middle managers has a significant impact on the victim.

4. A local solution of bullying and single cases of harassment as symptoms is ineffective without systemic changes within the organization. After the analysis of the theoretical aspects of bullying and harassment and the evaluation of the results of the researches, the proposed model makes it possible to: *first*, deal with individual cases in an integrated way; *second*, organize the system of prevention, which would reduce the possibility of taunting and its escalation to the level of bullying; and *third*, requires to correct management mistakes and improve the organization management processes. The model is based on the five stages, where the managerial decision-making is based on the situation analysis and monitoring of the implementation. The model includes such stakeholders as the higher education institution staff, students, and the management of the organization. Therefore,

highlighting of specific problems relevant to individual organizations, flexibility of solutions, implementation of the solutions, and support; and control of the created system are ensured. Moreover, after resolving the organizational issues, there occurs the opportunity to do all the system of organizational management more functional not only in dealing with the problem of bullying. This enables to evaluate the model in the aspects of value added.

The main conclusion that can be drawn from the analysis of the quantitative and qualitative research is that, the changes in management as the component of the organizational culture, ensuring the control of decision making on the middle level of management are required. Interferences of internal communication allow using informal communication against victims, conditionally restrict the victim's freedom of action when looking for help. After resolving organizational problems, it is possible to expect the weakening of unethical power centers, formed in the lower level of management, and reducing the abuse of power as one of the conditions that enable the victim to take advantage of the available competence in resolving conflicts.

References

Ananiadou, K., and P.K. Smith. November 2002. "Legal Requirements and Nationally Circulated Materials Against School Bullying in European Countries." *Criminology and Criminal Justice* 2, no. 4, pp. 471–91.

Ashforth, B. June 1997. "Petty Tyranny in Organizations: A Preliminary Examination of Antecedents and Consequences." *Canadian Journal of Administrative Sciences* 14, no. 2, pp. 216–40.

Ayoko, O.B., V.J. Callan, and Ch. E.J. Härtel. April 2003. "Workplace Conflict, Bullying, and Counterproductive Behaviors." *International Journal of Organizational Analysis* 11, no. 4, pp. 283–301.

Baillien, E., I. Neyens, and H. De Witte. December 2011. "Organizational Correlates of Workplace Bullying in Small- and Medium-Sized Enterprises." *International Small Business Journal* 29, no. 6, pp. 610–25.

Bartlett, J.E., II, and M.E. Bartlett. February 2011. "Workplace Bullying: An Integrative Literature Review." *Advances in Developing Human Resources* 13, no. 1, pp. 69–84.

Bishop, V., and H. Hoel. November 2008. "The Customer Is Always Right? Exploring the Concept of Customer Bullying in the British Employment Service." *Journal of Consumer Culture* 8, no. 3, pp. 341–67.

Blase, J., and J. Blase. December 2002. "The Dark Side of Leadership: Teacher Perspectives of Principal Mistreatment." *Educational Administration Quarterly* 38, no. 5, pp. 671–727.

Blase, J., and J. Blase. August 2003. "The Phenomenology of Principal Mistreatment: Teachers' Perspectives." *Journal of Educational Administration* 41, no. 4, pp. 367–422.

Blase, J., J. Blase, and F. Du. September 2008. "The Mistreated Teacher: A National Study." *Journal of Educational Administration* 46, no. 3, pp. 263–301.

Brown, J.R., M.C. Aalsma, and M.A. Ott. February 2012. "The Experiences of Parents Who Report Youth Bullying Victimization to School Officials." *Journal of Interpersonal Violence* 28, no. 3, pp. 494–518.

Bubelienė, D., and G. Merkys. 2012. "Pedagogų streso socialinis konstravimas ir jo atspindžiai profesinėje spaudoje [Teacher Stress Social Construction and Its Reflections in the Trade Press]." *Acta Paedagogica Vilnensia* 29, pp. 100–09, in Lithuanian.

Bulotaitė, L., R. Bliumas, and B. Pociūtė. 2008. "Universitetų dėstytojų darbo ir streso ypatumai [University Lecturers Work and Stress Peculiarities]." *Acta Paedagogica Vilnensia* 21, pp. 208–19, in Lithuanian.

Carnero, M.A., B. Martínez, and R. Sanchez-Mangas. August 2012. "Mobbing and Workers' Health: Empirical Analysis for Spain." *International Journal of Manpower* 33, no. 3, pp. 322–39.

Casimir, G., D. McCormack, N. Djurkovic, and A. Nsubuga-Kyobe. 2012. "Psychosomatic Model of Workplace Bullying: Australian and Ugandan School Teachers." *Employee Relations* 34, no. 4, pp. 411–28.

Cemaloglu, N. August 2011. "Primary Principals' Leadership Styles, School Organizational Health and Workplace Bullying." *Journal of Educational Administration* 49, no. 5, pp. 495–512.

Chirila, T., and T. Constantin. July 2013. "Understanding Workplace Bullying Phenomenon Through Its Concepts: A literature Review." *Procedia-Social and Behavioral Sciences* 84, no. 9, pp. 1175–79.

Damskis, O., B. Banevičienė, M. Labeikytė, A. Razmantienė, A. Valevičiūtė, J. Vaščėga, and R. Zungailienė. 2012. *Lietuva. Švietimas regionuose. Indėlis, procesai, rezultatai [Lithuania. Education in the Regions. Input, Processes, Outcomes]*. Vilnius: Education Supply Centre, in Lithuanian.

DeSouza, E.R., and J. Ribeiro. September 2005. "Bullying and Sexual Harassment among Brazilian High School Students." *Journal of Interpersonal Violence* 20, no. 9, pp. 1018–38.

Duffy, M., and L. Sperry. October 2007. "Workplace Mobbing: Individual and Family Health Consequences." *The Family Journal* 15, no. 4, pp. 398–404.

Duffy, M., and L. Sperry. 2012. *Mobbing: Causes, Consequences, and Solutions.* New York: Oxford University Press Inc.

Einarsen, S. January 1999. "The Nature and Causes of Bullying at Work." *International Journal of Manpower* 20, nos. 1–2, pp. 16–27.

Einarsen, S. July–August 2000. "Harassment and Bullying at Work: A Review of the Scandinavian Approach." *Aggression and Violent Behavior* 5, no. 4, pp. 379–401.

Einarsen, S., and B.I. Raknes. February 1997. "Harassment in the Workplace and the Victimisation of Men." *Violence and Victims* 12, no. 3, pp. 247–63.

Einarsen, S., and A. Skogstad. June 1996. "Bullying at Work: Epidemiological Findings in Public and Private Organizations." *European Journal of Work and Organizational Psychology* 5, no. 2, pp. 185–201.

Harvey, M.G., J.T. Heames, R.G. Richey, and N. Leonard. Summer 2006. "Bullying: from the Playground to the Boardroom." *Journal of Leadership & Organizational Studies* 12, no. 4, pp. 1–11.

Heames, J., and M. Harvey. January 2006. "Workplace Bullying: A Cross-Level Assessment." *Management Decision* 44, no. 9, pp. 1214–30.

Heinemann, P.P. 1972, cited in P.K. Smith, Y. Morita, J. Junger-Tas, D. Olweus, R. Catalano, and P. Slee. 1999. *The Nature of School Bullying: a Cross-National Perspective.* London: Routledge.

Katrinli, A., G. Atabay, G. Gunay, and B.G. Cangarli. September 2010. "Nurses' Perceptions of Individual and Organizational Political Reasons for Horizontal Peer Bullying." *Nursing Ethics* 17, no. 5, pp. 614–27.

Kolodej, C. 2005. *Mobbing: Psychoterror am Arbeitsplatz und seine Bewaltigung.* Wien: Wuv.

Lazutka, R., and D. Skuciene. 2009. "Socialinės garantijos Lietuvos mokslininkams." [Social Guarantees Lithuania Scientists]. Filosofija. Sociologija 20, no. 2, pp. 144–53, in Lithuanian.

Lee, Ch.H. January 2009. "Personal and Interpersonal Correlates of Bullying Behaviors Among Korean Middle School Students." *Journal of Interpersonal Violence* 25, no. 1, pp. 152–76.

Leymann, H. Summer 1990. "Mobbing and Psychological Terror at Workplaces." *Violence and Victims* 5, no. 2, pp. 119–26.

Leymann, H. 1993. *Mobbing: Psychoterror am Aabeitsplatz und wie man sich dagegen wehren kan.* Reinbek bei Hamburg, Rowohlt Taschenbuch Verlag.

Leymann, H. 1996. "The Content and Development of Mobbing at Work." *European Journal of Work and Organisational Psychology* 5, no. 2, pp. 165–84.

Leymann, H., and A. Gustaffson. January 1996. "Mobbing at Work and the Development of Post-traumatic Stress Disorders." *European Journal of Work and Organizational Psychology* 5, no. 2, pp. 251–75.

Leon-Perez, J.M., G. Notelaers, A. Arenas, L. Munduate, and F.J. Medina. May 2013. "Identifying Victims of Workplace Bullying by Integrating Traditional Estimation Approaches into a Latent Class Cluster Model." *Journal of Interpersonal Violence* 29, no. 7, pp. 1155–77.

Lewis, M. 2004. *Bullying in Nursing, the Perspectives of Clinical Nurses and Nurse Manager* [Doctoral Research]. Manchester: Manchester Metropolitan University.

Liefooghe, A.P.D., and R. Olafsson. January 1999. "'Scientists' and 'Amateurs': Mapping the Bullying Domain." *International Journal of Manpower* 20, no. 2, pp. 39–49.

Lohro, F., and U. Hilp. 2001. *Mobbing am Arbeitsplatz. European Parliament— Directorate-General for Research—Working Papers of the European Parliament, SOC I 108*. European Union: European Parliament.

Lorenz, K.Z. 1966. *On Aggression*. San Diego: Harcourt Brace.

Melia, J.L., and M. Becerrill. November 2007. "Psychosocial Sources of Stress and Burnout in the Construction Sector: A Structural Equation Model." *Psicothema* 19, no. 4, pp. 679–86.

Meschkutat, B., M. Stackelbeck, and G. Lagengoff. 2002. *Der Mobbing-Report. Repräsentativstudie* für die Bundesrepublik Deutschland. Schriftenheire der Bundesansstalt für Arbeitsschutz und Arbeitsmedizin – *Forscung, Fb 951*. 2nd ed. Bremerhaven: Wirtschaftsverlag NM.

Messinger, H., and W. Rüdenberg. 1977. *Langenscheidts Grosses Schulwoerterbuch. Englisch-Deutsch*. Muenchen: Langenscheidt Wien.

Mikkelsen, E.G., and S. Einarsen. March 2002. "Basic Assumptions and Symptoms of Posttraumatic Stress Among Victims of Bullying at Work." *European Journal of Work and Organizational Psychology* 11, no. 1, pp. 87–111.

Moon, B., and S.J. Jang. August 2014. "A General Strain Approach to Psychological and Physical Bullying: A Study of Interpersonal Aggression at School." *Journal of Interpersonal Violence* 29, no. 12, pp. 2147–71.

Niedl, K. 1996. "Mobbing and Well-Being: Economic and Personnel Development Implication." *European Journal of Work and Organizational Psychology* 5, no. 2, pp. 203–14.

Parzefall, M.R., and D. Salin. March 2010. "Perceptions of and Reactions to Workplace Bullying: A Social Exchange Perspective." *Human Relations* 63, no. 6, pp. 761–80.

Petrylaite, D. January 2011. "International Legal Standards of Regulation of Mobbing at Work." *Issues of Business and Law* 3, pp. 121–33.

Premper, V. March 2002. "Mobbing am arbeitsplatz—eine Folge ungerklärter Konflikte." *Report Psichologie* 27, no. 3, pp. 182–90.

Prosch, A. 1995. *Mobbing am Arbeitsplatz. Literaturanalyse mit Fallstudie*. Konstanz: Hartung-Gorre Verlag Konstanz.

Rayner, C., H. Hoel and C.L. Cooper. 2002. *Workplace Bullying: What We Know, Who Is to Blame and What Can We Do?* London: Taylors and Francis.

Resch, M. July 1997. "Mobbing und Konflikte am Arbeitsplatz." *Deutscher Gewerkschaftsbund Bundesvorstand Informationen zur Angestelltenpolitik* 3, no. 97, pp. 142–49.

Richard, J.F., B.H. Schneider, and P. Mallet. August 2011. "Revisiting the Whole-School Approach to Bullying: Really Looking at the Whole School." *School Psychology International* 33, no. 3, pp. 263–84.

Rigby, K. August 2004. "Addressing Bullying in Schools: Theoretical Perspectives and Their Implications." *School Psychology International* 25, no. 3, pp. 287–300.

Riley, D., D.J. Duncan, and J. Edwards. January 2011. "Staff Bullying in Australian Schools." *Journal of Educational Administration* 49, no. 1, pp. 7–30.

Salin, D. November 2005. "Workplace Bullying Among Business Professionals: Prevalence, Gender Differences and the Role of Organization Politics." *Pistes-Perspectives Interdisciplinaires sur le Travail et la Santé* 7, no. 3, pp. 2–12.

Salin, D. September 2008. "The Prevention of Workplace Bullying as a Question of Human Resource Management: Measures Adopted and Underlying Organizational Factors." *Scandinavian Journal of Management* 24, no. 3, pp. 221–31.

Samier, E.A., and T. Atkins. August 2010. "Preventing and Combating Administrative Narcissism: Implications for Professional Programmes." *Journal of Educational Administration* 48, no. 5, pp. 579–94.

Somunoğlu, S., A. Gedik, D.E. Kurt, G. Eygi, Ş. Gebedek, Y. Ilhan and Z. Sağ. June 2013. "Mobbing in Health Sector: Sample of University Hospital." *Journal of Health Management* 15, no. 2, 169–75.

Tam, F.W.M. August 2013. "A Study of Workplace Aggression as Related to Pedagogical Reform in Hong Kong Secondary Schools." *International Journal of Educational Management* 27, no. 6, pp. 578–93.

Tepper, B. April 2000. "Consequences of Abusive Supervision." *Academy of Management Journal* 43, no. 2, pp. 148–90.

Thomas, M. July 2005. "Bullying Among Support Staff in a Higher Education Institution." *Health Education* 105, no. 4, pp. 273–88.

Vartia-Vaananen, M. January 1996. "The Sources of Bullying—Psychological Work: Environment and Organizational Climate." *European Journal of Work and Organizational Psychology: Mobbing and Victimization at Work* 5, no. 2, pp. 203–14.

Vartia-Vaananen, M. 2003. *Workplace Bullying—A Study on the Work Environment, Well-Being and Health* [Doctor of Psychology dissertation]. Helsinki: University of Helsinki.

Vickers, M.H. November 2009. "Bullying, Disability and Work: A Case Study of Workplace Bullying." *Qualitative Research in Organizations and Management: An International Journal* 4, no. 3, pp. 255–72.

Vickers, M.H. September 2013. "Workplace Bullying as Workplace Corruption: A Higher Education, Creative Nonfiction Case Study." *Administration & Society* 46, no. 8, pp. 960–85.

Vveinhardt, J. 2009. *Mobingo kaip diskriminacijos darbuotojų santykiuose diagnozavimas siekiant gerinti Lietuvos organizacijų klimatą [The Diagnostics of Mobbing as Discrimination in Employee Relations Aiming to Improve the Organizational Climate in Lithuanian Organizations].* [Doctoral Dissertation: Social Sciences, Management and Administration]. Kaunas: Vytautas Magnus University, 238 pp. in Lithuanian.

Vveinhardt, J. March 2011. "Mobingas švietimo organizacijose: konsultavimo paslaugų poreikis." *Studijos šiuolaikinėje visuomenėje* 2, no. 1, pp. 193–201.

Vveinhardt, J., and P. Žukauskas, P. 2012. *Mobingas darbuotojų santykiuose: individas, organizacija, sociumas.* Kaunas: Vytautas Magnus University.

Westhues, K. 2006. *The Remedy and Prevention of Mobbing in Higher Education: Two Case Studies.* Lewiston, NY: The Edwin Mellen Press.

Yildirim, D., A. Yildirim, and A. Timucin. July 2007. "Mobbing Behaviors Encountered by Nurse Teaching Staff." *Nursing Ethics* 14, no. 4, pp. 447–63.

Zabrodska, K., Sh. Linnell, C. Laws, and B. Davies. October 2011. "Bullying as Intra-Active Process in Neoliberal Universities." *Qualitative Inquiry* 17, no. 8, pp. 709–19.

Zapf, D. January 1999. "Organisational, Work Group Related and Personal Causes of Mobbing/Bullying at Work." *International Journal of Manpower* 20, nos. 1–2, pp. 70–85.

Zapf, D. Summer 2002. "Emotion Work and Psychological Wellbeing: A Review of the Literature and Some Conceptual Considerations." *Human Resource Management Review* 12, no. 2, pp. 237–68.

Zapf, D., S. Einarsen, H. Hoel, and M. Vartia. 2003. "Empirical Findings on Bullying in the Workplace." In: *Bullying and Emotional Abuse in the Workplace: International Perspectives in Research and Practice*, eds. S. Einarsen, H. Hoel, D. Zapf, and C. Cooper. London: Taylor & Francis.

Zapf, D., C. Knorz, and M. Kulla. January 1996. "On the Relationship Between Mobbing Factors and Job Content, Social Work Environment and Health Outcomes." *European Journal of Work and Organizational Psychology* 5, no. 2, pp. 215–37.

Žukauskas, P., and J. Vveinhardt. September 2013. "Mobbing and Bullying within the Organization: Socio-demographic Portrait of the Victim." *Krytyka Prawa* 5, no. 1, pp. 693–716.

Zuschlag, B. 1994. *Mobbing: Schikane am Arbeitzplatz.* Goettingen: Verlag fuer Angewandte Psychologie.

CHAPTER 7

The Dark Side of Higher Education Administration: The Untold Story of Women in Leadership

Marjorie L. McInerney and Deanna D. Mader

Marshall University

Introduction

The dark side of higher education is not a new discovery. Murder mysteries have even used the dark side of higher education as the central theme (Jones 1993). Sadly, harmful, hateful, and incompetent behaviors among the ivory towers have been in existence, in all likelihood, since the first ivory towers were erected. However, although not a new discovery, discussion of such behaviors among the cap and gown membership has remained a whisper and relegated to corner tables in coffee shops and offices with doors closed. Nowhere is this near-silence more evident than in the impact of the dark side of higher education administration on women in leadership, the topic of this chapter. Career paths must be kept clean, untarnished images are required, and the flow of large sums of money from donors must not be ebbed. Needless to say, fear of reprisal goes a long way in keeping mouths shut.

A glimpse of the dark side of higher education administration is provided through descriptions and vignettes of women administrators at the department chair, associate dean, and dean levels of administration.

Data were collected using personal interviews via convenience sampling, thereby allowing for the collection of stories from colleagues on campuses and at conferences. The experiences selected for this chapter represent a range of experiences shared with the authors by the women.

The practice of silence and the very real fear of reprisal are worth noting again. The women who came forward to share their administrative experiences with the "dark side" agreed to do so only if their names and universities remained anonymous. It was very clear no one would speak of their negative experiences unless anonymity was guaranteed. The use of descriptions and vignettes here allow the authors to share those experiences without mentioning the individual players and settings. This experiential approach is often used in classrooms when the names of companies or corporate officials would put whistleblowers in professional danger.

Literature Review

Articles addressing the dark side of higher education in general, for the most part, make the comparison of faculty status and administrative posts within the popular cultural framework of sarcasm (i.e., crossing over to the dark side). The articles focus on a few dominant themes, and provide food for thought to those considering a move into administration.

Regarding transitioning from faculty to administrator, Olson (2009) suggests that there are steps one can take to better prepare for the move into administration. He recommends taking on roles to gain experience, such as working on various university committees, participating on faculty senate, and assisting in strategic planning for the university. Palm (2006) also discusses the transition from faculty to administrator and states for some, as in her case, the transition can appear to be deceptively easy. The willingness and eagerness to accept committee work and leadership roles can lead to part-time administrative roles, which then lead to full-time administrative roles, which then lead to higher-level administrative roles. Glick (2006) views actively participating in university committees and faculty senate as the logical first steps in moving into higher education administration. Once in the senate, the attention of the Provost can be obtained and assignment in academic affairs can begin.

Several authors agree, the perspective of an administrator is not, nor should be, the same as faculty. Willis (2010) comments that rather than being a human silo, administrators must look outside their own program and area of research, and view the university from a broader perspective that encompasses all disciplines contained in the university. Palm (2006) also discusses the transition from faculty to administration, and reviews the need for administrators to gain a broader perspective of the university. Likewise, Olson (2009) discusses the need to broaden one's faculty focus from individual discipline to overall university perspective. In achieving this broader perspective, learning about issues such as budgets, legal, and political issues are critical to administrative problem solving.

Another theme in the literature deals with the life of an administrator in higher education. Specifically, administrators face too much work and not enough time, and often, the position is short in duration relative to the tenure of a faculty position. Glick (2006) states that any attempt by administrators to conduct creative research is nearly impossible to achieve due to the time commitment of the job. He adds that the power as an administrator will ebb and flow, so opportunities for change should not be wasted. Palm (2006) suggests that administrators who can balance administrative responsibilities with traditional faculty expectations in teaching and research will maintain a moral leadership position with faculty. However, taking on an administrative role to serve the institution adds work to a finite number of hours in the day, necessitating personal choices as to how one's time will be focused. Palm also notes the shorter time frame in which most administrators keep their jobs, as opposed to the tenure of faculty positions, thus the need to concentrate on limited goals and setting realistic expectations for administrators.

A final theme, faculty–administrator relationships, also finds similar thought among several authors. Mumford (2010) discusses the tendency of administrators to forget the responsibilities of faculty. The tension between faculty and administrators is often exasperated due to an "us versus them" mentality that exists in many organizations. Rather than seeing how different jobs and levels within the organization make for efficient operations, people will view their job and their level as the highest-producing unit. The value of others in the organization is discounted, ignored, or cheapened. Dowdall and Dowdall (2005) state that friends and colleagues may view an individual very differently, following her move into administration. The administrator may feel like the same person, but being asked to leave a faculty meeting, for example, indicates a different perspective by a faculty. The authors further state that this divided relationship between faculty and administrators can be exacerbated when collective bargaining is involved. Glick (2006) stated that once the move into administration is complete, the former faculty member will lose faculty colleagues as friends, as they will not understand the job of an administrator.

Beyond the popular cultural framework of sarcasm, there is a truly dark side in higher education administration (Sullivan 2008). A college or university, whether public or private, is an organization like any other public or private organization. All organizations have warts as well as beauty marks. Before warts can be removed, they must be recognized.

One predominant wart, if you will, concerns higher education management and the barriers to women seeking administrative positions, as well as the treatment of and attitudes toward women in those positions. Unfortunately, this particular area of the dark side of higher education is both persistent and global (Carvalho and Santiago 2010; Lindsey 2012; Odhiambo 2011).

The Dark Side Descriptions and Vignettes

Some Associate Deans Can Pull Off Wearing a Lampshade

Barbara was the Division Chair; new to the position and eager to make a difference as most new administrators are. She maintained a positive working relationship with her faculty colleagues, but had little social interaction other than the occasional lunch because her family characteristics and interests were different from most of theirs. She was honored to be elected the chair, and was determined to further the goals and image of the college.

Division chairs at this particular university were required to attend social functions they previously could ignore as faculty members. Barbara quickly learned there weren't enough hours in the day for work and social obligations, and a lot of her time was no longer her own. The last thing she wanted to do was attend a student organization meet-and-greet to recruit new members, but she went.

The function was held on a Friday evening at an area hotel, and Barbara arrived several minutes late. She was pleased to see the meet-and-greet had drawn a good crowd of students, although very few faculty or administrators were in attendance. The student organization had hired a DJ and alcohol was in abundance. Not long after her arrival, the Associate Dean came up to her and threw his arm around her shoulder. Clearly, as measured by his slurred speech and 100-proof breath, he had started drinking well before the event, and he was still drinking—glass in hand. Barbara moved out of the conversation quickly saying she needed to mingle with the students. Sometime later, loud singing and laughter drew her and others' attention. Across the room, there was the Associate Dean wearing a lampshade like a hat and dancing on an end table! Another male administrator moved over to that part of the room, and with some amount of difficulty, coaxed the Associate Dean down. Barbara made her apologies to the students and left the event. The embarrassment and disgust bothered her for the remainder of the weekend.

Back at work, Barbara made an appointment to speak to the Dean about the incident. The Dean had not attended the meet-and-greet. To Barbara's dismay, he chastised her for making a big deal out of the incident, and was told those in attendance were just having a good time. She was told the Associate Dean is a productive researcher and all the students like him. The Dean warned Barbara not to discuss the behaviors witnessed at off-campus social events. She later learned from a couple of faculty, who pleaded for anonymity, the Associate Dean came into his current position by virtue of being a close friend of the Dean. The two had been colleagues, as well as drinking and golfing buddies, at another institution earlier in their careers. There also were rumors, later confirmed, of the Associate Dean having numerous affairs with female students enrolled in his classes. Faculty assumed the Dean knew, but didn't care.

At the end of that same semester, Barbara received a written reprimand from the Dean for giving a female student, who had been hospitalized, a grade of *Incomplete* and was informed a copy had been placed in her personnel file. Barbara remained Division Chair for four years and then left to take an academic position elsewhere. Prior to her departure, the Associate Dean became Dean at another university.

Unfortunately, cultural gender stereotypes still prevail. In a study by de Visser and McDonnell (2012), the authors found gender double-standards for alcohol consumption persist. Although actual consumption activities (e.g., frequency of consumption, binge drinking, and experiences of drunkenness) were similar between males and females, the differences in male and female perceptions of the activities were observed. Specifically, both genders perceived drinking behaviors as masculine, and both genders were more condemning of women than men who drank excessively or got drunk. Similarly, gender stereotyping has been reported in the workplace (Evans 2011; Brescoll and Uhlmann 2008), and specifically, in higher education (Bird 2011; Carr et al. 2003; Cress and Hart 2009; Easterly and Ricard 2011; Pearson and Trent 2004; Settles et al. 2006). In summary, gender stereotypes exist and present barriers to women's careers.

Barbara's story, other stories from women administrators, and the extant research tell us gender discrimination is still alive and well in academia. Even though the types and ramifications of discrimination are taught in courses across campuses, apparently, it is not necessary to practice what one preaches. Barbara's story begs the question, what would have happened to her immediate and long-term academic career had Barbara been the one drunk and wearing a lampshade?

Friends and Allies Today, Tomorrow—Not So Much

Larry, Morris, and Lucia, faculty in the same college, formed a friendship with similar teaching and research interests. They often went to lunch and would discuss issues at length in their office suite. Everything from curriculum, to recruiting, to committee activities and more were discussed with openness and shared insights. There were never fears of anger or back-stabbing. The three shared a level of trust and professionalism, which allowed them to agree, or disagree, and raise the bar of critical thinking to make the college better.

When Lucia was presented with the opportunity to move into the Associate Dean's position for a year, Larry and Morris gave their full support. Not long after Lucia moved into the Associate Dean's office, the lunches and good-natured discussions quickly stopped. Larry and Morris stopped arranging meetings or lunches, and when Lucia made the invitation, the other two were often busy. Larry would only stop by Lucia's office to complain about administrative decisions, while Morris would stop by on occasion to say hello, but then would quickly depart. She thought it strange that these same friends who carried on long in-depth conversations seemed not to want to be seen speaking to her now. When they did stop by her office, it was at odd times when few people were around, and they talked in whispered tones so as not to be heard by anyone outside Lucia's office.

Needless to say, Lucia was disappointed to discover via the gossip grapevine that on more than one occasion, Larry and Morris had each been critical of Lucia's appointment and her decisions thus far as an administrator. The two also had commented to others they were surprised she was even still in the Associate Dean's position. Lucia didn't want to believe the gossip, but on one particular day, she got confirmation the rumors were true. Morris stopped by to discuss a policy matter. The issue was quickly resolved, but he continued to talk about trivial matters. Suddenly Morris said, "Well, I am surprised you are still Associate Dean. I thought you would be gone by now."

It is a tough lesson to learn, but new administrators learn it quickly and they learn it well. Some friends and colleagues who are early supporters of the move to administration will quickly fade away. In their eyes, the administrator leaves the "us" and becomes one of "them." In addition, for some, there is a certain amount of jealousy among those not appointed or elected to administration. Lucia's story exemplifies the findings of Dowdall and Dowdall (2005), Glick (2006), and Mumford (2010), and cited earlier in the chapter, as well as the findings of Mabokela (2003). Specifically, one of the common themes brought forward from Mabokela's interviews with six senior women administrators in South African institutions of higher education was the disappointing adversarial stance by other women. One of the administrators interviewed called this the "P.H.D. syndrome," that is to say the "Pull Her Down" attitude (138).

Perhaps of greater concern is the issue of gender stereotyping again. According to a study by Catalyst, women are seen as leaders who are almost there, but never quite ready to lead (Evans 2011). Women have to continually prove themselves, whereas men are perceived as born leaders who possess all the right characteristics (Hamzelou 2014). Gender stereotypes dictate that male leaders should be assertive, but assertive women are viewed as masculine or worse (Barletta 2006; Evans 2011).

It is important to note, however, as discussed in the literature earlier and as told to us by Lucia, not all friends and colleagues are deserters. Analogous to personal friendships outside the office, one's true professional friends remain one's friends.

Experience Required—Not Really

Sheena, a full-time professor, had several years of administrative experience in higher education as the Division Head and Associate Dean prior to being asked by the Provost to serve as interim dean. The upper administration was dissatisfied with the current Dean and was suspicious of unethical activities, though not criminal. The Provost told her she could select her own team and he had complete trust in them to fix the problems in the college and move it forward. Sheena and her team worked tirelessly achieving goal after goal and reunited an otherwise splintered faculty. Everyone knew from the outset a national search for the Dean's position would be conducted, and Sheena was promised she could apply.

Sheena believed she had a good working relationship with the Provost and open communication. She and her team handled all student, personnel, curriculum, and development matters in the college, but felt comfortable seeking his input when unexpected serious issues arose from her predecessor's tenure. She and her team received positive feedback from him, and conversations were always cordial. When the ad was posted, the faculty encouraged Sheena to apply and she did.

The Provost told Sheena's experience as Dean was his number one priority for the job. As the campus interviews approached, Sheena was happy to receive word that she was one of the finalists. The campus interview started off well with a visit to the search committee and college faculty. By lunchtime, however, Sheena felt something was "off" and asked the next interviewer, the Provost, some pointed questions about the position. He assured Sheena that she remained a top candidate based on her years of administrative experience in the college.

When the selection process was complete, it was announced the new Dean was a male. The individual had overseen several grants, but had no academic administrative experience or managerial experience. When Sheena met the Provost, she was told the President had decided to take the university in a different direction toward more grant funding.

A female administrator from another university had a similar story. Like Sheena, Clarice had previous administrative experience in higher education and applied for the Dean's position while serving as an interim dean. Also like Sheena, she received positive feedback from the upper administration and faculty, and was a finalist in the search. Clarice was told administrative experience was a critical asset for the position, and it was included in the posted ad. Up to the point of the announcement, the search committee maintained silence as instructed by the Provost. Following the announcement, the members, both internal and external to the college, were angered at the choice and could not believe this person, a male from outside the state, had been hired. He had no administrative experience in higher education, or anywhere for that matter. The search committee members admitted they feared the worst when his application did not make the final cut, and then was put back on the list by the committee chair.

Research suggests moving up the ladder one rung at a time through university committees, faculty senate, and administrative posts is a logical and necessary path to leadership in higher education (Glick 2006; Olson 2009; Palm 2006). Learning to be an administrator through administrative experience, much like apprenticing, helps one to understand the complexities of higher education and how the system works. The process produces leaders with the knowledge and confidence to lead effectively. Similarly, Sternberg (2007) states an effective, positive educational leader gains practical intelligence from experiences, and is able to synthesize intelligence, creativity, and wisdom. Apparently, based on Sheena's and Clarice's career disappointments, there are differences in opinion as to whether experience is really necessary.

Administrators often withhold important information from other administrators. They may share part of the information, but not the entire story. The omitted pieces are often critical to the understanding of why a decision is made, and the controlling information is power. Without direct and honest communication, only speculation is possible. Sheena and Clarice might have been offered the interim positions based on the fact that their Provosts would not promote any current faculty member into the Dean position. The Provosts might have thought by picking a female faculty member for the interim post, disorder in the college would be created, which, in turn, would lessen hostility when the new Dean was appointed. One or both may have appointed the women to clean house to get ready for the next occupant. They may have appointed Sheena and Clarice to give the impression, if only temporarily, to other female faculty that women are valued at the university, and it is possible to climb the administration ladder. Whatever the reason, or reasons, for the poor communication or manipulation, it resulted in trust being broken and trust is an essential factor in effective leadership (Clark, Kokko, and White 2012; Gaiter 2013).

Bullies Welcome

Phyllis had been happy as a faculty member. She enjoyed teaching her classes and doing her research. She quickly became a favorite faculty member to invite on committees because she was extremely efficient in getting work completed on time. When the college Associate Dean decided to retire, the Provost decided to intervene and told the Dean to move Phyllis into the vacant position. The Dean had no choice, but to comply with the request.

Phyllis began to notice problems in the Dean's office and was not surprised when the Provost asked the Dean to step down, and a new Dean, Felix, was named. Felix came from another university and began his job by delegating his work to Phyllis. When Phyllis tried to acquaint him with tasks and policies, recognizing he was new, Felix would tell her to handle it because he was too busy. It seemed the more work Phyllis did, the more work the Dean gave her. She was signing all forms, handling all student and personnel issues, attending meetings on his behalf, and managing the day-to-day activities of the college. Over several months, Phyllis developed a new set of acquaintances, the evening custodial staff, because she worked late every weeknight.

One day following a meeting across campus, the Provost stopped Phyllis to ask how things were going. Phyllis thought it was a good time to advise the Provost about the Dean delegating too much work to her. Obviously, things were not going to get better on their own. In fact, her workload had increased further, and to make matters worse, the Dean now felt comfortable yelling at her and the staff. The Provost listened and thanked her for the information.

At the next meeting of the college leadership team, Felix was late and visibly agitated. His tone was terse, and he challenged the group on several points. He got more and more agitated, when suddenly he pounded his fist on the table and yelled, "There can only be *one* voice for the college and that is *my* voice. No one will be allowed to speak for the college except *me* and no one will speak to the Provost except *me*!" Phyllis knew the next time the Provost asked how things were going, she would simply say, "Fine."

Phyllis' experiences point out two major problems for women managers in higher education: horrendous workloads with little recognition or respect for their efforts, and bullying. One senior female administrator in a study by Mabokela (2003) used the metaphor "Donkeys of the University" to describe her condition and that of other women in senior administrative positions in higher education. She stated the term was actually coined by women senior administrators in a group activity and the consensus was the term was very appropriate. The women felt they had tremendous workloads, spent long days at their job, and did their job extremely well, yet received little recognition or respect—like a donkey.

Bullying is not confined to elementary and secondary schools—it is also found in the workplace (Corbell 2015; Lewis, Hall, and Richardson 2014; Mansi 2007; Omari and Paull 2014; Sutton 2010). Specific to higher education, bullying is an increasingly common problem (Sedivy-Benton et al. 2015). In a study of 204 women, senior administrators in two Australian institutions of higher education (Tessens, White, and Web 2011) indicated the women felt men were permitted to engage in more bullying behavior before it was considered unacceptable, and they believed learning how to deal with bullying would be a beneficial topic in a women's leadership program. In a survey of 175 universities, Hollis (2012) found higher incidences of bullying experienced in higher education than was reported in other places of business. Specifically, 62 percent of the employees surveyed in higher education, compared to 37 percent of the general workforce, reported witnessing or experiencing bullying in the past 18 months. Most reports of being victimized by bullies were among lower-level and mid-level managers, such as program directors and department heads. In other words, most victims were those whose line ran to the provost and president. According to Hollis, institutions of higher education (a.k.a. ivory towers) lend themselves to higher occurrences of bullying because they employ people who are trained to be experts in their fields and who work on their research largely in isolation in their office and the library. Add to this, a hierarchical structure and individuals with big egos, and you have a recipe for bullying. The emphasis now placed on fund-raising and grants only adds to the problem. Lest one believes the problem is relegated to only a few universities or departments, think again. Webinars are now offered to train those in academia to address bullying tactics, including slander, physical threats, and unrealistic workloads (Inside Higher Ed 2014).

We've Got Your Back; Unless, Of Course, Your Battle Is with a Higher-Ranking Officer

Some of the first congratulatory e-mails Carlotta received upon her appointment as the Interim Associate Dean were from women who were senior administrators. They often wrote they were available for consultation or a friendly ear. When Carlotta ran into some resistance from the Provost on a few policy matters, she asked the women administrators what to do. To Carlotta's surprise, the very women who were supportive and eager to help backed away from a potential confrontation with top administration.

The lack of support from other women might have been the result of a fear of making the Provost angry and the resulting repercussions. It might also have been one of the types of gender bias barriers Williams calls *Tug of War* (Hamzelou 2014). In this type of situation, women remove themselves from other women or undercut their female colleagues to get ahead. In areas where the numbers of women are few, such as in science, the findings indicate that the Tug of War tends to be a real factor in preventing professional women from getting ahead.

Women might also find themselves pulled to the dark side by circumstances out of their control. They might feel (or were told) that if they want to remain in administration, they must either join the "old boy's network" or at least not oppose them in public. One of the predominate features of this "old boy's network" is the posse of individuals that gather around one dominant male. Administrators often notice this network at meetings and social gatherings. The network gathers around the dominant male and displays a unity of purpose—often they mimic what the dominant male says. In the past, females have developed their own networks to support their members as they move through administrative posts. Palm (2006) went further to suggest that administrators need to develop networks among students, alumni, and faculty.

When Carlotta first began her academic career, she was invited to join a network of women on campus whose expressed purpose was to promote its members into university committee assignments and administrative positions. They jokingly referred to themselves as an "old girl's network." The network eventually found its members in positions such as department chair, vice-president for student affairs, provost, faculty senate president, and director of a prestigious university center. For many years, these women were a dominant force in university administration, but power fades over time, as new administrators come on campus. Carlotta moved into her administrative position several months after the last of this "old girl's network" had retired. Unfortunately, the current group of women administrators had not formed into a network, so no such support was available when Carlotta needed it.

Lessons Learned

Darkness Is Reality

One of the key lessons learned by many female administrators is the realization that the "light" is an illusion and the "darkness" is reality. While faculty move into administrative positions with altruistic fervor, they soon encounter the dark side of administration. Job titles often symbolize more power and authority than actually exists. Within a university campus, the position of Dean might denote the final authority for all decisions made within the college; when in reality, the authority might reside with either the Associate Dean for the college or the university Provost. People can only see where the power resides when they have entered into the administrative arena. As Phyllis learned from her administrative experience, the Dean can shift all the paperwork and decision making to an Associate Dean who has no alternative, but to complete both the delegated work as well as her own work load. If Phyllis were to resign the Associate Dean's position, she would be seen as incapable of completing her work, and the opportunity to move into administration at a future date could be lost.

As power becomes apparent, the abuse or misuse of that power brings out the dark side of administrators. While some people believe they are using power for the good of the organization, their desire to control situations and outcomes can lead to serious loss of trust and productivity from subordinates. Buchanan's (2012, 2013) writings on the qualities of good leaders in business are applicable to administrators, as well. She reported that rather than leaders taking an all-powerful all-knowing all-controlling posture, true leaders are, among other things, inclusive, seek help when necessary, collaborative, generous, listen well, and flexible in using either masculine or feminine characteristics as the situation requires. Needless to say, darkness is real, but not necessary, in administrative positions. Those who want to cross over into the academic administrative arena must recognize the dark side and avoid it.

Trust Is Lost When Communication and Ethics Go Out the Window

Another key lesson learned is that the lack of communication, ethics, and trust is not only alive within the darkness, but can be overwhelming and enveloping. Without ongoing honest communication among administrators, opportunities can be lost due to lack of knowledge and trust suffers. When Sheena was made Interim Dean, the Provost was not honest about her appointment. It became clear through the selection process that Sheena was used as a position-holder until a male Dean could be selected. While a "show" was made that a female was actually being seriously considered for the Dean position, the reality was much darker. Clarice experienced the same type of situation at her university when she was also asked to be Interim Dean. While both Sheena and Clarice applied for the Dean's position in good faith, the lack of communication from top administrators was missing. Both women felt the decision not to appoint them was made well before they actually applied for their respective positions. Perhaps each Provost feared complete honesty would lead to a formal grievance. However, honesty should have prevailed, and a grievance avoided, by telling the women in serving as Interim Dean they could not apply for the Dean's position. Trust would have been strengthened, and each Provost would have been perceived as a leader instead of much worse.

Administrators should be honest about administrative jobs and the career path people should pursue to obtain those positions. Administrators need to be effective leaders of organizations, and honest, open communication is a hallmark of strong leadership. While leaders cannot and should not disclose all information to everyone, essential information should be disclosed to those who need it.

Communication is all-inclusive, and as such, it is important to remember all levels of the organization experience some type of gossip. Administrators are not exempt from the temptation to listen to or tell stories of human intrigue. One Department Chair recalled being called into the Provost's office periodically to report on college gossip. The Department Chair felt this was an important step into a higher level of administration and would make sure a regular quota of gossip was ready for their next meeting. At the same time, the Provost reproached the Deans on more than one occasion for discussing issues, without having total and accurate information. The ability to gossip appears to be limited by job title with that Provost.

People in Masks

A third lesson learned is that people are not always what they seem to be. Friends and allies may actually be the proverbial wolves in sheep's clothing. New administrators will learn that jealousy will rise to the surface when former colleagues now become subordinates within the organizational structure. While the majority of faculty is not fazed by administrators in general, when "one of theirs" moves into an administrative position, they can react with envy. They may praise you to your face and then stab you in the back.

Some administrators have learned early lessons about "people in masks," and they will often retreat into themselves during meetings or administrative events. Do not be put off by people who are quiet—they can become important allies in your struggle to survive the dark side. Become open and honest in your communication with others and they will eventually drop their masks and show their true selves.

One caveat about this lesson: people may not be willing to drop their masks in public. Lucia, the Associate Dean, learned that Department Chairs would only be honest with her if they met off-campus. She would have to plan lunchtime meetings at local restaurants that were far enough off campus that other administrators would not likely frequent them. Even when the college Dean was out of town on business, the Department Chairs would refuse to meet in college offices or conference rooms because someone in an adjoining room might hear the conversation through the vents.

Stay in the Light

Finally, and maybe the most important lesson learned is that one does not have to go to the dark side to be a good administrator. One has to *understand* the game playing and manipulation of the dark side in order to be successful, but one can elect not to play the game. It is important that administrators equip themselves with knowledge of how organizational politics are run in their institution. In order to be successful at the game, it is important to understand how the game is played and who controls the rules.

Advice to Those Venturing into the Administrative Realm of Higher Education

Higher education, like any other organization, needs good leaders. To be a good administrator in higher education, we offer the following advice.

(1) Self-assess and get feedback from others in the "light." Know yourself well. Determine your moral compass and follow it. Life is not a straight line, but you shouldn't make a U-turn to the dark side. If you're already on the dark side, then make the U-turn!

(2) Be aware of your social and political surroundings and be judicious in sharing information. Carefully assess who your allies and enemies are, then proceed wisely and cautiously. Realize several, or many, people below you in the organization structure covet your title—and some of them are willing to do whatever it takes to push you out of the way.

(3) Maintain honest and frequent communication with your closest allies. This is critical for your job performance, but just as critical for dealing with job stress, keeping your sanity, and staying true to your moral compass.

(4) Don't run away from an administrative position. Instead, be aware of the dark side, face it, and be a change agent. It is a well-worn phrase, but still true—change does not happen overnight, but it has to start somewhere.

(5) Be confident and determined to win some battles. However, also be realistic in knowing you won't win them all, and you are very likely to get some cuts and bruises along the way. You can become an outstanding administrator if you stay on the light side and focus on the positive outcomes for your institution.

References

Barletta, M. 2006. *Marketing to Women: How to Increase Your Share of the World's Largest Market.* New York: Kaplan.

Bird, S. 2011, March. "Unsettling Universities' Incongruous, Gendered Bureaucratic Structures: A Case-Study Approach." *Gender, Work and Organization* 18, no. 2, pp. 202–30.

Brescoll, V.L., and E.L. Uhlmann. 2008. "Can an Angry Woman Get Ahead?" *Psychological Science* 19, no. 3, pp. 268–75.

Buchanan, L. June 2012. "13 Ways of Looking at a Leader." *Inc. Magazine* 34, no. 5, pp. 74–76.

Buchanan, L. June 2013. "Between Venus and Mars: 7 Traits of True Leaders." *Inc. Magazine* 35, no. 5, p. 64+.

Carr, P.L., L. Szalacha, R. Barnett, C. Caswell, T. Inui. 2003. "A 'Ton of Feathers': Gender Discrimination in Academic Medical Careers and How to Manage It." *Journal of Women's Health* 12, no. 10, pp. 1009–18.

Carvalho, T., and R. Santiago. June 2010. "New Challenges for Women Seeking an Academic Career: The Hiring Process in Portuguese Higher Education Institutions." *Journal of Higher Education Policy and Management* 32, no. 3, pp. 239–49.

Clark, T., H. Kokko, and S. White. June 1, 2012. "Trust: An Essential Element of Leaders and Managers." *American Journal of Health-System Pharmacy* 69, no. 11, pp. 928–30.

Corbell, T. 2015. "21 Tips to Avoid the Dark Side of Management." In *The Biz Coach*. Retrieved from www.bizcoachinfo.com/archives/5720

Cress, C.M., and J. Hart. 2009. "Playing Soccer on the Football Field: The Persistence of Gender Inequities for Women Faculty." *Equity & Excellence in Education* 42, no. 4, pp. 473–88.

de Visser, R.O., and E.J. McDonnell. May 2012. "That's OK. He's a Guy: A Mixed-Methods Study of Gender Double-Standards for Alcohol Use." *Psychology & Health* 27, no. 5, pp. 618–39.

Dowdall, G., and J. Dowdall. September 23, 2005. "Crossing Over to the Dark Side." In Chronicle of Higher Education. Retrieved from http://chronicle.com/article/Crossing-Over-to-the-Dark-Side/45066/

Easterly, D.M., and C.S. Ricard. 2011. "Conscious Efforts to End Unconscious Bias: Why Women Leave Academic Research." *Journal of Research Administration* 42, no. 1, pp. 61–73. Abstract: EbscoHost Academic Search Premier AN 65207489.

Evans, D. 2011. "Women in the Business World." *National Civic Review* 100, no. 2, pp. 62–64.

Gaiter, D. 2013. "Facets of Leadership." *Neurodiagnotic Journal* 53, no. 4, pp. 323–27.

Glick, M.D. 2006. "Becoming 'One of Them' or 'Moving to the Dark Side'." *New Directions for Higher Education* 134, pp. 87–96.

Hamzelou, J. 2014. "Be a Player, Hate the Game." *New Scientist* 222, no. 2969, pp. 48–49.

Hollis, L.P. 2012. *Bully in the Ivory Tower: How Aggression and Incivility Erode American Higher Education*. Wilmington, DE: Patricia Berkly, LLC.

Inside Higher Ed. November 13, 2014. Bullying in Academia: Prevention and Response. Webinar.

Jones, D.J.H. 1993. *Murder at the MLA*. Athens, GA: The University of Georgia Press.

Lewis, S.E., R.R. Hall, and R. Richardson. 2014. "An Analysis of College Students' Perceptions of Workplace Bulling." *Academy of Business Research Conference*. New Orleans, March 26–28.

Lindsey, U. February 3, 2012. "Arab Women Make Inroads in Higher Education, But Often Find Dead Ends." *Chronicle of Higher Education* 58, no. 2, pp. A12–14.

Mabokela, R.O. 2003. "Donkeys of the University: Organizational Culture and Its Impact on South African Women Administrators." In *Higher Education*. Retrieved from http://ezproxy.marshall.edu:2111/ehost/pdfviewer/pdfviewer?vid=107&sid=e3f2b284-7f8a-498d-a09e-324af93d8eb5%40sessionmgr4001&hid=4204

Mansi, A. 2007. "What Is the 'Dark Side' of Management?" In *Worklife Management*. Retrieved from www.worklifemanagement.com/page8/page8.html

Mumford, C. 2010. "The Dark Side: A Year as Clinical Director." *Practical Neurology* 10, no. 6, pp. 355–58.

Odhiambo, G. December 2011. "Women and Higher Education Leadership in Kenya: A Critical Analysis." *Journal of Higher Education Policy and Management* 33, no. 6, pp. 667–78.

Olson, G.A. 2009. "A Guide to Joining the Dark Side." *Chronicle of Higher Education* 56, no. 17, pp. D23–24.

Omari, M., and Paull, M. 2014. "Shut Up and Bill: Workplace Bullying Challenges for the Legal Profession." *International Journal of the Legal Profession* 20, no. 2, pp. 141–60.

Palm, R. 2006. "Perspectives from the Dark Side: The Career Transition from Faculty to Administrator." *New Directions for Higher Education* 134 (Summer), pp. 59–65.

Pearson, J., and J. Trent. 2004. "Communication, Women, and Leadership." *Communication Studies* 55, no. 2, pp. 400–6.

Sedivy-Benton, A., G. Strohschen, N. Cavazos, and C. Boden-McGill. 2015. "Good ol' boys, Mean Girls, and Tyrants: A Phenomenological Study of the Lived Experiences and Survival Strategies of Bullied Women Adult Educators." *Adult Learning* 26, no, 1, pp. 35–41.

Settles, I.H., L.M. Cortina, J. Malley, and A.J. Stewart. 2006. "The Climate for Women in Academic Science: The Good, the Bad, and the Changeable." *Psychology of Women Quarterly* 30, no. 1, pp. 47–58.

Sternberg, R.J. 2007. "A Systems Model of Leadership." *American Psychologist* 62, no. 1, pp. 34–42.

Sullivan, S. 2008. "The Dark Side of Catholic Colleges." *Chronicle of Higher Education* 54, no. 41, pp. B25–B26.

Sutton, R. 2010. "Tales from the Dark Side of Management." *Inc. Magazine* 32, no. 8, pp. 120–22.

Tessens, L., K. White, and C. Web. December 2011. "Senior Women in Higher Education Institutions: Perceived Development Needs and Support." *Journal of Higher Education Policy and Management* 33, no. 6, pp. 653–65.

Willis, C.L. 2010. "To the Dark Side and Back: The Administrative Odyssey of an Academic Sociologist." *American Sociologist* 41, no. 2, pp. 190–209.

CHAPTER 8

Conspiratory Maneuverings: Tackling Them in Educational Institutions

Kamal Tandon

NCRD's Sterling Institute of Management Studies

Soma Kamal Tandon

Shipping Corporation of India Ltd.

Introduction

Abraham Lincoln once said, "*I would rather be a little nobody, then to be an evil somebody.*" This chapter discusses the "evil somebody" and attempts to understand the concept of conspiracy at work. An attempt will be made to identify the reasons for conspiracy, the types of conspiracy, and the impact thereof. The chapter will culminate with ways to tackle these conspiracies with instances of conspiracy in educational institutions.

What Is Conspiracy at Work?

Conspiracy at work is unethical strategy adopted for personal and professional gains. It is not a myth, but is a tool, which results in malfunctioning of institutions and disintegration of working teams. It is commonplace and exists in every institution waiting to raise its head at the opportune moment. It can manifest itself in various ways, like passing untrue information, taking credit for someone else's work, giving negative reference after volunteering, forgetting to give important messages, which can create trouble, and reneging on a commitment or passing of confidential information. Studies have shown that a sizeable number of employees have indulged in conspiracy at least once in their professional life, which could have taken various forms like theft, fraud, vandalism, sabotage (Harper 1990), lying (DePaulo and DePaulo 1989), spreading rumors (Fox, Spector, and Miles 2001), withholding effort (Kidwell and Bennett 1993), and absenteeism (Johns 1997). The misdeeds of conspiracy at work have varied nomenclature like employee deviance (Robinson and Bennett 1995), counterproductive work behavior (Spector et al. 2006), antisocial behavior (Giacalone and Greenberg 1997, Robinson and O'Leary-Kelly 1998), misbehavior in organizations (Sagie, Stashevsky, and Koslowsky 2003), dark side of organizational behavior (Griffin and O'Learly-Kelly, 2004), organizational misbehavior (OMB) (Vardi and Wiener 1996), noncompliant behavior (Puffer 1987), organization aggression (Spector 1978), Retaliation (Skarlicki and Folger 1997), revenge (Bies, Tripp, and Kramer 1997), workplace incivility (Andersson and Pearson 1999), and cyber loafing (Lim 2002). Such negative employee behavior is estimated to cost the U.S. businesses between $6 and $200 billion annually (Murphy 1993).

Reasons for Conspiracy—Why Does It Happen?

Conspirators are governed by psychological reasons for quick personal or professional gains. People who play conspiracy games are usually insecure and riddled with doubts. The seed of conspiracy could be sown through various factors like jealousy, inferiority or superiority complex, revenge, insecurity, attempt to gain unfair advantage, social or political mileage, power clash, ambition, discontent, or simply lethargic nature. Let us take a look at these factors.

Jealousy: Jealousy is a negative reaction to achievements or advantages of others. It could be at a professional level, like envying unprecedented promotion and accolades. On the other hand, personal achievements could also incite jealousy in terms of acquisition of expensive assets. Jealousy could also be owing to looks, behavior, or appearance, which increase popularity and give personal advantage or attributable to family or friendly ties, being of the same race or sharing the same mother-tongue with seniors.

Complex: The psychological state of mind wherein a person gets a feeling of failure or elevation in comparison to the achievements of others is considered as a complex. Inferiority complex could be a result of differences in communication skills due to primary education in vernacular or English medium, looks, family background, ethnic and minority, and is a consequence of jealousy. By contrast, pride results in a superiority complex.

Revenge: Revenge is a form of retaliation. A situation where the contribution of a less-qualified person is acknowledged above a highly qualified person, owing to better productivity, could result in the non-promotee creating problems by gossiping using the grapevine, defaming the management.

Insecurity: Insecurity is the feeling of failure or the thought of losing in the future. It could be manifested in physical or financial terms. Late duty hours, traveling for seminars and conferences could lead to physical insecurity, especially when the attitude of the management is revealed in their actions like sending to unsafe locales, transfers to remote places, or giving train fare instead of airfare. Financial insecurity creeps in with the fear of losing the job, losing incentives, or timely promotions.

Attempt to gain unfair advantage: Taking advantage in an unethical manner is another form of conspiracy. An example would be a person close to the management gives unethical information, discloses weaknesses of employees to management, or does the personal work for the top management during office hours.

Discontent: Unresolved grievances could be a major cause. An employee may be disgruntled for various reasons. Management usually tries to resolve a dispute between employees amicably, evading resolutions that suggest punishment. This may not satisfy the aggrieved party. In a situation where a faculty slaps or insults another, an apology letter may be okay for the management, but not for the offended faculty member, who expects a stronger punishment. It may seem like a compromise to him/her. Revenge could be in the form of the disgruntled faculty member destroying databases, which are highly crucial for placement. The case of Tim

Lloyd, a trusted employee, who planted a software time-bomb to destroy the hub of the network and brought a global enterprise supplying instrumentation to NASA and the U.S. Navy, to its knees, is a warning to tackle disgruntled employees on time (Gaudin 2000).

Ambition: The urge of success that results in conspiracy is a state described aptly by Erikson (2005): "Ambition is not a dirty word. Go for the throat." Portraying intelligence using somebody else's work, showing off, or trying to gain an increment or promotion superseding somebody using unethical means are all illustrations of ambition.

Social desirability: Behavior governed by the craving for social fame, which is termed as "social desirability" in the field of social psychology, could also sow the seed for conspiracy. This causes a person to do irrational things like taking somebody else's credit to appear in a newspaper article or making unnecessary expenditures, throwing parties, or giving personal gifts, in order to create a good impression.

Power: Political aspirations can also be a reason for conspiracy. This could happen when a person is accepted as a leader without professional designation. A person could try to lead a group of people by using the age-old policy of "divide and rule" by creating groups, causing fights between them and then act as the arbitrator and win confidence of both the groups. Two or more persons trying to acquire the same position could be disastrous to the workplace. A case in point would be two faculty in almost similar positions, like the academic head and the director of an institute, who are at loggerheads, try to thrust their decisions on the mass.

Lethargy: Unwillingness to work hard by the virtue of personal commitments or by natural instinct (inherently lazy) could also result in conspiracy. Such persons shirk or withhold efforts or pursue their self-interest (Peterson 2002). To ensure that their lethargy is not identified in the crowd, they won't let others work, which could result in lowering the overall productivity.

Types of conspiracy

Conspiracy has been classified by Robinson and Bennett (1995) into "minor and serious" as well as "personal and organizational." Spector et al.

(2006) came up with two categories behaviors targeting the organization and behaviors targeting individuals in the organization (Spector et al. 2006). The authors would like to consider two types of conspiracies: professional and personal.

Professional conspiracy: Professional conspiracy is related to career and professional growth. Instances would be misrepresentation of performance, data misuse, and manipulated report submission. It manifests itself in the form of non-cooperation, groupism, finding minor faults, data manipulation, parallel reporting, breaking line of command, insubordination, delaying promotions and incentives, discouragement, and false cases.

Non-cooperation: Lack of involvement or withholding contribution to an assigned job is non-cooperation. Slow work, work not in the right direction, not following the process flow defined, absenteeism without valid reason, and wasting time, are all instances of non-cooperation.

Groupism: Groupism is a state when two or more people come together for a cause and form groups, social or issue-based, for retaliation. This group could be on the basis of caste, religion, or work based and used to retaliate against management decisions in a bid to weaken the management. Trying to stop a transfer of a person on the grounds that a person belongs to the group could be an example.

Finding minor faults: A person could also indulge in highlighting insignificant issues, for example, pointing out grammatical mistakes, draw the attention of the management to minor quality issues. The purpose is to belittle and disgrace the person. These faults may not have major professional impact, but it undermines the person's capability.

Parallel reporting: Parallel reporting would be a case of reporting to other heads of department informally besides one's own boss. With informal reporting, confidential information could also be leaked out. Breaking the line of command is a conspiracy to eliminate the middle person. Reporting to super boss, avoiding the direct boss, and taking instructions directly is disrespectful to the direct boss and weakens him/her. If instructions from super boss are contrary to the instructions from the boss, following such instructions could be detrimental.

Delaying promotions and incentives: Deliberately delaying the deserved promotion and recognition by using wrong or undervalued confidential reports could also be a form of conspiracy. Implicating a person under false cases like forgery, bribery by using other people is another approach. The power of the employee's union could be used against a group of people or person in a false and unethical manner.

Distorting reality: Distorting reality by manipulating data like sales or expenses is another tool. In an educational institution, wrong reporting, submission of wrong projections, or wrong costing, for instance, inflated admission numbers, could have a devastating impact.

Insubordination: Demanding change in the nature of work or doing the work in a manipulated way or accepting assignments and instructions and then not doing it or giving excuses for not completing it are all forms of professional revolt. Denying orders is a more blatant approach whereby a subordinate refuses to do the assigned work, like not taking lectures on Sunday for executive MBA, or refusing to travel citing family reasons. Another approach could be creating hurdles by counter-questioning every decision, major or minor. Instructions are challenged at every step, even if they are accepted at a later stage. This frustrates the decision maker, and may create doubts about his decision making, if it is repeatedly done. Adopting a negative approach toward assignments is another approach where any new and innovative ideas are discouraged. Demotivation sets in like poison, which weakens the organization.

Personal conspiracy: Personal conspiracy, on the other hand, pertains to the individual image of a person. Tarnishing the personal image of a person, creating a situation of personal conflict with others, and personal attacks are components of personal conspiracy. It is adoption of unethical strategies on the basis of personal issues for personal gain. It could tantamount to workplace bullying in terms of being rude, misbehaving, condescending attitude toward subordinates, gossiping and spreading malicious rumors, sabotaging projects, or even physical assault, behaving unethically with a person as in abusing, ignoring, teasing with gestures and social ostracism, leaking personal information, negative or personal favor exposure, and worst of all, character assassination.

The major tools for personal conspiracy are gossip, rumors, false allegations, and character assassination. At this juncture, it is essential to differentiate between gossip and rumors and false allegations vis-a-vis character assassination. Exaggerated discussion about individual behavior of a person or against informal nature of a person with the intention to malign the person is gossip. Rumor is spreading false information with mala fide intention. Gossip is a continuous discussion on a topic, while rumor is event-based. A rumor would be the sighting of two faculty members at the beach. Gossip would be discussing this event in an exaggerated manner to make it sound like an affair between the two. Gossip may or not be based on a rumor. The root is rumor, growth on the roots is gossip. A rumor could be that a person is quitting the organization, gossip could turn the person into an evil person who has been asked to quit by the management.

Instances of making false personal allegations would be pointing out deviation from duties, less dedication to work, or that the person was playing games on the computer during office hours. But, the worst kind of personal conspiracy is character assassination, whereby a false attack is made on the moral and ethical values of the person. Character assassination is an attempt to tarnish a person's reputation, which could result in rejection by family, colleagues, and society. Sexual or moral allegations are instances of character assassination. Making false allegations acts as a distraction, while character assassination is destructive.

Conspirators may even adopt ways and means to belittle a person by divulging personal information, which is not known to others with an intention to defame. Such behavior may not affect the organization much, but could be done more for a cheap thrill or for applying psychological pressure. Negative exposure is also adopted by propagating any personal trait, habit, or behavior in a derogatory manner. Personal favors exposure is another way to create a hostile environment. This would include exposing personal favors given outside the professional limits, like personal favoritism to an individual or a group.

Impact of Conspiracy

Conspiracy at the workplace plays a dual role. It has a negative as well as a positive impact. The impact of conspiracy is manifold. Conspiracy can have impact in any organization, including educational institutions. The intensity of the impact can be measured on the basis of the damage caused to the individual or organization. An organization can lose business or image, and an individual can lose job, money, and reputation. The destructive nature of this scheming can lead to the collapse of an organization and a decline in public confidence in the institution and its leaders. It results in many negative outcomes, tangible and intangible. For example, in terms of cost, employee workplace theft has been estimated to range between $10 billion and $120 billion annually (Bourke 1994; Murphy 1993). The victims of conspiracy may quit, have stress-related problems, decreased productivity, and low morale. Thus, conspiracy has an impact on productivity, discipline, employee retention and recruitment cost, brand image, and the psychological mindset of employees.

The organization suffers losses due to conspiracies. People spend time in resolving issues, which are unproductive in nature. This has a negative impact on the productivity. Continuous deliberate absenteeism, by a person or group of people, for false or inadequate reasons, done with the intention of creating unrest in the organization, results in indiscipline and lower productivity. Dissatisfaction and low morale in employees propagate negativity about the organization in the market, and could result in low enthusiasm while serving customers, for example, faulty replies given for enquiries for admission. Both these contribute to tarnishing the brand image. There are also additional costs incurred through the negative effect on performance (Dunlop and Lee 2004), lowered quality, lost work time, medical and legal expenses, and a damaged public perception (Litzky, Eddleston, and Kidder 2006; Van Fleet and Griffin 2006). Dissatisfied employees tend to leave the organization, resulting in high turnover, which has impact on two costs—employee retention and employee recruitment cost. Damaged self-esteem, increased fear, insecurity at work, and psychological and physical pain (Griffin, O'Leary-Kelly, and Collins 1998) could result in psychological unrest among the employees and absenteeism. Psychological unrest among the employees may be real or perceived. With the removal of an employee, fear and insecurity in employees is ignited, if cause of removal is not projected properly by the union leaders. Sometimes, the grapevine can create problems, for example, with several employees reporting sick, a rumor is floated that the drinking water is contaminated and the management does not care for hygienic conditions, which has resulted in people falling ill. The actual reason may be a simple change in weather.

Thus, conspiracies disrupt operations, leading to the downfall of personal and professional productivity. Studies have shown a negative link between dysfunctional employee behaviors and company turnover (Kacmar and Carlson 1998), company growth and, eventually, market share (Laabs 1999). Business suffers and the economic condition deteriorates. This can lead to a nation suffering at a macro level, as in the case of India, even after 65 years of independence, not a single Indian university has made it to the world ranking of top universities, despite being known for its education system. Informatively, the world's oldest university was at Nalanda, India, which functioned from 500 to 1300 AD.

The silver lining to this dark cloud is the resulting positive impacts. During conflicts and conspiracies, the higher management can distinctly identify the people who are pro and anti-company policies. This also helps the management to take appropriate and effective decisions and actions. Conspiracies and conflicts help the management to take cautious and favorable decisions, keeping in mind the impact of implementation in the existing situation. Removal of one person is stalled if the management knows that it could result in mass resignation. In such a case, a hasty decision would be fatal. Hence, the management should take such an action with caution.

Conspiracies compel management to do process re-engineering, which could be manifested in process monitoring, process change, process deletion, and even process addition. A process is the well-defined flow of activities to accomplish a goal. For instance, if a document goes to a person for signing, and the person takes bribes, the management could make it online, so that the bribes could be stopped. Similarly, if a person delays repeatedly, the flow of activities could be changed to bypass the person. If a person makes mistakes intentionally, introduction of a maker-checker concept would resolve the problem. Process re-engineering could also be in the form of automation, like making fees, document submission online. Deliberate mistakes committed repeatedly can be resolved through automation. If people's internal conspiracy is creating too many problems and less productivity, it would be essential to give the pink slip, and the management could opt for outsourcing at lower costs.

Tackling Conspiracy

It is essential to take quick decisions and have contingency plans handy to tackle conspiracies. Let us consider the instance of a function coordinator who sends out the invitations, and expediently forgets to book the auditorium or creates a situation where the chief guest backs out at the last moment. One should be able to tackle such situations by advancing the event, if the invitees are from within the institution. Having a list of people who can be called as chief guest at a short notice would also be helpful. The ideal approach would be not to rely on one person solely for the event and randomly cross-check crucial points.

Keeping your eyes and ears open and having your own people in various groups could help in avoiding crisis situations. If the institutional head, through his network, finds out that a faculty member has incited students to sabotage a function, the best way to handle such a situation would be to make the conspiring faculty officially responsible for student behavior and even invite him on dais for the function. In a situation where students won't deposit fees, it would perhaps help to have a notice signed by the instigator stopping all cultural functions and industrial visits. It would be difficult to handle a situation where an individual is not able to take disciplinary action against a subordinate due to the fact that his boss chooses to support the subordinate. Other subtle measures would have to be adopted in such circumstances.

Conspiracy can be curtailed by providing a conducive and ethical work environment, ensuring safety and security, proper communication, employee engagement, and motivation. Conspirators can be counseled, and if, all else fails, the management would have to resort to harsher measures like disciplinary action or termination. Various steps can be taken at macro (organizational) and micro (personal) levels.

Employee Intent

Employee intent plays a vital role in conspiracy. Vardi and Wiener (1996, 151) define *OMB* as "any intentional action by the members of organizations that violates the core organizational and/or societal norms." According to Griffin, O'Leary-Kelly, and Collins (1998), employee intent is an important part of this definition. Adams' equity theory (1965) postulates that a person compares his balance of ratio of output to input with the balance of ratio of a "referent" other. Input is derived in terms of time, effort, ability, loyalty, tolerance, flexibility, integrity, commitment, reliability, heart and soul, personal sacrifice, and so on, while output is calculated in terms of pay, bonus, perks, benefits, security, recognition, interest, development, reputation, praise, responsibility, enjoyment, and so on. If there is an imbalance in the ratios compared, the person is demotivated and works toward restoring equity. Demotivated people are more prone to adopt conspiratory methods to restore this equity as perceived by them. Thus, motivation is a major tool that can be used to eradicate conspiracy.

Work Environment

Work environment plays a crucial role in incubating conspiracy, and this may be regardless of the individual characteristics. At the same time, the propensity of conspiracy can be influenced by personality traits such as sensation seeking or risk taking (Henle 2005). Safety and security on the personal and infrastructure front is one aspect, which should be taken care of. In terms of employees, professional job, non-hazardous environment, work-related physical security round the clock, security norms to be followed, personal and infrastructure, no late sitting for female employees, traveling norms, safe travel, and air ticket even if not entitled are some of the measures that could be adopted. A cohesive conducive work environment encourages the feeling of safety and security. From the organizational perspective, adequate data security should be maintained like regular backups, not depending on a single person for data administration. Insiders who know exactly where information is stored and what strikes can hurt the most, can play havoc.

Ethical Climate

An ethical climate would also make employees feel more secure and enhance ethical behavior. Vidaver-Cohen (1998) suggests that an organization may be most successful in creating an ethical climate by addressing the behavior exhibited by senior leadership. Prior studies have suggested that ethical behavior of employees is influenced by the ethical climate of an organization (Deshpande, George, and Joseph 2000; Fritzsche 2000; Litzky, Eddleston, and Kidder 2006.). The issue of ethics should be addressed while conducting orientation programs for new entrants. Imbibing high moral and ethical values with the use of lecture series of moral leaders, yoga, and meditation could also be another approach.

Employee Engagement

Effective and efficient team can be built up with employee engagement as the core value where employees are actively involved in the activities. The *State of the American Workplace: Employee Engagement Insights for U.S. Business Leaders* (Gallup 2013) report highlights findings from Gallup's ongoing study of the American workplace from 2010 through 2012. It describes three kinds of employees: "engaged" employees who drive innovation and move the organization forward, "not engaged" employees who are "emotionally disconnected" about their work, and "actively disengaged" employees who are unhappy and work in a negative way to undermine the accomplishment of their engaged co-workers. The research also found that managers play an important role in employee engagement levels. The keyword is *emotional engagement*, which could be done by adopting a humanitarian approach by celebrating birthdays, anniversaries, or awarding major and minor achievements. Employee welfare activities, like taking care of employees' accommodation, crèche for the children of women employees. It can be also done at the professional level by involving employees in interdisciplinary decision or activities other than routine work. Interdisciplinary transfers could also broaden perspective of employees. Regular trainings on various aspects in terms of workshops and seminars would go a long way. An offshoot of effective engagement is a sense of belongingness. A study by Duffy et al. (2012) of the University of Minnesota shows that envy on its own is not necessarily a negative thing in the workplace. Persons who reported feelings of envy and low levels of identification with their workgroups were significantly more likely to report committing acts of sabotage when they belonged to groups, which reported high rates of sabotage as a whole. In this context, it is essential to discourage unproductive discussions. Informal discussions should be avoided or restricted, as they lead to waste of time and energy. An unproductive employee, besides wasting his/her own time, wastes the time of others also.

Management Policies

Excessive managerial interference or pressure tactics can contribute to deviant behavior by employees. It is imperative that managers recognize the triggers and take adequate steps to curtail them. Well-defined work policies that are updated regularly and are in tandem with the market would go a long way in ameliorating the triggers that encourage conspiracy. In a study examining both prosocial and noncompliant behavior, Puffer (1987) found noncompliant behavior to be inversely related to the need for achievement and confidence in management. Most of the decisions should be unbiased, and it should be known to the concerned parties, preferably with the reasoning. Closed-door meetings should be avoided as far as possible, barring some crucial issues. Issues should be resolved by taking people into confidence. An open-door policy is more conducive to the working environment than an iron-curtain policy. There should be no ambiguity in communication. It should be timely, proactive, and in writing, wherever possible, giving detailed explanation where needed. The line of instruction should be followed.

Counseling and Disciplinary Action

When none of the mentioned measures work, the management is left with no other choice but to adopt a harsher stand, which may be in the form of disciplinary action. This action of the management has to be taken according to well-defined rules or societal moral norms. It is a harsh way to treat conspiracies and should be used with caution. It should be used as the last resort in an institution. It is a negative tool. Adopting personal and professional counseling should be the initial step. Counseling could be done on the basis of personal issues like marital issues, children, distance of home from workplace, health or professional issues based on work, contribution, organization environment, nature of work, working hours, promotion, increment, and incentives. It could be done on a one-to-one basis or it could be in the form of tripartite counseling, group counseling, or even mass counseling. Tripartite counseling would be intervention by a third party when two people cannot come to an agreement. Group counseling could be used when a selected problem group is agitating. Mass counseling would entail counseling the entire organization. The human resources department should play a vital role in this process. Internal committees could be set up or the entire process could be outsourced.

Conclusion

As the human brain works in both directions, positive and negative, the elimination of origin of conspiracies is not possible. But, on a positive note, conspiracies can be used as organizational and individual checking points for loose ends and loopholes. It is imperative that conspiracy is tackled to avoid disruptions at work and the downfall of the institution. The first is to acknowledge what is happening and confront the perpetrator. The general tendency is to avoid it, but this only helps to breed it further. All types of conspiracies can be handled with the right managerial strategies, and it works as an eye opener for the management, thus having a high positive impact on management decision-making.

References

Adams, J.S. 1965. "Inequity in Social Exchange." In *Advances in Experimental Social Psychology*, ed. L. Berkowitz, 267–99. 2nd ed. New York: Academic Press.

Andersson, L.M., and C.M. Pearson. 1999. "Tit for Tat? The Spiraling Effect of Incivility in the Workplace." *Academy of Management Review* 24, no. 3, pp. 452–71.

Bies, R.J., T.M. Tripp, and R.M. Kramer. 1997. "At the Breaking Point: Cognitive and Social Dynamics of Revenge in Organizations." In *Antisocial behavior in organizations*, eds. R.A. Giacalone, and J. Greenberg, 18–36. Thousand Oaks, CA: Sage.

Bourke, A.J. 1994. "Get Smart About Getting Ripped Off." *HR Focus* 71, p. 18.

DePaulo, P.J., and B.M. DePaulo. 1989. "Can Deception by Salespeople and Customers be Detected Through Nonverbal Behavioral Cues?" *Journal of Applied Social Psychology* 19, no. 18, pp. 1552–77.

Deshpande, S.P., E. George, and J. Joseph. 2000. "Ethical Climate and Managerial Success in Russian Organizations." *Journal of Business Ethics* 23, no. 2, pp. 211–17.

Duffy, M., K. Scott, J. Shaw, B. Tepper, and K. Auino. 2012. "A Social Context Model of Envy and Social Undermining." *Academy of Management Journal* 55 no. 3, pp. 643–66. doi:10.5465/amj.2009.0804

Dunlop, P.D., and K. Lee. 2004. "Workplace Deviance, Organizational Citizenship Behavior, and Business Unit Performance: The Bad Apples Do Spoil the Whole Barrel." *Journal of Organizational Behavior* 25, no. 1, pp. 67–80.

Erikson, S. 2005. *The Gardens of the Moon.* New York: Tor Fantasy. Reprint edition.

Fox, S., P.E. Spector, and D. Miles. 2001. "Counterproductive Work Behavior (CWB) in Response to Job Stressors and Organizational Justice: Some Mediator and Moderator Tests for Autonomy and Emotions." *Journal of Vocational Behavior* 59, no. 3, pp. 291–309.

Fritzsche, D.J. 2000. "Ethical Climates and the Ethical Dimension of Decision Making." *Journal of Business Ethics* 24, no. 2, pp. 125–40.

Gallup Inc. 2013. *The State of the American Workplace: Employee Engagement Insights for U.S. Business Leaders.* USA: Gallup, Inc.

Gaudin, S. 2000. "Case Study of Insider Sabotage: The Tim Lloyd/Omega Case." *Computer Security Journal* 16, no. 3, pp. 1–8.

Giacalone, R.A., and J. Greenberg, eds. 1997. *Antisocial Behavior in Organizations.* Thousand Oaks, CA: Sage Publications.

Griffin, R.W., and A. O'Leary-Kelly. 2004. *The Dark Side of Organizational Behavior.* San Francisco: Jossey-Bass.

Griffin, R.W., A. O'Leary-Kelly, and J. Collins. 1998. "Dysfunctional Work Behaviors in Organizations." In *Trends in Organizational Behavior*, eds. C.L. Cooper, and D.M. Rousseau, 66–82. Vol. 5. New York: John Wiley.

Harper, D. 1990. "Spotlight Abuse—Save Profits." *Industrial Distribution* 79, no. 3, pp. 47–51.

Henle, C.A. 2005. "Predicting Workplace Deviance from the Interaction between Organizational Justice and Personality." *Journal of Managerial Issues* 17, no. 2, pp. 247–63.

Johns, G. 1997. "Contemporary Research on Absence from Work: Correlates, Causes, and Consequences." In *International Review of Industrial and Organizational Psychology*, 12, eds. C.L. Cooper, and I.T. Robertson, 115–74. London: John Wiley & Sons.

Kacmar, K.M., and S.C. Dawn. 1998. "A Qualitative Analysis of the Dysfunctional Aspects of Political Behavior in Organizations." In *Dysfunctional Behavior in Organizations*, eds. R.W. Griffin, A.M. O'Leary-Kelly, and J. Collins, 195–218. Stamford, CT: JAI Press.

Kidwell, R.E., and N. Bennett. 1993. "Employee Propensity to Withhold Effort: A Conceptual Model to Intersect Three Avenues of Research." *Academy of Management Review* 18, no. 3, pp. 429–56.

Laabs, J. 1999. "Employee Sabotage: Don't Be a Target." *Workforce* 78, no. 7, pp. 32–42.

Lim, V.K.G. 2002. "The IT Way of Loafing on the Job: Cyberloafing, Neutralizing and Organizational Justice." *Journal of Organizational Behavior* 23, no. 5, pp. 675–94.

Litzky, B.E., K.A. Eddleston, and D.L. Kidder. 2006. "The Good, the Bad, and the Misguided: How Managers Inadvertently Encourage Deviant Behaviors." *Academy of Management Perspectives* 20, no. 1, pp. 91–103.

Murphy, K.R. 1993. *Honesty in the Workplace*. Belmont, CA: Brooks/Cole.

Peterson, D. 2002. Deviant Workplace Behavior and the Organizations Ethical Climate." *Journal of Business and Psychology* 17, no. 1, pp. 47–61.

Puffer, S.M. 1987. "Prosocial Behavior, Noncompliant Behavior, and Work Performance Among Commission Salespeople." *Journal of Applied Psychology* 72, no. 4, pp. 615–21.

Robinson, S.L., and R.J. Bennett. 1995. "A Typology of Deviant Workplace Behaviors: A Multi-Dimensional Scaling Study." *Academy of Management Journal* 38, no. 2, pp. 555–72.

Robinson, S.L., and A.M. O'Leary-Kelly. 1998. "Monkey See, Monkey Do: The Influence of Work Groups on the Antisocial Behavior of Employees." *Academy of Management Journal* 41, no. 6, pp. 658–72.

Sagie, A., S. Stashevsky, and M. Koslowsky. 2003. *Misbehaviour and Dysfunctional Attitudes in Organizations*. New York: Palgrave Macmillan.

Skarlicki, D.P., and R. Folger. 1997. "Retaliation in the Workplace: The Roles of Distributive, Procedural, and Interactional Justice." *Journal of Applied Psychology* 82, no. 3, pp. 424–43.

Spector, P.E. 1978. "Organizational Frustration: A Model and Review of the Literature." *Personnel Psychology* 31, no. 4, pp. 815–29.

Spector, P., S. Fox, L. Penney, K. Bruursema, A. Goh, and S. Kessler. 2006. "The Dimensionality of Counter-Productivity: Are All Counterproductive Behavior Created Equal?" *Journal of Vocational Behavior* 68, no. 3, pp. 446–60.

Van Fleet, D.D., and R.W. Griffin. 2006. "Dysfunctional Organization Culture: The Role of Leadership in Motivating Dysfunctional Work Behaviors." *Journal of Managerial Psychology* 21, no. 8, pp. 698–708.

Vardi, Y., and Y. Wiener. 1996. "Misbehavior in Organizations: A Motivational Framework." *Organizational Science* 7, no. 2, pp. 151–65.

Vidaver-Cohen, D. 1998. "Moral Climate in Business Firms: A Conceptual Framework for Analysis and Change." *Journal of Business Ethics* 17, no. 11, pp. 1211–26.

About the Authors

Paolo Canonico is an associate professor of organizational studies at the University of Napoli Federico II, Italy, where he currently teaches Organization of information systems and Staff administration. He holds a PhD in business administration; he obtained a Master of Science in Information Systems from the London School of Economics, and has been a visiting scholar at the Department of Management and Engineering at Linkoping University, Sweden.

Stefano Consiglio is a full professor of organizational studies at University of Napoli Federico II, Italy. His main research interests are human resource management, employment agencies, innovation, and creativity. Since 2012, he is a scientific coordinator for the project Smart Cities Orchestra—Smart Cities and Communities and Social innovation.

Ernesto De Nito is an associate professor of organizational studies at the University of Catanzaro "Magna Graecia," Italy, where he teaches Organization Studies and Organizational Behavior. He gained a PhD in business economics at the University of Naples Federico II, with a thesis entitled "Knowledge management as a tool to manage information."

Fabiola Gerpott is a PhD student in business administration and psychology in the joint PhD program at Jacobs University Bremen, Germany, and VU University Amsterdam, Netherlands. Her research concentrates on learning and leadership in the context of societal changes, and has been published in a wide range of national and international journals.

Rosalie Holian is an associate professor in Management Decision at the School of Management, RMIT University, Melbourne. Her main research interests are organizational psychology, human resource management, organizational development, management education, action research, and insider research. She is a Certified Professional Member of the Australian Human Resources Institute (CHARI), Member of the Australian

Psychological Society, (MAPS), Member of Coaching Psychology Interest Group, Registered Psychologist at the Psychology Board of Australia, and Member of the International Association of Applied Psychology.

Raimondo Ingrassia is an associate professor (with tenure) at the Department of Economics, Management and Statistics—University of Palermo. He wrote books on Professional in Organizations, Workloads in Organizational Theory, Organization and Communication of Public Administration, and several articles. His research focuses on mismanagement, human resource management, organizational behavior, and public administration and management.

Kamal Tandon is Director of the NCRD's Sterling Institute of Management Studies. He has 13 years of academic experience (Business Development & Operations) coupled with 15 years of experience in FMCG, IT, and ITES industry and experience of business operations in several countries (Australia, Belgium, Holland, Hong Kong, Bahrain, Kuwait, UAE, Qatar, Burundi, Ethiopia, and Zaire). His areas of interest lie in developing community leadership and bringing about social change using academic leadership, social innovation, and entrepreneurship through public and private partnerships.

Soma Kamal Tandon has a versatile background of IT, HR, and CSR. She is working in a Public Sector Undertaking. She received her PhD in Management Studies from SNDT University, India. She has written several articles and book reviews in Indian journals and book chapters in three international publications on varied topics Her main research interest is leveraging literature as a management-teaching tool. She has written chapters on this subject in two international publications. She has also written a book chapter about CSR in India.

Deanna D. Mader received her PhD from the University of Georgia, and currently serves as a senior associate dean. She is responsible for undergraduate programs in the Lewis College of Business at Marshall University. She has 31 years of teaching and administrative experience in public higher education. Among other topics, Dr Mader's publications and presentations include business education, online shopping, and ethics.

Marjorie L. McInerney received her PhD from the Ohio State University, and has 31 years of teaching and administrative experience in public higher education. She currently serves as an associate dean for graduate programs in the Lewis College of Business at Marshall University. Dr McInerney has published and presented her research in a number of areas including business ethics, healthcare management, role of managers, and business education.

Lorenzo Mercurio is an assistant professor in Business Administration at University of Naples "Parthenope"—Italy. He holds a PhD in organization theory and management from Università del Molise. His main research interests are public administration, public utilities, knowledge management, management education, and heritage management. He is member of scientific and organizing committees in national and international conferences and academic associations focused on organizational and managerial studies.

Andrea Tomo is a post-doc research fellow at the Department of Economics, Management, Institutions, University of Naples Federico II, Italy. He holds a PhD in Business Economics from University of Naples Federico II, Italy. He has been visiting doctoral student at Leuphana Universität of Lüneburg in Germany. His main research interests are governance in the public sector, professional services, information systems, and public transportation (especially railways and their regulation).

Sven C. Voelpel is the founding director of the WISE Research Group (Wisdom, Innovation, Strategy, Energy) and professor of Business Administration at Jacobs University Bremen, Germany. He is interested in leadership, innovation, strategy, change processes, and knowledge management, and has contributed more than 200 book and journal publications to these domains, including outlets such as the Academy of Management Journal.

Jolita Vveinhardt works in two Universities in Lithuania: as a chief researcher, professor in Lithuanian Sports University and associate professor in Vytautas Magnus University. She is a member of the editorial boards of nine scientific journals. She is engaged in volunteer activities providing consultations to the victims of bullying. J. Vveinhardt as an author and co-author has published more than 100 scientific publications in Lithuanian and foreign journals. J. Vveinhardt is the author and co-author of five books. The main areas of research interest are mobbing in employee relations, climate of the organization, nepotism as a management anomaly, favoritism, cronyism, protectionism, values congruence, and human resource management.

Index

This book is a publication in support of the United Nations Principles for Responsible Management Education (PRME), housed in the UN Global Compact Office. The mission of the PRME initiative is to inspire and champion responsible management education, research and thought leadership globally. Please visit www.unprme.org for more information.

The Principles for Responsible Management Education Book Collection is edited through the Center for Responsible Management Education (CRME), a global facilitator for responsible management education and for the individuals and organizations educating responsible managers. Please visit www.responsiblemanagement.net for more information.

—Oliver Laasch, University of Manchester, Collection Editor

- *Personal and Organizational Transformation Towards Sustainability: Walking a Twin Path* by Dorothea Ernst
- *The Human Side of Virtual Work: Managing Trust, Isolation, and Presence* by Laurence M. Rose
- *Corporate Social Responsibility: A Strategic Perspective* by David Chandler
- *Designing Ethical Workplaces: The Moldable Model* by Donald D. Dunn
- *Responsible Management Accounting and Controlling: A Practical Handbook for Sustainability, Responsibility, and Ethics* by Daniel A. Ette
- *Responsible Governance: International Perspectives For the New Era* by Tom Cockburn, Khosro S. Jahdi, and Edgar Wilson
- *Stop Teaching: Principles and Practices for Responsible Management Education* by Isabel Rimanoczy
- *Teaching Ethics Across the Management Curriculum: A Handbook for International Faculty* by Kemi Ogunyemi
- *Teaching Ethics Across the Management Curriculum: Principles and Applications, Volume II* by Kemi Ogunyemi
- *Teaching Ethics Across the Management Curriculum: Contributing to a Global Paradigm Shift, Volume III* by Kemi Ogunyemi

Announcing the Business Expert Press Digital Library

Concise e-books business students need for classroom and research

This book can also be purchased in an e-book collection by your library as

- a one-time purchase,
- that is owned forever,
- allows for simultaneous readers,
- has no restrictions on printing, and
- can be downloaded as PDFs from within the library community.

Our digital library collections are a great solution to beat the rising cost of textbooks. E-books can be loaded into their course management systems or onto students' e-book readers.
The **Business Expert Press** digital libraries are very affordable, with no obligation to buy in future years. For more information, please visit **www.businessexpertpress.com/librarians**. To set up a trial in the United States, please email **sales@businessexpertpress.com**.

www.ingramcontent.com/pod-product-compliance
Lightning Source LLC
Chambersburg PA
CBHW071653200326
41519CB00012BA/2508